Child Care in the 1990s
Trends and Consequences

Edited by

Alan Booth

Pennsylvania State University

LEA

1992

LAWRENCE ERLBAUM ASSOCIATES, PUBLISHERS
Hillsdale, New Jersey   Hove and London

Lawrence Erlbaum Associates, Inc., Publishers
365 Broadway
Hillsdale, New Jersey 07642

Library of Congress Cataloging-in-Publication Data

Child care in the 1990s : trends and consequences / [edited by] Alan
   Booth.
      p.   cm.
   Papers from the National Symposium on Child Care in the 1990s held
June 19–20, 1991 at the University of Nebraska.
   Includes bibliographical references and index.
   ISBN 0-8058-1060-9. — ISBN 0-8058-1061-7 (pbk.)
   1. Child care services—United States—Congresses.   I. Booth,
Alan, 1935–   .
HQ778.7.U6C49   1992
362.7—dc20   92-1110
                                                    CIP

Printed in the United States of America
10   9   8   7   6   5   4   3   2   1

Child Care in the 1990s
Trends and Consequences

Contents

PART II
WHAT CHILD-CARE PRACTICES AND ARRANGEMENTS LEAD TO POSITIVE OUTCOMES FOR CHILDREN? NEGATIVE OUTCOMES FOR CHILDREN?

PART III
WHAT ARE THE CONSEQUENCES OF CHILD-CARE PRACTICES AND ARRANGEMENTS FOR THE WELL-BEING OF PARENTS AND PROVIDERS?

PART IV
WHAT POLICIES ARE NECESSARY TO MEET THE NEED FOR HIGH-QUALITY CHILD CARE, AND HOW CAN THE POLICIES BE REALIZED?

List of Contributors

Jay Belsky • Human Development and Family Studies, Pennsylvania State University, University Park, PA 16802

Alan Booth • Sociology Department, Pennsylvania State University, University Park, PA 16802

Barbara T. Bowman • Erikson Institute, Chicago, IL 60610

Andrew Cherlin • Sociology Department, The Johns Hopkins University, Baltimore, MD 21218

Alison Clarke-Stewart • Psychology Department, University of California-Irvine, Irvine, CA 92717

Laura Duberstein • Population Studies Center, University of Michigan, Ann Arbor, MI 48106

Ellen Galinsky • Families and Work Institute, New York, NY 10001

Ron Haskins • U.S. House Committee on Ways and Means, Washington, DC 20515

Sandra L. Hofferth • Urban Institute, Washington, DC 20037

Rebecca A. Maynard • Mathematica Policy Research Inc., Princeton, NJ 08540

Eileen McGinnis • Mathematica Policy Research Inc., Princeton, NJ 08540

Sharon M. McGroder • Health and Human Services, Washington, DC 20201

Patricia P. Olmsted • High/Scope Educational Research Foundation, Ypsilanti, MI 48198-2898

Karen Oppenheim Mason • East-West Population Institute, East-West Center, Honolulu, HI 96848

Deborah A. Phillips • Psychology Department, University of Virginia, Charlottesville, VA 22903

Harriet B. Presser • Department of Sociology, University of Maryland, College Park, MD 20742

William Prosser • Health and Human Services, Washington, DC 20201

Sandra Wood Scarr • Psychology Department, University of Virginia, Charlottesville, VA 22903-2477

Kathy Thornburg • Department of Human Development and Family Studies, University of Missouri-Columbia, Columbia, MO 65211

Preface

The family is in the midst of many changes. These include increasing numbers of mothers becoming involved in the labor force, high rates of divorce and remarriage, and declining family income. Related to these changes is the increasing demand for and provision of child care. The National Symposium on Child Care in the 1990s was held June 19–20, 1991, at the University of Nebraska, to bring together the best minds in the country to focus on four questions related to child care:

- What are the factors that affect the demand and supply for child care, and what will be the demand in the 1990s?
- What child-care practices and arrangements lead to positive and negative outcomes for children?
- What are the consequences of child-care practices and arrangements for the well-being of parents and providers?
- What policies are necessary to meet the need for high quality child care, and how can the policies be realized?

The planning for the symposium was accomplished at several levels. Members of the University of Nebraska Departments of Human Development and the Family, Psychology, and Sociology were involved in the early definition of the topic. It was further developed by an advisory committee appointed by the National Council on Family Relations. The design that emerged was a two-day symposium that entailed four sessions, one focused on each question. Each session had a lead speaker who presented a paper on the question. Each paper had three discussants, each of whom was responsible for reviewing the lead speaker's paper and bringing to bear his or her own work, as well as that of others, on the question. Following the symposium, each lead speaker had an opportunity to prepare a rejoinder to the discussant's comments. Two did so. The lead papers, review papers, and rejoinders constitute the contents of this volume.

The lead speakers were chosen because of their current involvement in research projects dealing with the topic. The discussants were selected for their prominence as policy or program experts or because they had done research on the topic. An attempt was made to obtain persons who would provide divergent points of view on each question. Our goal was to provide the reader with current information and a review of issues intended to provoke new ways of thinking about child care.

There are many people to thank for assisting in the organization of this national symposium. We are indebted to the Woods Charitable Fund, who provided the majority of the funds for the symposium, and to John Yost (then University of Nebraska Vice Chancellor for Research), who marshalled university resources behind the project. Members of the University of Nebraska Department of Human Development and the Family, the Sociology Department's Family Study Group, and the Psychology Department, especially the Center on Children, Families, and the Law helped with the initial planning of this symposium. The National Council on Family Relations, a cosponsor of the symposium, appointed an advisory committee consisting of Katherine Allen, David Demo, Richard Fabes, Mark Fine, Deborah Godwin, Sandra Hofferth, Robert Joseph Taylor, Elizabeth Thomson, and Alexis Walker, who spent considerable time reviewing symposium proposals and suggesting key speakers and discussants. I offer very special thanks to one member of that committee, Sandy Hofferth, whose intimate knowledge of child care helped me numerous times throughout the planning process; the special balance of people involved in this symposium is in no small way due to her guidance and counsel. Thanks to Becky Bean and Susan Ptacek and members of the City–County Child Care Advisory Committee, for helping with symposium proceedings. Joleen Deats, the symposium coordinator, added immeasurably to the success of the Symposium. Professors Paul Amato, John DeFrain, Ross Thompson, and Lynn White presided over the sessions and contributed greatly to the flow of ideas.

—Alan Booth

I

What Are the Factors that Affect the Demand and Supply for Child Care, and What Will be the Demand in the 1990s?

The Demand for and Supply of Child Care in the 1990s

SANDRA L. HOFFERTH
The Urban Institute

In the late 1970s the movement of women into the work force was touted as a major revolution, albeit a "subtle" one (Smith, 1979). A large proportion of these women were mothers, and many had very young children (under age 1). By the late 1980s enormous changes in the way children were being cared for constituted a second revolution. Of course, parents still provided the majority of care for children, yet as mothers spent longer hours and more years in the work force, care for younger and younger children for relatively significant quantities of time was, to a large extent, increasingly assigned to nonrelatives and institutions. Even when mothers are not in the work force, children spend time in early education and care, albeit for smaller amounts of time.

Recent legislation has increased the potential demand for child-care services. The Family Support Act of 1988 requires welfare parents with children age 3 or older (at the state's option, age 1 or older) to work or engage in job training under the new JOBS program. To carry out this aspect of welfare reform, states are required to provide child care for participants. This has greatly increased government responsibility for child care.

Recent legislation has also increased the potential sources of federal subsidies for child care. Important policy debates in the United States, at the federal and state levels, over the past several years led to the enactment in October, 1990 of child-care legislation to assist low- and moderate-income working families with their child-care and other household expenses, to increase the supply, to improve the quality of programs, and to expand Head Start.

Although extrafamilial child care has recently become a subject of concern and legislative action, it has historically served a variety of purposes. At first (starting in the late 1800s), child care served as a welfare service for the care and protection of low-income and immigrant children while their mothers could not care for them, primarily because they worked outside the home (Nelson, 1982; Phillips & Zigler, 1987; Young & Nelson, 1973). The nursery school movement of the 1920s then focused on developing children's abilities and skills. Which particular tradition dominated at any particular time has depended on a variety of historical and political factors. For example, during World War II, substantial funds were provided under the Lanham Act to establish child-care centers for the children of mothers working in the war industries. The Great Society spawned Head Start, with its emphasis on the educational aspect of child care, following research that had suggested that programs such as Head Start would help prepare poor children for school and compensate for their economic disadvantage. In the 1970s, the increased participation of women in the labor force raised concern that there would not be enough spaces for their children and that many would have to care for themselves. Increased use of child care in centers was acceptable as long as no evidence was found of harm to children. Thus, in the 1970s, the focus of child-care debate was primarily on the employment consequences for parents of the availability and use of child care. In the 1980s, attention increasingly focused on the consequences of maternal employment and types of nonparental child care for children and for society. This culminated in a series of debates over whether nonparental care was helpful or harmful to children, first, during their older preschool years, and then, during the first year of life (Belsky, 1986; Clarke-Stewart, 1989; Phillips, McCartney, Scarr, & Howes, 1987).

As a consequence of this revolution in the way children were being cared for in the late 1980s, an unprecedented amount of federal attention focused on child care, reflecting a consensus that a major reevaluation of services and programs was needed. This led to substantial debate about the nature of the problem, and the form any solutions should take.

Part of what occurred during this debate was a clarification of the issues. Prior to the late 1980s, the "child-care problem" had not been clearly laid out. In particular, there were several problems that reformers were aiming to resolve, and the solutions to them were not necessarily mutually compatible. For example, quoting Hofferth and Phillips (1991), "is the problem the inability of some mothers to obtain affordable child care for their children, so that they can work and be economically self-sufficient? Is it the poor quality of programs for children? Or is it the inability to get and keep good child-care providers in the field?" (p. 2). Finally, what are the roles of federal, state and local governments in resolving these issues?

> Employed mothers, whose salaries are generally modest, need care that is low enough in cost to make their employment profitable. Providers need to make enough money to remain economically viable and to attract people who are committed to providing high quality, stable care for children. Children need the highest quality of care possible. To promote maternal employment (particularly among low-income welfare mothers), the price of child care needs to be moderate. To promote the development of children, the quality of care needs to be improved, which is likely to raise its cost substantially. (Hofferth & Phillips, 1991, p. 5)

The conflict between price and quality is the crux of the child-care debate.

This volume is organized around these four different constituencies: children, parents, providers, and federal/state policymakers. This is no accident. It was during the debates in Washington that the importance of identifying these groups was first clearly articulated. Policies developed for the purpose of assisting one group might have an unintended negative impact on another. However, separating these groups and their interests is not possible either, because the groups overlap. Parents (and relatives) are also providers. Parents are interested not only in their own well-being but also that of their children. Ideally, by clarifying the issues, research evidence can be used to design a more rational and effective set of solutions to the problems identified.

THE ISSUE OF UNMET NEED

During these debates, one of the questions I was asked over and over is whether there was a discrepancy between demand for and supply of child care, and, therefore, an unmet need. The answer, in brief, is "No, probably not." Although this was the important issue in the 1970s, when increased maternal labor force participation led to predictions of a crisis in child care, and in the early 1980s, when the Reagan Administration began its steady retreat from policies of the Great Society, it is not an important issue today. My reasoning for laying this issue to rest is as follows: If the number of spaces per se were a problem, we would see three important consequences: First, the number of spaces in child-care centers and nursery schools would not have kept up with the number of children of employed mothers.[1] Because of this, a large number of preschool children would be found caring for themselves.

---

[1] Care in centers is used here to illustrate the responsiveness of supply to demand pressures because, being licensed or registered in all states, they are most easily counted.

Furthermore, the price of child care would be increasing as parental demand puts pressure on the existing supply.[2] None of these, however, appears to be the case. Consistent with this story, we have seen an enormous increase in the number and capacity of child care centers, an increase that parallels the large increase in the number of children. Although utilization rates are high, spaces are available, especially in family day care. The evidence suggests that supply is very responsive to increased demand. There is always one person out there who is willing to care for another child. Second, few preschool children are left to care for themselves. Children gradually begin caring for themselves at about age 9 or 10, and by the teenage years the great majority care for themselves for part of the day. Finally, trends from 1975 to the present show only a slight rise in prices for child care in centers and no rise in the price of care in family day-care homes. Families pay about the same proportion of their incomes on child care as they did 15 years ago. What *has* risen is the price of care by a babysitter in the child's home; that has almost doubled over the past 15 years.

That does not mean, then, that there are no legitimate and important concerns that can be addressed, such as the accessibility of specific types of programs and services, the price of care, and whether parents are getting what they want and children what they need. First I consider demand, then supply, then I put them together. Finally, I address four important concerns: the accessibility, cost, and quality of care, and parental preferences.

SOURCES OF DATA

The data I report come from two sources: the National Child Care Survey 1990 (NCCS), a nationally representative survey of 4,392 households with children under age 13 (Hofferth, Brayfield, Deich, & Holcomb, 1991; Fig. 1.1), and the Profile of Child Care Settings Study (PCS), a nationally representative survey of child-care centers and family day-care providers (Kisker, Hofferth, Phillips, & Farquhar, 1991; Fig. 1.2).

The objectives of the NCCS were (a) to obtain a comprehensive picture of how families care for their children, (b) to examine how families make their child-care choices, and (c) to describe the characteristics of nonregulated and informal care arrangements for children. NCCS researchers contacted by telephone a random sample of households located in 100 counties and groups

---

[2]In a competitive market, if the downward sloping demand curve shifts upward (reflecting increased demand), the price will rise. How much it rises depends on the slope of the upward sloping supply curve. If supply is not very elastic (almost vertical), an upward shift in demand will raise the price considerably. If supply is elastic (almost horizontal), an upward shift in demand will raise the price only slightly.

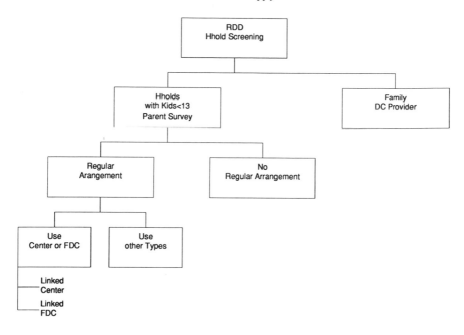

FIG. 1.1 Design of the National Child Care Survey, 1990. Note: FDC means Family Day Care.

of counties throughout the United States to identify families with children under age 13 or households in which child care was provided to other families. Between October 1989 and May 1990, 4,392 parents (primarily mothers) were interviewed about the early education and care arrangements used for children under age 13 and about their activities, employment, and demographic characteristics. In addition, 162 family day-care providers, identified during the screening process, and 250 providers who cared for children of NCCS parents were interviewed with the identical questionnaire used by the PCS. Previous studies have identified the child-care arrangements of only employed mothers while they were employed, thus excluding arrangements for child development and other purposes by employed or nonemployed mothers (U.S. Bureau of the Census 1987, 1990).[3] With these new data, we can now examine the child-care arrangements of both employed and nonemployed mothers. Standardized sample weights were used to adjust for

[3]The only previous study to include children of all types of parents (Rodes & Moore, 1975) did not present results separately by age of the child and employment status of the mother, and primary and secondary arrangements were not ascertained. Therefore, it is difficult to compare results. Because Census Bureau data from the same period were available, we have used them instead.

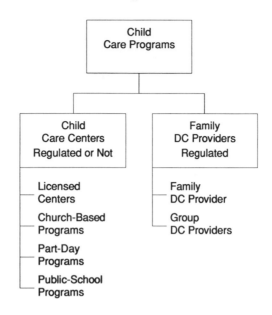

FIG. 1.2   Design of a Profile of Child Care Settings.

differential probabilities of sample selection and nonresponse (see Abt Associates, Inc., 1990; Hofferth et al., 1991).

The major objective of the PCS was to obtain national estimates of the level and characteristics of early childhood programs available in 1990 for young children in the United States. Center-based programs and regulated family day-care homes were randomly selected from state and county licensing and registration lists in the same nationally representative counties and county groups used by the NCCS. Interviews were conducted from October, 1989 to February 1990 using computer-assisted telephone interviewing methods. The final sample includes 2089 center directors and 583 regulated family day-care providers (Kisker et al., 1991).

Because both the NCCS and the PCS used the same first-stage sample of counties and county groups and were conducted at the same time, these two studies together give a reasonable representation of the supply and demand for child care in the same nationally representative American communities in early 1990.

DEMAND FOR CHILD CARE

The number and ages of children and the number of mothers who are employed outside the home are key determinants of demand for child care.

The number of children has been increasing since 1980. In 1990 there were 47 million children under age 13 in the United States. By 1995 the projection is for 22.5 million children under age 6 and 30.6 million children age 6 to 13 (Hofferth & Phillips, 1987). In addition, the number of children with mothers in the work force has been increasing. If trends continue as they have been since 1970, I have projected there will be 14.6 million preschool children under age 6 with mothers in the labor force in 1995 — about 2 out of 3 — and 23.5 million school-age children 6 to 13 with a mother in the labor force — about 3 out of 4 school-age children.

Will this happen? The labor force participation of mothers certainly cannot keep increasing indefinitely. We have seen a slowdown in the past several years, most of which occurred among divorced, never married, and separated mothers (U.S. Department of Labor, 1988). Some of these mothers will be affected by welfare reform. If the Family Support Act of 1988 is successful, the labor force participation of these mothers should rise. Finally, fertility has been higher than anticipated. So, it is still too early to tell how accurate these projections will be.

On hearing these figures, many people immediately jump to the conclusion that in 1995 all 14.6 million children of employed mothers will need out-of-home nonrelative care, and when they compare this with the number of spaces, they conclude that a great discrepancy exists. How can we determine how many children will need out-of-home nonrelative care? Our best guess would be that the same proportion of children in 1995 as in 1990 will need such care. This assumes that although the number of children may change, their distribution across arrangements will remain the same.

In 1990, 26% of preschool children with an employed mother were in a center-based program, 19% were in family day-care, and a small proportion of children (4%) were in the care of a nonrelative in the child's home as their primary arrangement (Fig. 1.3). Half of all preschool children whose mothers were employed were cared for either exclusively by their own parents (30%) or by relatives (18%) as the primary arrangement.

There have been substantial changes in the use of various arrangements since 1965. The proportion of youngest, preschool-age children with employed mothers enrolled in center-based programs as a primary arrangement increased more than fourfold, from 6% in 1965 to 28% in 1990 (Fig. 1.4). Given the trend in center-based programs (Fig. 1.4), using 1990 proportions may underestimate the proportion in center-based programs and overestimate the proportion in other forms of care. Accompanying the increase in the proportion enrolled in center-based programs has been a decline in the proportion cared for by in-home providers and relatives. Parental care as a primary arrangement for employed mothers appears to have grown somewhat over the past 15 years, perhaps reflecting an increased ability or desire of parents to share care when the mother is employed. The use of family day care relative to other

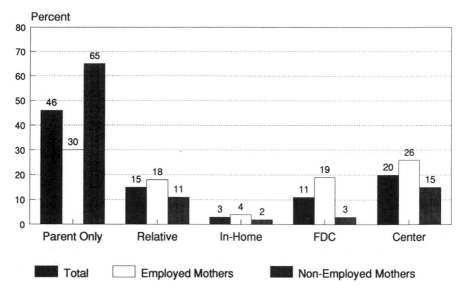

FIG. 1.3 Primary child-care arrangements of all preschool children. From Hofferth et al. (1991). Copyright 1991 by The Urban Institute Press. Reprinted by permission.

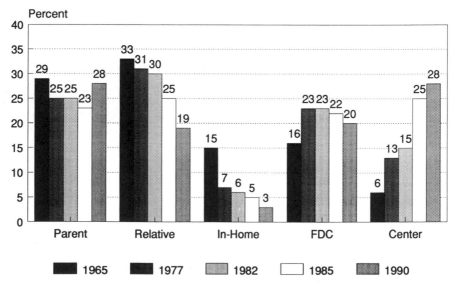

FIG. 1.4 Primary care, youngest preschool child, employed mothers, 1965–1990. From Hofferth et al. (1991). Copyright 1991 by The Urban Institute Press. Reprinted by permission. (Additional data from Low and Spindler, 1968; U.S. Bureau of Census, 1982, 1983, 1987.)

arrangements has remained constant over the period, but, as have other forms, enrollments have increased because of the increased number of children with employed mothers.

However, there is another source of demand for preschool programs. There has been a rapid increase in center-based enrollments to enhance the development of young children regardless of whether their mothers are employed. This consists of nursery school and preschool programs for children of middle- and upper-income families, as well as compensatory programs for disadvantaged children. For example, between 1970 and 1989, the proportion of 3- to 4-year-old children enrolled in school or in a preschool program doubled from 21% to 39% (U.S. Bureau of the Census, 1991). According to the NCCS, by 1990, 52% of 3- to 4-year-old children (41% of 3-year-olds and 61% of 4-year-olds) were enrolled in a preschool program (day-care center, nursery school, Head Start) or kindergarten, (Fig. 1.5). For this age group, there is little difference in enrollment between children of employed and nonemployed mothers.

In addition, care for school-age children before and after school is becoming a more important source of demand for programs. In 1990, 11% of

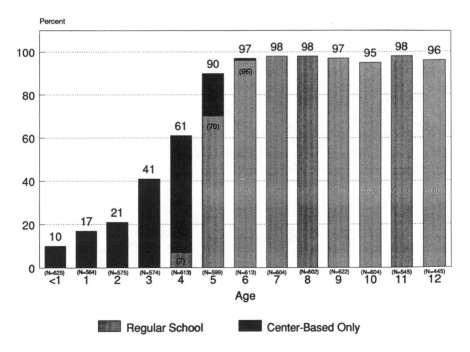

FIG. 1.5 Proportion of children enrolled in regular schools or center-based programs, by age. From Hofferth et al. (1991). Copyright 1991 by the Urban Institute Press. Reprinted by permission.

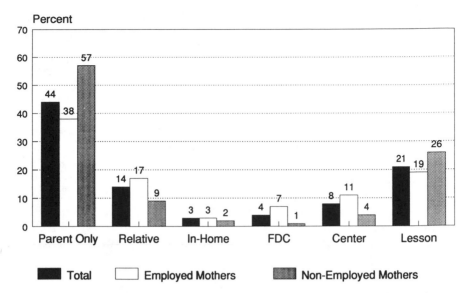

FIG. 1.6 Primary child-care arrangements of all school-aged children. From Hofferth et al. (1991). Copyright 1991 by The Urban Institute Press. Reprinted by permission.

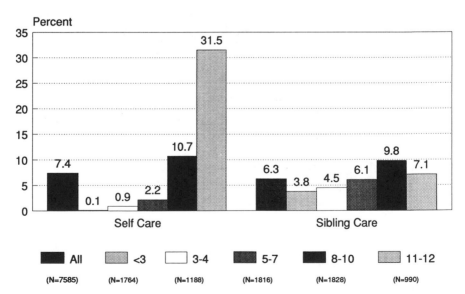

FIG. 1.7 Percentage of all children ever in self care or sibling care. From Hofferth et al. (1991). Copyright 1991 by The Urban Institute Press. Reprinted by permission.

school-age children with an employed mother were in center-based programs, 7% were in family day care before and after school, 19% participated in lessons and sports, 3% were cared for by a nonrelative in their own home, 3% cared for themselves, and 2% were in other arrangements (Fig. 1.6). Self-care, though not the primary arrangement, becomes important as a supplemental arrangement for older children (Fig. 1.7). By age 12, 32% care for themselves at some time during the day.

Estimate of Demand for Care

Based on the NCCS, 7.6 million children under age 13 — 5.1 million preschool children and 2.5 million school-age children — were enrolled in centers as their primary or secondary child-care arrangement in 1990, and 4 million children were enrolled in family day-care as their primary or secondary arrangement. This accounts for the major ways children are cared for during a week.

THE SUPPLY OF CHILD CARE

According to the PCS and the NCCS, at the beginning of 1990 there were approximately 80,000 center-based early education and care programs serving preschool children in the United States. Based on comparisons of the PCS findings with earlier studies, there were three times as many center-based programs in early 1990 as there were in the mid-1970s, and four times as many children were enrolled in such programs. As a consequence the average number of children per program increased 39%.

According to the PCS, in 1990 there were approximately 118,000 regulated family day-care providers serving 700,000 children. Based upon the number of children enrolled in family day care as a primary or secondary arrangement, we estimate that in 1990 there were between 550,000 and 1.1 million nonregulated family day-care providers in the United States caring for 3.3 million children. Thus, there were between 668,000 and 1.2 million family day-care providers caring for 4 million children, and between 10% and 18% were regulated (See Willer, Hofferth, Kisker, Dinne-Hawkins, Farguhar & Glantz, 1991).

THE MATCH BETWEEN SUPPLY AND DEMAND

Apparently, the number of children enrolled in early education and care is substantial and has increased dramatically over the past 15 years. So, what might be meant by an unmet need for child care? It could mean (a) care is not available for special types of care or certain groups of children: for example, a deficiency of licensed spaces, lack of access to spaces for infants in centers, a geographic mismatch between supply and demand, such that the spaces are in one place and the children are somewhere else; (b) care is not affordable; or (c) care does not meet parents' wants (or children's needs).

In this presentation I focus primarily on describing what we know about the availability, cost, and quality of care in the United States today.

Availability

Licensed Slots.   The discussion so far has identified about 3.3 million children in nonregulated family day care. (Center-based programs are either licensed, not required to be licensed, or regulated by a different agency, e.g., public schools.)

Whether this many children in nonregulated family day care is desirable or undesirable depends on the characteristics of family day care and state regulations. First, just because a family day-care home is not licensed does not mean it violates state regulations. Small family day-care homes caring for fewer than 4 children are not required to be licensed in 21 states (Hayes, Palmer, & Zaslow, 1990). Second, there are few studies of nonregulated family day care, so we have not previously been able to compare it with regulated care. New data from the NCCS show that nonregulated family day care is very similar to regulated family day care. Nonregulated family day-care homes differ from regulated family day-care homes in expected and predictable ways. They are smaller, they are more available (but harder to locate), they charge lower fees, they make less money, they care for children for fewer hours per week, and they offer more family-like services (e.g., they are more likely to care for sick children). They are also less likely to consider themselves professional providers. In other ways they do not appear to differ markedly from regulated family day-care homes. Of course, this survey probably underrepresents large providers, those providers who are in violation of the law, and those who are providing poor care. How many of these there are is unknown.

Infant Care.   An increasing proportion of mothers are at work within the first year after the birth of a child (U.S. Bureau of the Census, 1990), and need someone to care for that child. Fifty-seven percent of infants are cared for by relatives or by parents sharing the care between themselves; 20% of infants are in family day care, and 14 percent are placed in a center. Although parents not using center-based care may want it for their very young children, they may not be able to find programs to take them. Only slightly more than half of center-based programs accept children who are not toilet trained (compared with almost all family day-care providers). Perhaps even more critical, fewer than 10% of the vacancies in centers could be filled by children younger than 1 year old.

Geographic Distribution of Care.   Across the United States the supply of day-care centers and family day-care homes generally mirrors the number of children in the area (Table 1.1). However, there are relatively more spaces than children in centers in the South and relatively fewer spaces than children in the West. For family day care, regulated providers are relatively more concentrated in the Midwest and West and relatively less concentrated in the Northeast and South, reflecting differences in regulatory coverage. Nonregulated family day care is more concentrated in the Midwest and less concentrated in the South and in the Northeast.

Center-based programs, regulated family day, and nonregulated family day care are all distributed in urban areas in proportion to the population. Approximately three fourths are located in metropolitan areas, and one fourth are in nonmetropolitan areas.

Vacancies and Advertising.   Centers are more likely to advertise than are regulated family day-care providers, and regulated family day-care providers are more likely to advertise than are nonregulated family day-care providers, who do little to fill a vacancy. Not surprisingly, a higher proportion of spaces are occupied in center-based programs (90%) than in family day care, and regulated providers have a higher proportion of spaces filled (83%) than do nonregulated providers (65%).

Parental Expenditures and Budget Shares

Parental Expenditures on Care.   Not all parents pay for child care. In 1990, just over half of employed mothers paid for child care (Fig. 1.8). Almost 70% of full-time employed mothers, compared with 33% of part-time employed mothers and only 14% of nonemployed mothers, paid for care for their youngest preschool-age child.

The percent who pay also varies substantially by type of arrangement. Almost all parents pay when care is in a family day-care home or by an in-home provider (Fig. 1.9). Whereas the majority of parents pay for care in a center, nonemployed mothers are less likely to pay for it (57%) than employed mothers (90%). Fewer than half of mothers (40% of employed, 12% of nonemployed mothers) pay for care by a relative.

In 1990 employed mothers with a preschool-age child spent an average of $63 per week on child care for all of their children, or about $3150 per year (50 weeks). How much they spend depends on the type of arrangement and the age of the child. Not all children need care for the same number of hours, because parents do not all work the same number of hours per week and some children are in school most of the day. The type of care used is closely tied to the hours it is used.[4] Therefore, to compare expenditures across different

---

[4]For example, children spend more hours in centers and family day care than in other forms of care.

TABLE 1.1

Distribution of Preschool Children, Erly Childhood Programs, and Program Spaces by Region and Urbanicity (by Percent)

	Children Younger Than 5[a]	Centers	Space in Centers	Regulated Family Day-Care Homes	Spaces in Regulated Family Day-Care Homes	Non-Regulated Family Day-Care Homes	Spaces in Non-Regulated Family Day-Care Homes
Region							
Northeast	19	18	16	14	11	16	20
South	35	41	42	21	20	30	44
Midwest	24	23	23	29	32	30	26
West	23	19	19	36	37	23	10
Urbanicity							
Metropolitan	75	76	83	77	77	72	72
Nonmetropolitan	25	24	17	23	23	28	28

Note. From Hofferth et al., 1991; Kisker et al., 1991.

[a]The distribution of children younger than age 5 by region is estimated from projections of 1980 census data to 1988. The distribution of children younger than age 5 by urbanicity is estimated as the distribution of the population by urbanicity in 1980.

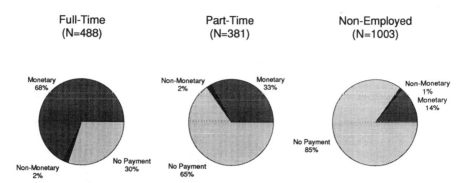

FIG. 1.8 Distribution of Payment arrangement by maternal employment status, youngest child under five. From Hofferth et al. (1991). Copyright 1991 by The Urban Institute Press. Reprinted by permission.

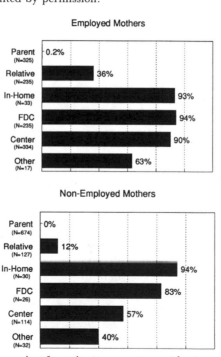

FIG. 1.9 Percentage paying for primary arrangement by type of arrangement and maternal employment status, youngest child under five. From Hofferth et al. (1991). Copyright 1991 by The Urban Institute Press. Reprinted by permission.

types of arrangements, we created a measure of expenditure per hour. Having an in-home provider is the most expensive arrangement for a mother with a preschool-age child ($2.30 per hour; Fig. 1.10). Of those who charge, relatives provide the least expensive care ($1.11 per hour), and family day care ($1.35 per hour) and center-based programs ($1.67 per hour) fall in

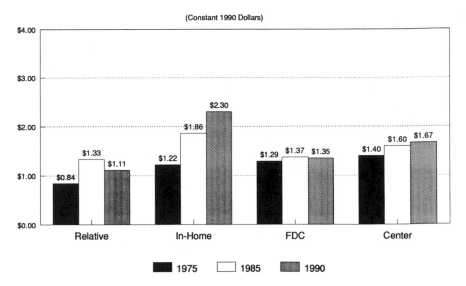

FIG. 1.10   Mean hourly payment for youngest child under 5-years-old, Employed mothers paying for child care, 1975–1990. From Hofferth et al. (1991). Copyright 1991 by The Urban Institute Press. Reprinted by permission. (Additional data from Rodes & Moore, 1975; Hofferth, 1988.)

between. In real terms expenditures on center-based programs and (regulated and nonregulated) family day care have risen very little over the past several decades. Adjusted for inflation, average hourly expenditures on center-based care rose 19% between 1975 and 1990, and average hourly expenditures on family day care rose 5% over the same period (Fig. 1.10). Average expenditures for care by a relative rose only 7%. In contrast, hourly expenditures for in-home providers rose by 180% over the period.

Although these figures provide a good idea of what parents can expect to pay for child care, they do not indicate how child care compares to other family expenditures. What is the share of the family budget that child care represents? Over all families, child care takes 10% of the family budget. It constitutes only a small proportion of the budget for wealthy families (6%), but as much as 22% to 25% of the family income among poor families who pay for care (Fig. 1.11). Whereas 10% is comparable to expenditures on food, 22% to 25% is comparable to expenditures on housing.

Quality

Quality of Care Provided.   Trends suggest that the quality of care in both center-based and home-based settings has improved, as measured by the increased education and training of providers. The average levels of educa-

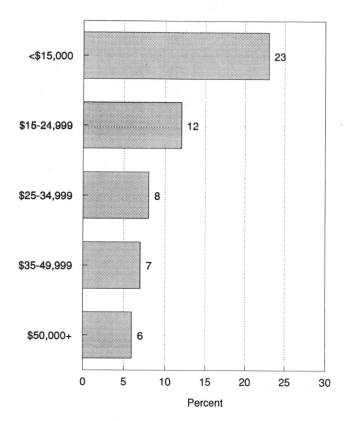

FIG. 1.11 Mean percentage of family income spent on child care by family income, employed mothers with youngest child under five paying for care only. From Hofferth et al. (1991). Copyright 1991 by The Urban Institute Press. Reprinted by permission.

tion and training received by regulated and nonregulated family day-care providers and center-based staff have increased substantially since the 1970s. For example, in 1990, 42% of teachers in center-based programs had 16 or more years of education, compared with 29% in 1976 to 1977. The average schooling of family day-care providers, though lower than center-based teachers, has also risen, from high school in 1976 to one year of college in 1990. About half of family day-care providers have had some college education. There is no significant difference between regulated and nonregulated providers in level of schooling. Not only has the education of providers increased, but it has continued to exceed general increases in the level of education among all women. Providers today, as they were in the 1970s, continue to be better educated than the population as a whole.

However, as a result of increased enrollments and only small increases in staff, the size of groups in center-based care has increased (from about 14 to

16) and the average number of children per staff member in center-based care has grown (from about 7 to 9), such that group sizes and ratios now tend to hover in the upper end of the ranges of group sizes and ratios recommended by early childhood professionals, particularly for groups of infants and toddlers. Average group sizes increased by approximately 16% and the average child-staff ratio rose 25% between 1976 to 1977 and 1990. Average group sizes in regulated family day-care homes have increased from about 4 to 6 children, although it is important to note that average group sizes in family day-care homes are still small. Average group sizes in nonregulated family day care homes have stayed about the same, at about 3 children. Child–staff ratios have not increased in regulated family day care, primarily because the proportion of regulated providers with helpers has increased. Thus, because training and education levels have increased, the quality of family day care has improved.

Perhaps as a consequence of the actual decline between the mid-1970s and 1990 in the wages and salaries of these well-educated providers, we have seen an increase in staff turnover in centers. The PCS documents a 27% increase in teacher turnover in comparable center-based programs between 1976 to 1977 and 1990.

In sum, family day care has fared favorably over time. On the three indicators used—education and training of provider, group size, and child-staff ratio—there has been either no change or an improvement. For centers, however, the picture is mixed. The education and training of teachers has improved; however, group sizes and child-staff ratios have increased. Teacher turnover rates have also increased. We do not know the extent to which increased training and education offset the burden of caring for more children and increased staff turnover.

Quality of Care Demanded.   What do parents want? Do parents select their programs using these same standards, and what characteristics of care do parents consider when choosing an arrangement? According to the NCCS, approximately 60% of parents who used center programs or family day care volunteered one aspect of the quality of care as the most important factor in their choice of arrangements (Fig. 1.12). Availability, location, or hours was mentioned by 22% of those using family day care and 29% of those using centers; fewer than 10% (6% of center users and 8% of family day-care users) mentioned cost as their most important consideration. Of those who felt quality of care was important, 6 out of 10 mentioned a characteristic of the provider, such as a warm and loving style, reliability, training, or experience as most important, and of these, a warm and loving manner was most frequently cited. Child-related characteristics of care, such as child-staff ratios, group size, and appropriate age ranges were each cited by 14% to 19% of parents. Characteristics of facilities cited by another 10% of parents

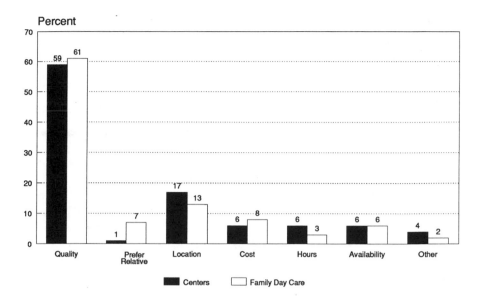

FIG. 1.12 Most important factor in choice of current arrangement, Parents Using Centers or Family Day Care. From Hofferth et al. (1991). Copyright 1991 by The Urban Institute Press. Reprinted by the permission.

include a home-like environment, safety, and equipment. Program goals, such as school preparation, promoting child development, and religious instruction, were cited by 18% of users of centers and only 2% of users of family day care.

To what extent do parents' choices reflect their preferences and to what extent do they represent what is available? The measurement of parental preferences is not straightforward (see Sonenstein, 1991, for a more complete discussion of these issues). I have so far discussed only the actual arrangements parents use. This approach assumes that parents purchase the care that best fits their needs, given cost and other constraints. If the market operates optimally, then parents who are dissatisfied quickly change arrangements and the actual arrangements parents select should reflect their preferences. Reported levels of parental satisfaction are always found to be high, which is consistent with this approach. A second approach assumes that parents' choices are so constrained that they may not be able to use their preferred arrangements. Parents may reduce guilt and stress by convincing themselves they are satisfied even if they are not. Or, they may be satisfied they have chosen the best among the options available. Preferences are ascertained by asking a hypothetical question about what parents would prefer under ideal circumstances (Presser & Baldwin, 1980). Of course, there is no way to know whether parents would behave as they state under such circumstances.

In the NCCS two types of questions were asked to get at underlying preferences: whether parents were satisfied, and whether they would prefer another type or combination of arrangements. Parents appeared content: Nine out of 10 parents reported satisfaction with their current child-care arrangements. However, 1 out of 4 would like to change arrangements. Among those parents who wanted to change, the majority wanted to switch to a center-based program. Although parents' motivations for desiring a change are partly linked to the growth and development of their children — with increased desire for a center-based program for older preschoolers — age alone cannot explain the massive shift of children from relative care and family day care into center-based programs since the early 1970s. This shift implies increased parental preference for center-based care. Other data support this conclusion. One study found that whereas only 30% to 40% of welfare mothers with a child under age 3 using a relative and 2% using a family day-care provider or babysitter were using their first choice of child care, 7 out of 10 whose child was in a center were in their first choice (Sonenstein, 1991).

What is not known is the additional proportion of parents who would like center-based programs for their children but who cannot find or pay for them. The NCCS suggests that, relative to groups with lower or higher incomes, families in which the mother is not employed, whose incomes are just above the poverty line but still below the median income level for all families, are the least likely to use such programs. These families constitute the group most likely to increase their use of center-based programs over time if child-care subsidies draw mothers into the work force or if subsidized early childhood programs (which serve children regardless of maternal employment) are expanded to include these families because such education is considered a public good.

Another group of importance consists of mothers of infants. Parents who are caring for their children themselves are least likely to want to change arrangements. However, their choices are limited. About half of mothers took some leave after the birth of their youngest child, with a median length of 16 weeks. Only about 3 out of 10 were paid during this absence from work. Of those who were paid, the majority were paid through a combination of annual leave, sick leave, and disability pay. About half kept their health insurance. Few mothers had paid parental leave available to them.

SUMMARY AND CONCLUSIONS

Early policy debates about child care were couched in terms of an overall shortage of care: that there was simply not enough child care for all the children in need. This conclusion was fueled by trends in births and in maternal labor force participation. However, analysis of the number of centers and family day-care homes and their enrollments, and increases over the past 15 years, does not suggest any evidence of a shortage, per se. Children are being cared for, supply has increased, and prices have risen very little relative to the cost of living. The advantage of eliminating number of spaces, per se, as an issue is that we can move on to determining what the real issues are. I have presented what I think these are: The cost of care is still a problem for the poorest American families, on several measures the quality of care in centers has been declining, and providers are underpaid.

What does the future hold? Maternal employment has been stable for the past several years. We do not yet know whether maternal employment will continue to rise; it depends on the success of welfare reform and recovery from an economic recession. It also depends on future childbearing in the United States.

One legislative approach that is gaining momentum is to increase the personal exemption in the income tax system or replace it with a refundable child tax credit. The credit would benefit families whose incomes are so low that they do not have to pay taxes. Research shows that the value of the exemption has declined in real terms over time, such that if it were increased to what it was worth in 1948, its value would be about $8,000 per year (National Commission on Children, 1991). Although such an increased exemption or credit would not be directed specifically at child care, it would assist families raising children by increasing the amount of earnings that they would keep after paying taxes.

I feel that the biggest policy debate as we enter the 21st century will be parental leave after childbirth, because care for infants is most expensive to provide, potentially most harmful to children, and, therefore, presents the strongest price–quality tradeoff. A bill that would mandate unpaid, job-protected leave for employees in companies with 50 or more employees, the Family and Medical Leave Act, was passed by both houses of Congress in 1990 and vetoed by President Bush. It was resurrected again in 1991 and probably will continue to be until it passes in some form. No legislation will resolve the basic conflict between the needs of the child and the employment needs of the parent until it addresses the issue of parental leave.

ACKNOWLEDGMENTS

The detailed comments of Bill Prosser and Sharon McGroder on an earlier draft are much appreciated. Ann Mitchell also provided helpful comments. Funding for this research was provided by the Administration for Children, Youth and Families, and the Assistant Secretary for Planning and Evaluation, U.S. Department of Health and Human Services, and by the National

Association for the Education of Young Children. The Opinions expressed herein do not necessarily reflect the position and policy of the U.S. Department of Health and Human Services, the National Association for the Education of Young Children, or the Urban Institute, and no official endorsement should be inferred.

REFERENCES

Abt Associates, Inc. (1990). *Final report on survey methods: National Child Care Survey 1990*. Cambridge, MA: Author.

Belsky, J. (1986). Infant day care: A cause for concern? *Zero to Three, 6*(5), 1–9.

Clarke-Stewart, K. A. (1989). Infant day care: Maligned or malignant? *American Psychologist, 44*, 266–273.

Hayes, C. D., Palmer, J. L., & Zaslow, M. J. (Eds.) (1990). *Who cares for America's children? Child care policy for the 1990's*. Washington, D.C.: National Academy Press.

Hofferth, S. (1988). Child care in the United States. American families in tomorrow's economy, *Proceedings of a hearing before the Select Committee on Children, Youth, and Families* U.S. House of Representatives, (pp. 168–187). Washington, D.C.: U.S. Government Printing Office.

Hofferth, S., Brayfield, A., Deich, S., & Holcomb, P. (1991). *National Child Care Survey 1990*. Washington, DC: The Urban Institute.

Hofferth, S., & Phillips, D. (1987). Child care in the United States: 1970 to 1995. *Journal of Marriage and the Family, 49*, 559–571.

Hofferth, S., & Phillips, D. (1991). Child care policy research. *Journal of Social Issues 47*(2), 1–13.

Kisker, E., Hofferth, S., Phillips, D., & Farquhar, E. (1991). *A Profile of Child Care Settings: Early education and care in 1990*. Princeton, NJ: Mathematica Policy Research.

Low, S., & Spindler, P. (1968). *Child care arrangements of working mothers in the United States*. Washington, DC: U.S. Department of Health, Education and Welfare, Children's Bureau; and U.S. Department of Labor, Women's Bureau.

National Commission on Children (1991). *Beyond rhetoric: A new American agenda for children and families*. Washington, DC: Author.

Nelson, J. R. (1982). The federal interagency day care requirements. In C. Hayes (Ed.), *Making policies for children: A study of the federal process* (pp. 151–205). Washington, DC: National Academy Press.

Phillips, D., McCartney, K., Scarr, S., & Howes, C. (1987). Selective review of infant day care research: A cause for concern. *Zero to Three, 7*,(3), 18–21.

Phillips, D., & Zigler, E. (1987). The checkered history of federal child care regulation. In E. Rothkopf (Ed.), *The review of research in education* (Vol. 14, pp. xx–xx). Washington, DC: American Educational Research Association.

Presser, H. B., & Baldwin, W. (1980). Child care as a constraint on employment: Prevalence, correlates, and bearing on the work and fertility nexus. *American Journal of Sociology, 85*(5), 1202–1213.

Smith, R. (Ed.). (1979). *The subtle revolution: Women at work*. Washington, DC: The Urban Institute.

Sonenstein, F. L. (1991). The child care preferences of parents with young children: How little is known. In J. Hyde & M. Essex (Eds.), *Parental leave and child care: Setting a research and policy agenda.* (pp. 337–353). Philadelphia: Temple University Press.

Rodes, T. W. & Moore, J. C. (1975). *National Child Care Consumer Study.* Washington, DC: Unco.

U.S. Bureau of the Census. (1982). Trends in child care arrangements of working mothers: June 1982. *Current Population Reports,* Series P-117, No. 23. Washington, DC: U.S. Government Printing Office.

U.S. Bureau of the Census. (1983). Child care arrangements of working mothers: June 1982. *Current Population Reports,* Series P-23, No. 129. Washington, DC: U.S. Government Printing Office.

U.S. Bureau of the Census. (1987). Who's minding the kids? Child care arrangements: Winter, 1984–85. *Current Population Reports,* Series P-20, No. 9. Washington, DC: U.S. Government Printing Office.

U.S. Bureau of the Census. (1990a). Who's minding the kids? Child care arrangements: Winter 1986–87. *Current Population Reports,* Series P-70, No. 20. Washington, DC: U.S. Government Printing Office.

U.S. Bureau of the Census. (1991). School enrollment — Social and economic characteristics of students: October 1989. *Current Population Reports,* Series P-20, No. 452. Washington, DC: U.S. Government Printing Office.

U.S. Department of Labor. (1988). Labor force participation unchanged among mothers with young children. *News,* 88–431. Washington, DC: U.S. Bureau of Labor Statistics.

Willer, B., Hofferth, S., Kisker, E., Dinne-Hawlans, P., Farquhar, E., & F. Glantz (1991). *The Demand and Supply of Child Care in 1990.* Washington, DC: National Association for the Education of Young Children.

Young, D. R., & Nelson, R. R. (1973). *Public policy for day care of young children.* Lexington, MA: D.C. Heath.

Child-Care Supply and Demand: What Do We Really Know?

HARRIET B. PRESSER
University of Maryland

I am delighted to be included as a discussant at this important symposium on child care in the 1990s. Let me say at the outset that if it were not for the availability of child care in the 1960s, I would probably not be a professional sociologist and demographer and thus would not be making this contribution. In 1960 — over 30 years ago — I entered graduate school at the University of North Carolina in Chapel Hill, as a single mother with a 2-year-old daughter. The decision to do graduate study, and my selection of UNC, related directly to the availability of a child-care center on the campus — a rare, if not unique, service at that time. The center was set up primarily to assist married *male* students, whose employed wives were helping to put them through graduate school. In 1960 there were very few wives in graduate school who had children. I believe I was the only single mother using this service, and perhaps the only single mother in graduate school at UNC at the time.

Times have definitely changed! A substantial proportion of graduate students are now themselves mothers (although I have never seen precise statistics on this), and many universities now have child-care centers. Moreover, the employment of women with young children has increased dramatically, along with an increase in the supply of child-care places for these children. Research on child care is on the rise, along with growing federal interest in this issue. There is an on-going debate as to whether we need to subsidize child care and, if so, how. This debate is a healthy sign that we are paying more attention to the welfare of our country's children, but a principal concern of mine is that we are letting policy issues narrow rather than broaden our child-care research agenda. Moreover, we are overstating what is known from existing data in order to support certain policy positions.

I have every expectation that after Sandra Hofferth and her colleagues have an opportunity to analyze in depth the rich data base they have generated, our knowledge base will improve considerably. Their data, understandably, cannot address all the relevant child care issues, but they should make an important contribution. My comments relate to our current policy perspective and to the nature of the existing knowledge that supports it, including the preliminary data Hofferth includes in her presentation.

It is in this context that I address the issue of the relationship between supply and demand for child care, the theme of this session. Sandra Hofferth and others (e.g., Hayes, Palmer, & Zaslow, 1990) contend that supply seems to be in line with demand, and thus there is probably no "unmet need" for more providers. I take some comfort in this position, because as a sociologist, I have never liked framing the child-care debate in such strict economic terms, and I would like to dismiss the issue. But, as I elaborate in this commentary, we really do not have an adequate enough understanding of the child-care market to say with any confidence, one way or other, whether supply equals demand.

Sandra Hofferth also tells us that the conflict between price and quality is now the crux of the child care debate. She is probably right. This debate, however, is limited to the *formal* child care market, with minimal attention given to the extensive use of informal care. Moreover, even when focusing on the formal market, our knowledge about the relationship between quality and price is limited.

Our narrow perspective and lack of data result from the fact that we have so seriously neglected child-care research in the past. How do we go about broadening our perspective? This entails, first of all, that we expand the concept of child care to include all such care.

I like the definition of Karen Mason and Laura Duberstein (this volume): "In the most general usage, child care refers to a division of labor through which dependent children are reared" (p. 128). But how is child care operationalized in our studies? Typically, researchers define child care to be care by someone other than the mother, specifically during the time the mother is employed.[1] In this context, if a mother is caring for her own child while employed (say, as a child-care provider), this is typically regarded as a form of child care, but if she is not employed and caring for her own child, this is not child care. Sometimes surveys ask about child care when the mother is attending school, but care for this purpose is rarely singled out, and it is typically ignored in discussions about demand and supply.

---

[1]When the mother is absent in the household, the father or other person who may be the principal caregiver is then generally substituted.

The National Child Care Survey 1990 (NCCS; Hofferth, Brayfield, Deich, & Holcomb, 1991) that Hofferth reports on is distinctive in that it asked about regular child-care arrangements for both employed and nonemployed mothers. Indeed, Hofferth showed that among *nonemployed* mothers, the large majority of regular care of preschool-aged children by nonmothers is by "parents," presumably the father. Although Hofferth defines this as child care — and I would too — she does not discuss in her paper, nor does anyone else, how such father care fits into the supply–demand equation. This is clearly not of interest to policy makers. But the participation or *lack* of participation of fathers and other relatives in child care, broadly defined, is essential to our understanding of the child care problem. Indeed, I would argue, we cannot understand the supply and demand for formal care without this informal component. We need this broad conception of child care to answer what I regard as the essential first question: How are young children today being cared for?

The omission of informal care is most evident in studies of child-care providers (as distinct from recipients). The Profile of Child Care Settings Study (PCS; Kisker, Hofferth, Phillips, & Farquhar, 1991), which Hofferth uses to estimate supply, exemplifies this. Because of noncooperation, probably due mostly to legal concerns, it is virtually impossible to survey a representative sample of unregulated child-care providers; moreover, we do not do surveys to measure the potential availability of relatives for child care. The PCS includes only child-care centers and regulated family day-care providers, and it is not clear in Hofferth's paper how linking the NCCS data (which include informal care) to the PCS data provides a reliable estimate of total supply of child care. One possibility is to use screening data on the NCCS to estimate unregulated care, but it is questionable how reliable this would be. If we cannot get good estimates, we cannot assess supply in relation to demand, even with a focus on formal care.

The fuzzy conceptualization of child care in the existing literature, and our minimal treatment of nonformal arrangements, reflects the problem we have more generally in conceptualizing caregiving in a market context. This, I would argue, is because caregiving is traditionally an unpaid female activity. Giving care to children is generally regarded as child care when women have a "good" reason to make alternative caregiving arrangements for their preschool age children or their school-age children during non-school hours, the good reasons being, for example, employment, schooling, or improving the child's development; it is not regarded as child care if it is providing women with leisure time (even when having leisure time away from kids may be needed more than extra income).

It would seem essential that we broaden our conceptualization of child care *before* we estimate supply and demand and assess the workings of the child-care market. Responding to pressure for policy answers, before we know the right questions, puts us on shaky ground.

This is exemplified by the recent report of the National Academy of Science Panel on Child Care Policy (Hayes et al., 1990), of which I was a member, as were several people in this audience. A key policy question was whether there was an unmet need for child care that might require government subsidization to either expand supply (such as subsidizing more child-care centers) or ease demand (such as subsidizing parents, typically mothers, to stay home full time). In a perfect market, economists tell us, supply would be equal to demand, but the panel acknowledged that the child-care market seems far from perfect:

> [It] fails to meet several of the economic conditions that characterize an efficiently operating market: lack of information available to consumers (parents); high transaction costs associated with changing child care arrangements; and resistance to profit maximization by some providers (not raising prices as demand increases). In addition, there are the costs or benefits of a program that are not (or cannot be) reflected in the price paid by individual consumers, "externalities." For example, the benefit to society as a whole of better education for 4-year-olds is not accounted for in the price of a preschool enrichment program. . . .

> [The child care market] in fact consists of many segmented, localized markets with little coordination and enormous turnover among providers and changing needs among consumers. It is also a rapidly expanding market and one in which many parents have difficulty obtaining adequate information about how to locate and arrange services that will meet their needs. (Hayes et al., 1990, pp. 227, 228)

The panel attributed our rudimentary knowledge of the child-care market to the "underdeveloped nature of the relevant analytic base" (p. 228), but nevertheless proceeded to draw some highly qualified conclusions based on the little we know. This focused primarily on formal types of child care.

The imperfect market applies to the issue of quality, as well as supply and demand. The little we know about the relationship between quality and price is unsettling.

For example, the work of Linda Waite and her colleagues (Waite, Leibowitz, & Witsberger, 1988), using standard measures of quality such as size of group, number of children per adult, and education of provider, suggest that paying more for care does not generally lead to higher quality. This finding obtains even when considering only those children cared for in centers and nursery schools. Although this conclusion is based on only one data source (the 1985 wave of the National Longitudinal Survey of Youth), there is no competing evidence to date from any other national data source. Hopefully, the NCCS can provide us with some insights in this regard.

Waite et al. have suggested that this lack of a direct relationship between price and quality may be due to the way we measure quality, in structural terms, versus the way consumers view it, in terms of process and outcome. The process characteristics include a secure and loving environment, and outcomes include emotional and intellectual growth. We tend to think it is relatives who are strongest on process and perhaps outcome, but they are the cheapest form of child care. (By the way, when we say "cheap" we mean in terms of the cost to the parent, not to the relative.)

Hofferth's study asked respondents what the most important factor was in choosing the current child care arrangement. The responses are coded separately for *quality* and *prefer relative*. This is a questionable distinction. I would guess that parents are thinking of quality when they say they prefer relatives. As researchers, we know far too little about the quality of care by relatives, or, for that matter, care by parents.

Take, for example, a scenario that may be quite widespread, but never, to my knowledge, addressed in the literature: mothers — or fathers — being home with their children, but not providing any supervision. I am not talking about parents who are employed at home, but rather parents who are sleeping during the day because they are employed in the evening or night. Their children are a special type of latch-key children, who are not counted as such in our surveys. There may be thousands of them, and many may be very young. If we were bold enough to investigate this issue, we would undoubtedly have to modify existing assumptions about the quality of parental care and expand our conceptualization of unmet needs to include unsupervised children who are in need of care.

As I have shown elsewhere, about one third of dual-earner couples in the United States with children have a spouse who works a different shift; that is, one works days, the other evenings, nights, or a rotating shift (Presser, 1989a). We know from survey data that in most cases, when one spouse is home while the other is employed, the spouse is the principal caregiver of the child during this time, but we don't know how these parents, mothers and fathers, are caring for their children. Is this not an issue of quality of care? Why do we ignore the quality issue when it comes to parental care?

These questions apply as well to care provided by relatives. I have shown that one third of grandmothers who provide child care to their preschool-aged grandchildren whose mothers are employed are themselves otherwise employed; that is, the grandmothers work different shifts than the child's mother; moreover, this type of arrangement is more common for single than married mothers (Presser, 1989b). If the children are sleeping while the grandmother is sleeping, and the mother works nights in this way, then this child-care mode may be satisfactory, but how is the mother caring for the child when she gets home and has had no sleep? To what extent are these children actually alone or being cared for by somewhat older siblings? With this question in mind, I was particularly struck by Hofferth's finding, relating to the percentage of children in self-care; when children are aged 8 to 10 and mothers are *not* employed, 7.3% of the children are reported to be in self-care; when children are aged 11 to 12, it is 21.9%. The percentage would undoubtedly be higher if we explicitly included children caring for themselves while their "caregivers" are sleeping.

My point is that we cannot assume that relative care is tantamount to high quality care in all or even most cases. We need to break the taboo of studying the quality of caregiving by parents and relatives, and expand our conception of quality beyond such structural dimensions as staff/child ratios, education of provider, and so forth.

With regard to the education of providers, Hofferth notes that providers continue to be better educated than the population as a whole. This does not necessarily mean that most providers are better educated than the mothers of the children they are providing care for. Even if this *were* true, however, would this mean such children were getting better quality care from these providers? From Head Start, maybe, but what about family day care? What do we know about how the quality of care relates to the education of mothers?

Hofferth concludes her paper with a specification of what she regards as the "real" child-care issues, followed by an assessment of where the focus of the policy debate will be in the 1990s. We might disagree over the ranking of issues, but the ones she raises are certainly important: the (high) cost of care for poor families, the (declining) quality of care in centers, and the low pay of providers. She then says that . . . "the biggest policy debate as we enter the 21st century will be on parental leave after childbirth, because care for infants is the most expensive to provide, potentially most harmful to children, and, therefore, presents the strongest price–quality tradeoff" (p. 23). I agree with her that infant care is the most expensive for the parent — when provided in the formal market — but I don't know if we know very much, empirically, about the quality of infant care, both informal and formal. At least here, we seem to be developing a body of research in this area that hopefully will permit us to soon say — with empirical evidence — how the quality of infant care varies by provider, including mothers versus fathers, and the effect of infant care versus toddler care on child development. Only then can we meaningfully assess the impact of parental leave — including its timing and duration — on children.

There is also the important question of whether *unpaid* parental leave is what most women — or men — want. This relates to issues discussed in my other commentary (this volume) on parental well-being, but let me note here that my own research (Presser, 1989a) suggests that most employed women with infants would not make use of such leave if they had this option; they do not want a reduction in income. I would also question how unpaid parental leave would help to solve the important issues Hofferth notes of the high cost of care for poor families, the declining quality of care in centers, or the low pay of providers. If there are linkages, they need elaboration.

I conclude by repeating that our state of knowledge about the supply and demand for child care is minimal and of limited value, given our narrow definition of child care. We cannot adequately assess changes in the price of care over time, given the difference in the measures that are used in the various studies since 1975. As for quality, our measures in national surveys tend to be crude and simplistic. Before we can capture adequately the complex realities of the interactions between supply and demand, and between price and quality, we need to broaden our conception of caregiving to include both its informal and formal aspects, we must go beyond structural measures of quality, and we must be clear about the weight of evidence that supports our convictions.

REFERENCES

Hayes, C. D., Palmer, J. L., & Zaslow, M. J. (Eds.). (1990). Who cares for America's children? Child care policy for the 1990s. Washington, DC: National Academy Press.

Hofferth, S., Brayfield, A., Deich, S., & Holcomb, P. (1991). *National Child Care Survey 1990.* Washington, DC: The Urban Institute.

Kisker, E., Hofferth, S., Phillips, D., & Farquhar, E. (1991). A profile of child care settings: Early education and care in 1990. Princeton, NJ: Mathematica Policy Research.

Presser, H. B. (1989a). Can we make time for children? The economy, work schedules, and child care, *Demography, 26,* 523–543.

Presser, H. B. (1989b). Some economic complexities of child care provided by grandmothers. *Journal of Marriage and the Family, 51,* 581–591.

Waite, L. J., Leibowitz, A., & Witsberger, C. (1988, April). *What parents pay for: Quality of child care and child care costs.* Paper presented at the annual meeting of the Population Association of America.

A Cross-National Perspective on the Demand for and Supply of Early Childhood Services

PATRICIA P. OLMSTED
High/Scope Educational Research Foundation

As Dr. Hofferth noted in her chapter, there are two major components of the demand for early childhood services in the United States: (a) the employment of mothers with young children outside the home and (b) parents' desires to enhance the development of their young children by enrolling them in early childhood education programs. Also, the findings Dr. Hofferth reported regarding the supply of early childhood services in the United States provide information about two types of early childhood settings: care-oriented settings and educational settings.

To provide a broader perspective within which to view the current situation in the United States, I discuss here the demand for and supply of early childhood care and education services in 11 nations or territories around the world. In 4 of these—Belgium (French), Hong Kong, the People's Republic of China, and Finland—I briefly describe the relationship between the demand for services and maternal employment and parental desire for early childhood education programs, and present information about the supply of early childhood care and educational services.

During the past several years, the High/Scope Educational Research Foundation has been serving as the International Coordinating Center for the IEA Preprimary Project, an ongoing cross-national study of early childhood services in 14 countries (International Association for the Evaluation of Educational Achievement [IEA], 1991). Eleven countries participating in the study have gathered information about the demand for and supply of early childhood services through the examination of available public records (e.g., government statistics regarding the percent of economically active women) as well as through household surveys of nationally representative samples of parents.

The nations participating in the IEA Preprimary Project were most interested in information about the early childhood services available to children in the last year before their entry into the formal educational system. Consequently, as a group the countries selected a common age-range of 3 years 6 months to 4 years 6 months for children of families in the household survey. This common age-range allows for cross-national data comparisons.

At present, High/Scope Foundation staff are conducting the cross-national data analysis for the IEA Preprimary Project household survey. Consequently, specific cross-national findings are not yet available. However, I present here some general categorical findings about the use of early childhood services for 3½- to 4½-year-old children for the 11 nations participating in the household survey. Table 1 presents the proportion of 3½- to 4½-year-old children attending early childhood services in 11 countries in four general categories. In addition, Table 1 illustrates the percentage of children in this age-range enrolled in educational services.

In general, the more developed nations participating in the IEA Preprimary Project have higher proportions of 3½- to 4½-year-olds enrolled in early childhood services than do the less developed nations. Also, in the more developed nations, a higher proportion of 3½- to 4½-year-old children attend early childhood educational settings. Although the proportion of children in

TABLE 1

Percent of 3½- to 4½-year-old Children in at Least One Extraparental Early Childhood Setting in 11 Countries and the Proportion for Whom the Primary Setting is Educational

Percent in Extraparental Settings	Percent for Whom the Primary Setting is Educational			
	0–25	*26–50*	*51–75*	*76–100*
76–100		Germany (FRG)	Spain	Belgium (French) Hong Kong Italy
51–75	Finland United States		Portugal	
26–50	Nigeria Thailand	China (PRC)		
1–25				

Note. *Primary Setting* refers to the extraparental setting in which the child spends the greatest amount of time in a typical week.

educational settings cannot exceed the proportion of children enrolled in any type of setting, a nation may have a high percentage of children attending early childhood settings, but only a low percentage in educational settings. Finland illustrates this latter pattern: a large proportion of children enrolled in early childhood settings in general, but only a small proportion attending primarily educational programs.

We look now at the demand for and supply of early childhood services in four specific countries or territories: Belgium (French), Hong Kong, the People's Republic of China, and Finland. I have selected these nations because the characteristics of supply and demand in each one offer a different perspective from which to view the situation in the United States.

EARLY CHILDHOOD SERVICES: FOUR PERSPECTIVES ON SUPPLY AND DEMAND

Belgium (French)

In French Belgium, a free, government-sponsored early childhood education program called the *école maternelle* is currently available to all 3- and 4-year-old children. This educational preschool program is generally housed in the local school building. Originally, Belgian early childhood services were care-oriented, but over the years they became more and more focused on providing early education activities, predominantly preacademic ones, for young children (Delhaxhe, 1989).

In 1988, more than 95% of 3½- to 4½-year-old children living in French Belgium attended the *école maternelle*. *Écoles maternelles* are open 4 ½ days per week for 5½ hours on full days and 3½ hours on half days, for a total of 25½ hours per week, but not all children attend the preschool full-time (Delhaxhe & Hindryckx, 1990; Olmsted, Delhaxhe, & Shi, 1991).

In the recently conducted IEA Preprimary Project household survey, Belgian researchers found that more than two-thirds of the 3½- to 4½-year-old children in the families surveyed spent over 30 hours in extraparental settings during a typical week. Therefore, the *écoles maternelles* alone do not meet the total needs of families for early childhood services. The challenge for most parents was to find care for their children during the "transitional" hours before and after preschool. The parents in the Belgian survey had two basic solutions to this challenge. Children from nearly half of the families spent these transitional hours in the care of grandparents; another group of nearly equal size spent the transitional hours in a *garderie* (a care-oriented setting) located in the same school building as the *école maternelle* (Olmsted, Delhaxhe, & Shi, 1991).

Because Belgium provides free, government-sponsored early childhood educational services for 3- and 4-year-old children, there is a sufficient supply of services for children of this age. However, because these educational services are available only 25½ hours per week, most employed parents with children in this age-range need additional early childhood services during a typical week. To improve the match between supply and demand, Belgian parents have requested an expanded time-schedule for the *écoles maternelles* that will more closely fit the schedules of working mothers. Also, because some parents will likely need to continue to use the *garderie,* the parents have been requesting a more stimulating program of activities in this early childhood setting. In summary, even in a nation in which free, government-sponsored early childhood educational services are widely accessible to families with 3- and 4-year-old children, the issue of match between supply and demand continues to be a problem.

Hong Kong

Hong Kong has two major types of early childhood services: half-day early childhood education programs (kindergartens) and half-day and full-day care programs (child-care centers). In contrast to Belgium's services, Hong Kong's services are only partially supported by the government, and parents assume the primary role in providing the financial support for the operation of the programs. Nevertheless, in Hong Kong, as in Belgium, nearly all 3- and 4-year-old children are enrolled in one or the other of the two early childhood programs, with 90% to 95% of children of this age attending kindergartens and the remaining 5% to 10% attending child-care centers (Opper, 1989a). In discussing the parental preference for early childhood education over child-care, Opper (1989a) wrote the following:

> This high proportion reflects the value that the Chinese traditionally attach to education, but it also reflects the economic and educational situation. Although a university degree has distinct economic advantages in Hong Kong, university places are only available for 2 percent of the population. Consequently university entrance competition is very keen, and success in previous schooling becomes a crucial factor. Formal schooling is an important avenue to social and economic mobility, and preschool is perceived as the first step along this avenue. (p. 120)

In Hong Kong, there is a sufficient supply of early childhood settings, and virtually all 3- and 4-year-old children are enrolled in these programs, even though only 35% of the mothers of these children participate in the labor force (Opper, 1989b). Thus, it appears that mothers' participation in the labor force is not a primary factor in the demand for early childhood services. A far stronger factor in the demand for services in Hong Kong is the family's desire for the child to receive an early beginning to his or her education.

People's Republic of China

In the People's Republic of China, the major form of early childhood services is the kindergarten, which enrolls 3- to 6-year-old children. In 1985, there were sufficient kindergartens for 20% of preschool-aged children. Local communities sponsored (i.e., financially supported) 75% of these kindergartens, and organizations, such as factories, the army, and academic institutions, supported another 20%. Boards of education sponsored the remaining 5%, which were attached to the local school system. In addition to kindergartens, the other form of child care that Chinese parents frequently use is care by relatives, particularly grandparents (Shi, 1989).

The IEA Preprimary Project household survey recently conducted in China found that over 97% of mothers with preschool-aged children were employed for pay either inside or outside of the home. In urban areas, nearly 90% of these mothers worked outside the home, compared with 20% of mothers in rural areas. In the rural areas, both mothers and fathers often spend several hours each day tending crops in the fields (Shi & Xiang, 1990).

In a nation in which nearly all mothers of preschool-aged children are employed for pay, it is clear that there is a need for extraparental early childhood services. However, the household survey data indicated that for more than half of families with preschool-aged children, such services were not available. In 1989, fewer than one third of families with a preschool-aged child had access to a kindergarten. During the past few years, there has been an increase in the number of kindergartens sponsored by factories and institutions. Consequently, kindergartens are generally available in urban areas, and most families with preschool-aged children use them. But, in China, the great majority of families with preschool-aged children live in rural areas where early childhood services are scarce, and very few families have access to services. In fact, in rural areas, many parents reported going to work in the fields and leaving their 4-year-old children near their homes, without supervision, for several hours. This is a common practice considered safe in rural areas of China, where the hazards of traffic and other dangers of industrialized areas do not exist.

Because of the high percentage of gainfully employed mothers with preschool-aged children, there is a great need for early childhood services in China, especially in rural areas. It was reported that the Ministry of Education of the Chinese central government was surprised by the household survey's finding of a very small number of kindergartens in existence in rural areas. During the next several years, the central government plans to strongly encourage rural villages to open kindergartens for the children in their communities. This verbal encouragement will be accompanied by very little in terms of central government financial resources, however.

Finland

The recent IEA Preprimary Project household survey conducted in Finland revealed that families enrolled their 3½- to 4½-year-old children in three major types of extraparental early childhood settings. Nearly equal numbers of children in this age-range were enrolled in family day-care homes and in day-care centers. A smaller percentage of the children attended day clubs or music clubs, which are in operation 1 to 2 days per week for 2 to 4 hours each day to provide a variety of activities (e.g., in art, music, social skills) for the children. The national government and the municipalities subsidize the day-care centers and family day-care homes. Families using these services pay only a small portion of the actual cost of the services, as determined by an income-based sliding fee scale. Day clubs and music clubs are sponsored by the Lutheran Church and charge only minimal fees (Ojala, 1990).

At the present time, the supply of early childhood services in Finland is inadequate. However, in 1973, the country passed legislation that "requires each municipality to provide publicly organized or supervised day care to such an extent and in such forms as the need demands (Law 36/1973)" (Ojala, 1989, p. 93). Because the supply of services is currently inadequate, priority in enrollment is given to children whose parents are gainfully employed outside the home, are students, or are ill, and to children requiring special education services. Finland has set a goal of adding 7,000 new places per year in day-care settings. If the country reaches this goal consistently, the supply and demand for day-care places will be in balance by the mid-1990s at the latest (Ojala, 1989).

In addition to focusing on meeting the growing demand for early childhood services, Finland is restructuring its national policies to enable parents to provide more home care for their young children. These actions include giving serious consideration to increasing the length of parental leave and decreasing the length of the workday for parents with children under the age of 5 (Ojala, 1989).

In Finland, children begin compulsory schooling at age 7. Before entering formal schooling, many children are enrolled in day-care settings that provide a wide range of activities and experiences in various areas of growth: physical, emotional, intellectual, aesthetic, ethical, and religious (Ojala, 1989). Prior to the 1973 Day Care Law, these day-care settings were called *kindergartens*. Since 1973, the change in name reflects the fact that the primary purpose of these settings has been considered to be child care; furthermore, intellectual activities are only one of the many types of activities that the children engage in while attending these programs.

Over 70% of 3½- to 4½-year-old children in Finland attend an extraparental early childhood setting. At present, the supply of early childhood services is not adequate to meet the demand; however, as just noted, by the mid-1990s, the nation plans to have a sufficient supply of day care spaces. The focus of the early childhood services is child care rather than education, and intellectual activities are only one of many different types of activities provided in early childhood settings. For several years, Finland has worked to integrate its child-care policies with other national policies (e.g., labor, education, family). A current example of this is the government effort to increase the amount of time that parents can provide at-home care for their own children while still meeting the needs of employers.

DISCUSSION

Information from the nations participating in the IEA Preprimary Project illustrates the large variation in the supply and use of early childhood services among nations. Among the major factors influencing this variation are the level of economic development in a country and the nature of involvement of the national government in the provision of early childhood services.

In general, the IEA Preprimary Project data indicate that there is a positive relationship between the level of economic development of a nation and the proportion of 3½- to 4½-year-old children who are enrolled in early childhood services. That is, the more developed nations have higher proportions of children in this age-range participating in extraparental early childhood settings than do the less developed nations. Among the countries participating in the IEA Preprimary Project, the proportion of children in this age-range attending extraparental settings ranged from approximately 30% to nearly 100%. However, some developing nations that were invited to participate in the study declined because their resource-poor governments were already overburdened by efforts to meet the basic needs of young children (i.e., health, nutrition). In these nations, the provision of early childhood services was not a subject of major concern. Consequently, the actual range of the proportion of preschool-aged children attending extraparental services is probably even larger than 30% to 100%.

The information presented also suggests that, in countries in which the national government is involved in service provision, there is a higher proportion of children attending extraparental early childhood services. For example, in Belgium, nearly every 3½- to 4½-year-old child attends the government-sponsored early childhood education program. However, there are different forms of government involvement at the national level that also seem to promote high rates of enrollment of preschool-aged children in early childhood services. For example, in Hong Kong, even though the parents provide the major financial support for the operation of early childhood services, the territorial government does supervise the operation of these services and regulates such program characteristics as curriculum and staff training. With this particular government–family division of responsibility for support and regulation of early childhood services, nearly every preschool-aged child in Hong Kong is enrolled in a program.

Finally, among the nations or territories with a high proportion of children attending extraparental early childhood services, there are some that view early childhood services as a single coordinated service system and others that have a dual system: child-care services and educational services. The United States would be an example of the latter group with regard to 3- and 4-year-old children. In part, a national emphasis on providing one type of service versus two types of service seems to be related to what purpose(s) parents, policymakers, and government officials see for these services and whether or not the views of the various groups are consistent. For example, in Belgium, there is general agreement among all groups that the primary purpose of the services is educational, whereas in Finland, there is general agreement that the primary purpose of the services is the provision of child care. Those countries like Belgium and Finland, in which the involved parties have reached a consensus about the general purpose and characteristics of early childhood services and in which there is at least a moderate level of involvement of the national government, have been able to centralize the administration of early childhood services in a single ministry and develop a coordinated set of guidelines for staff training, children's activities, and so forth.

A cross-national perspective on the demand for and supply of early childhood services can provide a broader context from which to view the current situation in the United States. Each nation participating in the IEA Preprimary Project portrays a unique relationship between demand characteristics, such as the rate of participation in the labor force for mothers with young children and families' desire for early education services, and supply characteristics, such as the support of the national government for the services and for the primary purpose of these services. These data, which illustrate the diversity of the supply–demand situation in various nations, may suggest alternative approaches for adjusting the supply–demand balance of early childhood services in the United States during the 1990s.

REFERENCES

Delhaxhe, A. (1989). Early childhood care and education in Belgium. In P. P. Olmsted & D. P. Weikart (Eds.), *How nations serve young children: Profiles of child care and education in 14 countries* (pp. 13–37). Ypsilanti, MI: High/Scope Press.

Delhaxhe, A., & Hindryckx, G. (1990). *IEA Preprimary Project: Phase 1. Results of the*

Belgian National Study. Unpublished report from the Belgian IEA Preprimary Project National Research Center, University of Liège, Belgium.

International Association for the Evaluation of Educational Achievement (IEA). (1991). IEA Preprimary Project. In W. Loxley (Ed.), *IEA: Activities, institutions, and people* (pp. 57–60). The Hague, the Netherlands: Author. (Available from IEA Preprimary Project International Coordinating Center, High/Scope Educational Research Foundation, 600 North River St., Ypsilanti, MI 48198)

Ojala, M. (1989). Early childhood training, care, and education in Finland. In P. P. Olmsted & D. P. Weikart (Eds.), *How nations serve young children: Profiles of child care and education in 14 countries* (pp. 87–118). Ypsilanti, MI: High/Scope Press.

Ojala, M. (1990). *IEA Preprimary Project: Phase 1. Results of the Finnish National Study.* Unpublished report from the Finnish IEA Preprimary Project National Research Center. Joensuu, Finland: University of Joensuu.

Olmsted, P. P., Delhaxhe, A., & Shi, H. Z. (1991, April). *Use of early childhood care and education services in Belgium and the People's Republic of China.* Paper presented at the annual meeting of the Society for Research in Child Development, Seattle, WA.

Opper, S. (1989a). Child care and early education in Hong Kong. In P. P. Olmsted & D. P. Weikart (Eds.), *How nations serve young children: Profiles of child care and education in 14 countries* (pp. 119–142). Ypsilanti, MI: High/Scope Press.

Opper, S. (1989b). *IEA Preprimary Project: Phase 1. Results of the Hong Kong Territorial Study.* Unpublished report from the Hong Kong IEA Preprimary Project Territorial Research Center. Hong Kong: University of Hong Kong.

Shi, H. Z. (1989). Young children's care and education in the People's Republic of China. In P. P. Olmsted & D. P. Weikart (Eds.), *How nations serve young children: Profiles of child care and education in 14 countries* (pp. 119–142). Ypsilanti, MI: High/Scope Press.

Shi, H. Z., & Xiang, Z. P. (1990). *IEA Preprimary Project: Phase 1. Results of the Chinese National Study.* Unpublished report from the Chinese IEA Preprimary Project National Research Center. Beijing: Central Institute of Educational Research.

The Supply of and Demand for Child Care: Measurement and Analytic Issues

WILLIAM R. PROSSER
SHARON M. McGRODER
U.S. Department of Health and Human Services

T he opening chapter by Sandra L. Hofferth is a descriptive piece building on information obtained from two recent studies of child care: The National Child Care Survey (Eisker, Hofferth, Phillips, & Farguhar, 1990; Hofferth, Brayfield, Deich, & Holcomb, 1991) and the Profiles of Child Care Setting Study (1990; Kisker, Hofferth, & Phillips, 1991). These data are the most recent nationally representative child-care data available.

We comment here on this chapter and focus our attention on its (federal) policy implications. We critique several of Hofferth's propositions and the evidence she uses to support them, comment on her discussion about potential policy issues, and mention what we believe might be significant policy concerns. We briefly discuss the following topics:

- Unmet need.
- Price faced by low-income parents.
- Quality of care.
- Demand for child care.
- "Latent" demand for child care.
- Parental leave.

For each of these major issues we consider: What are her hypotheses/ conclusions? What evidence has she marshaled to validate them? Do the data reported support her conclusions? If not, what would support them or what should she have done to present a more valid case? Do we agree with her criticisms of commonly used rhetoric? We conclude with what we believe are the major policy implications of the data presented, other major issues in the 1990s, and what data might inform the debate about them.

DISCUSSION

Unmet Need

The first major topic to explore is the issue of unmet need. Is there a discrepancy between demand for and supply of child care? Hofferth's answer is no, probably not. There is no shortage of child care, with the possible exception of infant child care in some localities.

We applaud her for helping to put to rest one of the often used arguments; it goes something like this: The number of licensed slots is substantially less than the number of young children with working parents; therefore, there are not enough child care slots. She points out that this logic is spurious; for example, parents and relatives, none of whom we would expect to be licensed, provide a substantial share of child care.

To the list of specious unmet needs arguments we would add the one that says center waiting lists show that there are not enough child-care center spaces. Walker (1990) uses a persuasive analogy: Colleges and universities use waiting lists to select a preferred mix of students and minimize excess vacancy problems, prospective students apply to a number of schools to assure entrance into at least one, and few people would argue that we need more college and university slots.

To support her conclusions that there is no supply problem, Hofferth uses the following reasoning and pieces of evidence:

First, center space supply has grown as fast or faster than the pool of preschool children of working mothers. Hofferth makes, for her, an unusual slip in framing the issue in terms of *child care* need and then discussing *center* spaces keeping up with preschool children of working women. It is important to consider all ages of children generally in care and all kinds of care: Center care accounts for less than a quarter of preschool children and less than one tenth of school-age children. (See Fig. 1.3, 1.6 of her paper.) Furthermore, one must consider latent demand: whether some serious potential labor-force entrants are prevented from entering the labor market because of lack of child-care supply. As we discuss further on, trying to estimate this latent demand accurately is difficult because it is virtually impossible to distinguish serious potential workers from people responding to questionnaires with what they think are socially acceptable answers to the interview questions. One solution is to look at whether the prevalence of latent demand responses has changed over the comparison time period in ways that are consistent with her conclusions.

Second, there does not seem to be a large number of young latchkey children. The validity of this assertion is difficult to assess. The data come from responses to questionnaires, and respondents are unlikely to admit leaving preschool children unattended. Again, comparing responses over time would help buttress her conclusion, if one believes that the propensity to tell the truth has remained more or less constant over time.

Finally, the hourly price of center care and family day-care has not increased dramatically since the mid-1970s. Center care cost about $1.40 per hour (constant 1990 dollars) in 1975 and about $1.65 in 1990. Family day care cost about $1.30 to $1.35 (constant 1990 dollars) over the same time period. To validly make this price comparison, one must compare identical units of child care. This would mean holding constant over time the following sorts of variables: the quality of care, the age of child in care, government subsidies, and other such factors that could affect the cost of providing care or parents' demand for it.

As Hofferth points out further on in her chapter, we know that several aspects of both center and family day care have changed. Group sizes and child–staff ratios have increased, which would generally lower current quality and costs; the education and training of the caregivers has increased, which would raise present wage rates somewhat and probably be passed onto child-care consumers. The net quality adjusted price for these two factors, we believe, would be higher in 1990 than in 1975.[1]

Since 1975, the average age composition of child-care centers has changed to include more infants, toddlers, and school-age children and have fewer 3- to 5-year-olds. The net effect of these age distribution changes may be to cancel out age change effects on prices.

When one considers prices for child care, whether obtaining the information from the consumer or the supplier, one must be aware of the extent to which government subsidies alter the true charges for that care in the absence of such subsidies. It is our belief that consumers report their before-tax out-of-pocket expenses, not the full cost of care nor their real net cost. Therefore, supply-side subsidies paid by the government directly to providers

---

[1]The increase in average center child to staff ratios of 6.8:1 (1976–1977) to 8.6:1 (1990) would decrease costs approximately 15%. The increase in ratio would decrease classroom staff costs approximately 25% to 30%; classroom labor costs are typically about 50% of total per child costs, which should be equate to unit hourly costs. The countervailing increase in education of classroom staff from an average of 13.5 years of education (1976–1977) to almost 15 years (1990) would increase per child costs only about 2% or 3%. Therefore, the net of the two changes would be to make comparable quality-adjusted prices higher in 1990 than in 1976–1977. The data for these comparisons come from Kisker et al. (1991).

would not be included in parents' reported expenditures because providers generally reduce their charges to parents by that amount. On the other hand, consumers report their out-of-pocket expenses and do not deduct the savings accrued if they take the child care tax credit, which they are entitled to claim when they calculate their taxes (see Table 1).[2] We have tried to piece together the total child-care market, including consumer expenditures and government subsidies. The child-care market was about $23.5 billion in 1990; approximately three times what it was in 1975 and about one third more in inflation-adjusted, constant 1990 dollars. Subsidies have also increased dramatically in the last few years. However, it is not clear to us at this time what these market expenditure changes mean for the validity of the unit price comparisons.

In our opinion the net result of all these factors, however, is to make price comparisons over time much more complex than Hofferth's analysis implies. Consequently, we call into question her conclusion about supply until further work is completed (see also Connelly, 1990).

On a more technical point, Hofferth presents neither rationale nor statistical significance tests to support her contention that these prices increased only very moderately. (We would need to know the standard errors for these estimates, and they are not presented.)

Price Faced by Low-Income Parents

Hofferth's next major conclusion is that the price paid by low-income parents is still too high. As evidence of her conclusion she shows that low-income families pay 22% to 25% of their budgets for child care, when they pay, and alleges that this budget share is comparable to (average?) expenditures on housing.

What is "too high"? We know of no value-free, scientific method for validating this conclusion. The fact that low-income families pay a larger share of their family budget on child care indicates that child care is what

---

[2]Because of this, when computing the entire child care market, one adds column 1 — not column 3 — to column 4. Note that the demand-side (tax) subsidies only include estimates of federal revenues lost from federal income taxes and not the additional revenues lost to states from child-care deductions and credits allowed by state income tax laws. Michalopoulos, Robins, and Garfinkel (1991) estimated a government tax subsidy rate of about 21% — 18% federal and 3% state. Therefore, consumers might be expected to overstate their net cost by about 21%.

On the other hand, consumer responses understate the full cost of care to the degree that providers, typically centers, receive program subsidies directly from the government, which do not pass through the consumer. Michalopoulos et al.'s calculations do not include program subsidies. Several scholars have put together estimates of total federal program subsidy time-series data (e.g., Besharov & Tramontozzi, 1990; Robins, 1990).

TABLE 1
The Child-Care Market: Total Expenditures (1965–1995) (Current $ in Billions)

Year	(1) Supply-Side	(2) Demand-Side (Tax)	(3) Total (1 + 2)	Consumer Expenditures (4)	Total Child-Care Market (1 + 4) / (5) (1 + 4)	(6) Subsidy Rate (3/5)
1965	$0.2	$0.03	$ 0.2[a]	$ 1.0[b]	$ 1.2	0.1
1972	0.6	0.2	0.8[c]			
1975	1.5	0.5	2.0[d]	6.1[c]	7.6	0.26
1980	1.7	1.0	2.7[d]	7.0[f]	8.7	0.31
1985	2.0	2.6	4.6[d]	14.0[g]	16.0	0.29
1988	2.6	3.9	6.5[d]	15.0[h]	17.6	0.37
1990	3.0	4.0	7.0[i]	20.5[j]	23.5	0.30
1995	6.8	4.9	11.7[i]			

Note. These estimates are very rough. They were derived from a number of sources. Details provide on request.

[a]Sources unknown: various old budget documents
[b]Low & Spindler (1968)
[c]Committee on Ways and Means, U.S. House of Representatives (1977)
[d]Robins (1990)
[e]Rodes & Moore (1975)
[f]Consumer Expenditure Survey (source unknown)
[g]U.S. Bureau of the Census (1987)
[h]Urban Institute, TRIM, personal correspondence (Roberta Barnes)
[i]The House Wednesday Group (1991)
[j]Hofferth et al., (1991)

economists call a necessity, rather than a luxury, not that it is too high. Food, housing, and (maybe surprisingly to some) alcohol and tobacco are examples of necessities, jewelry, entertainment, and dry goods are examples of luxuries, as measured by income elasticities. That is, higher income families spend a higher share of their expenditures on luxury items than do lower income families (Data Resources/McGraw-Hill, 1989; Prosser, 1972).

Furthermore, our analyses indicate that a lower percentage of employed parents are paying for child care in 1990 than in 1975. Hofferth reports that about 50% of employed mothers whose youngest child was under 5 in 1990 paid for child care, and about 15% of mothers not in the labor force who used child care for their young children paid for it. These percentages are down from the 1975 consumer study, when about 66% of employed mothers and 20% of mothers not in the labor force paid for child care (Rodes & Moore, 1975).

This would be consistent with the figures in Table 1 that indicate that the

TABLE 2
The Child-Care Market (Constant 1990 Dollars)

Year	(1) Govt. Subsidy ($billion)	(2) Consumer Expend. ($Billion)	(3) Total Child-Care Market ($Billion)	(4) Median House-hold Income	(5) Annual Average Child-Care Expenditure	(6) Average Budget Share (5/4)
1965	0.8	4.6	5.4	26,139	$2,110[a]	0.081
1975	4.9	14.8	18.5	28,662	2,521[b]	0.087
1980	4.3	11.0	13.8	28,088		
1985	5.7	17.3	19.8	29,186	2,584[c]	0.098
1990	7.0	20.5	23.5	28,586	2,534[d]	0.089

Note. Columns (1), (2), and (3) come from Table 1, and are adjusted to 1990 constant dollars. Colum (4) is from the 1990 Statistical Abstract of the U.S.

[a]Low & Spindler (1968)
[b]Rodes & Moore, Inc. (1975)
[c]U.S. Bureau of the Census (1987)
[d]Hofferth et al. (1991)

overall government subsidy rate (column 6) has increased over this time period.

Data indicate that fewer parents pay for care in 1990 than in 1975. This trend could be the result of sources other than parents subsidizing parents' child care. Moreover, if subsidies have increased over the years, then one could hypothesize that the kinds of care more often subsidized — and thus, cheaper to parents — would increase in prevalence. Since center care has traditionally and increasingly been subsidized by both government and perhaps by providers themselves,[3] one would expect an increase in the use of center care compared to the use of relative care. In fact, we do see an increase in the use of center care and a decline in the use of relative care, another form of care where parents often receive subsidies (free care) from their families. This lends evidence to the hypothesis that subsidies have indeed increased since 1975.

Table 2 shows constant-dollar child-care budget shares for median income families since 1965. We confirm Hofferth's statement that the average budget share spent on child care has remained pretty constant since the mid-1960s.

---

[3]Anecdotal evidence suggests that the production costs associated with center-based care have increased over the years, yet, providers are hesitant to increase charges to parents because they believe parents either are unwilling or unable to pay more for child care. To the extent providers fail to increase charges as their costs increase, then parents are effectively receiving a subsidy from the provider. The field could benefit from more systematic research in this area.

Quality of Care

Hofferth cites the increased education and training of both center and *regulated* family day-care providers and concludes that this implies that the quality of child care has improved.[4] She further explains, however, that because group sizes in center care have also increased and now hover at the upper range of "acceptable," center-care quality has actually declined. Nevertheless, she concludes with the observation that "we don't know the extent to which increased education and training offset the burden of caring for more children." Consequently, we are confused as to why she concludes in her summary that the quality of center-based care has declined.

Moreover, she cites that in regulated family day care, group sizes have also increased (but still remain "small"), but so has the number of helpers, implying that staff–child ratios have remained constant. Thus, with the increased education of providers, she concludes that the quality of family day care has improved. Her analyses indicate the complicated nature of assessing child-care quality, especially when only relying on a few structural or provider characteristics. Future research in this area will need to come up with ways of exploring what different "packages" of quality input indicators mean for overall quality. This is especially important when indicators seem to be moving in opposite, and possibly offsetting, directions.[5] Thus, researchers should guard against drawing conclusions on overall quality by relying on only one measure of quality.

Demand for Child Care

After exploring the quality of child care available, Hofferth asks whether parents select programs using quality input indicators, and what characteristics of care parents consider when choosing an arrangement. She begins her analysis by citing the finding that, among parents currently using nonparental care, 37% indicated *quality,* and another 30% indicated they *prefer a relative,* as the most important reason why they selected this care. She concludes that quality is the major factor parents consider when choosing child care.

Besides not addressing the potential response bias in citing quality as the major factor for having selected the current arrangement, she did not report on other characteristics that parents consider when choosing an arrangement. Blau (1990) suggested that economists have a broader view of quality than

---

[4]Discussion of quality in unregulated family day care is conspicuously missing from her discussion.

[5]We hypothesize that the child-care market may operate in such a way as to encourage providers to make explicit trade-offs among the quality input indicators, such as child-to-staff ratios, staff qualifications, and wage rates, in order to keep prices relatively stable for parents' sake.

child development experts. The latter look at the immediate environment of the child and consider child development outcomes based on quality factors, much like those we have already discussed. Economists would broaden the concept of quality to include other aspects, such as location and hours of operation. Parents do not select child care based solely on the quality of the services from their child's point of view, but they also make decisions based on these convenience factors. Indeed, the arrangement's location, availability, and hours (measures of the convenience of the available care) were cited by 20% of the respondents in the National Child Care Survey as the major reasons for having chosen the current arrangement, and another 9% indicated cost as the major reason.

Understanding the array of reasons for having selected a particular arrangement suggests what barriers may inhibit parents from obtaining a desired arrangement. Is it that quality care cannot be found, or is it available but unaffordable? Is it that finding *any* care for the number and schedule of hours needed is a problem? Although Hofferth is accurate in citing quality as the predominant reason reported for having selected the current arrangement, we cannot necessarily conclude that quality is the most important factor that parents consider when choosing child care. These data do not provide insight into the process by which parents make tradeoffs among cost, quality, and convenience considerations. Do parents maximize quality given cost and convenience limitations, or do they select the least costly among convenient and high-quality options? Future research on how child care is selected — and thus, to what extent barriers limit parents' options — will need to explore how the combination of quality and convenience factors drive parents' ultimate choice of arrangements.

Policy-makers care about parental preferences for child care because they are interested in enabling families to maintain self-sufficiency, which often depends on parents' abilities to find reliable, affordable, quality, nonparental child care. Policy-makers presume to know parental preferences for child care, because they propose policies aimed at ameliorating the barriers constraining low-income parents' choices. However, policy-makers often rely on anecdotal information or cite inadequate data (if they cite data at all) to support their assertions. We believe Hofferth, similarly, had difficulty supporting her conclusions on preferences and barriers when discussing parental preferences for child care throughout her chapter.

For example, at one point she asserts that many parents prefer to place their young children in family day care. She appears to substantiate this finding by citing that family day-care homes are more likely than center-based programs to accept infants and toddlers. Thus, she apparently believes that the availability of family day care for infants enables parents of young children to obtain their preference of family day care. Unfortunately, she does not cite any data that may more validly support this conclusion.

Next, she suggests that some parents want center-based programs for their very young children, but they may not be able to find programs to take them. To support this conclusion, she explains that only slightly more than half of center-based programs accept children who are not toilet-trained. She then concludes that there is shortage of spaces for infants in center-based programs. There are many sources of confusion over these statements. First, concluding that some parents want center care but can't find it suggests that parents prefer center care for their infants and toddlers, but availability is the constraint. This clearly contradicts the previous statement that parents prefer family day care for their young children. Finally, to conclude that there is a lack of infant care in centers, one should not look at the percentage of vacancies available for infants, the measure used by Hofferth, but should compare the total number of slots demanded with the number supplied: For how many infants is center care preferred and how many infant care slots are there? Without presenting any of these data or analyses, it seems inaccurate to conclude that the supply of infant care in centers is a problem.

Because she does not pose a model or present hypotheses on how parents make decisions about child care — what they prefer and what constraints they face — it is hard to draw conclusions regarding the extent to which parents are constrained in their search for child care. Without such models, researchers cannot inform policy-makers of the kinds of barriers preventing parents from obtaining a desired option.

We acknowledge the difficulty inherent in trying to ascertain parental preferences for child care (see methodologies in Brush, 1987; Kisker, Maynard, Gordon, & Strain, 1989; Mott & Baker, 1989; Sonenstein, 1989; and McGroder, 1991, for a review). And, once preference information is obtained, it is often unclear what it means.[6] An alternative to focusing on attitudinal information ("Assuming you could have any type of care arrangements you wanted, what would you prefer?") as an indication of whether

---

[6]The child care search and selection process is a dynamic one, consisting of identifying a "preferred" type of care, searching for it, encountering one or more barriers (price, availability, accessibility, etc.), and modifying preferences to accommodate what is available. Surveys that attempt to identify preferences are prone to capturing some degree of constraints in measures of preference, as parents pre-screen their responses to reflect what options are actually feasible. Consequently, researchers may never completely understand what parental preferences are by asking preference-type questions.

Similarly, it is invalid to conclude that parents are using a preferred option if they report that they are satisfied with their current arrangement. All this measures is how relatively happy they are given their current constraints and the anticipated likelihood of success in finding a better arrangement if they were to invest the time and energy to look. Satisfaction data do not provide any insight into the tradeoffs parents make in selecting their current arrangement and, therefore, do not indicate whether or how parents are constrained from obtaining a better option.

barriers exist, is asking behavioral questions about the child-care search and selection process. The National Child Care Survey 1990 (Hofferth et al., 1991) is unique in that it did just that: It asked what type of child care was first considered and why it was not selected. Moreover, it asked why the last arrangement ended, which indicates whether it was parent-initiated (e.g., to find more age-appropriate care) or provider-initiated (e.g., the provider stopped providing care). Presentation of some of these data would have strengthened Hofferth's argument on the extent to which parents are constrained from obtaining and maintaining a desired type of care.[7]

"Latent" Demand

Reviewing child-care utilization patterns among those currently using child care, the method employed by Hofferth, is one way to predict the future demand for child care. Still, there is likely to be latent demand for child care, which includes those not currently using early childhood education programs who may in the future. From a policy perspective, this is of particular interest when studying currently non-employed lower-income mothers for whom child care may be a necessary support service to securing and maintaining employment. Kisker, et al. (1989) showed that 19% of mothers of preschool children said they would seek employment if acceptable, affordable child care were available. (This is consistent with Ditmore & Prosser, 1973, who estimated a latent demand of 10% to 15%.) Unfortunately, Hofferth does not discuss the preferences among mothers not currently using child care nor explore how many mothers said they would work if child care were available.

Hofferth *does* suggest that lower-middle-income families with a non-employed mother are the least likely to use (center-based) care and may be the group most likely to increase their use over time if subsidies were available. It is unclear whether she is addressing this latent demand issue — suggesting that subsidies for center care would enable these women to secure employment — or whether she generally believes that increasing the use of center care is, in and of itself, a desired outcome, and that subsidies are the way to do it.

CONCLUSION

We find Hofferth's paper a useful descriptive summary of data on child care as we know it in 1990, although we do have some concerns and suggestions for the analytical portions of her presentation.

---

[7]Hofferth, Brayfield, Deich, & Holcomb (1991) also obtained information on the extent to which problems with child care led to changes in employment (lost time from work, reduction in the number of hours, quit or lost job). Future studies of parental preferences and of hypothesized barriers should explore responses to these questions to ascertain the likely success of alternative policy options in ameliorating these child-care barriers to employment.

When she looks to the future of child care during this decade, Hofferth prophesies that parental leave will be the major issue because non-parental care for infants is most expensive to provide and is potentially harmful to children, presenting the strongest price/quality tradeoff.[8]

Regardless of the driving force (parental preference for maternal care or the price of infant care), we agree that the parental leave debate *is* likely to continue. What is interesting to us, and what Hofferth implies by discussing parental leave as a child-care issue, is how the discussion of child-care issues has broadened since the early 1980s. Both the (liberal) advocates of parental leave and the (conservative) opponents to categorical child-care legislation have used the argument that the child-care debate should include the option of facilitating parents who want to stay home with their children. In our opinion, the conservative, "pro-family" advocates were the first to link child care to an equity consideration: Why should parents who make sacrifices so that one member of the couple (primarily two-parent middle-class families) can stay home and care for their children pay taxes to subsidize child care for families who choose not to stay home? These pro-family advocates argued for tax credits and child allowances for either one- or two-parent working couples rather than child-care subsidies like those proposed in the Act for Better Child Care (ABC) bill. On the other hand, some of these same people opposed parental leave bills that give parents of newborns some extended leave to stay home to take care of their infants. Their opposition, however, was based on commercial considerations related to small business complaints that such provisions would be expensive to them and cost jobs.

We recognize that, in the end, parental leave is only viable for middle- and upper-income, dual-earner parents who can afford the time off and can live on one paycheck. Although we do not foresee the Bush Administration supporting mandated parental leave any time soon, we do believe that there is a role for various groups, such as government, employer associations, and labor organizations, to encourage and explore policies that help employees balance their work and family responsibilities, including allowing shift work, job-sharing, flex-time, part-time employment, and work-at-home options, and offering parental leave and assistance in finding and paying for child care.

So what *are* likely to be the major debates regarding child care and

---

[8]This assertion implicitly assumes that nonparental infant care is truly the preferred alternative to maternal care, but because it is so expensive (the constraint), mothers will choose the less costly and higher quality option of staying home. There are two unsubstantiated premises incorporated in this conclusion: (a) it assumes that mothers prefer (non-parental) infant care, and (b) it assumes that staying at home is less "costly" than expensive infant care, which disregards the opportunity cost of forgone earnings for the mother.

child-rearing options in the future? We believe that, from the federal government's perspective, the biggest on-going policy issue will be that of facilitating employment among low-income families and providing the necessary support services — including child care — to see that this happens.

We also believe that the Family Support Act constituted potential landmark legislation vis-à-vis child care for low-income families in that, for the first time, child care is provided as an entitlement for those who are in job training programs and for those who earn their way off Aid to Families with Dependent Children. This new child-care legislation also provides funding for child care for low-income employed parents and expands the Earned Income Tax Credit to enable working parents to keep more of their earned income. Implementing these new programs and seeing that they do, indeed, increase options available to low-income working parents will be a major focus of federal administrators over the next few years.

Finally, there is likely to be continued interest in broader family support policies. The Bush Administration has delineated four principles to guide its child-care policy, but these principles can apply equally to broader family policy:

1. Parents should be the ultimate decision-makers concerning their children.
2. Federal policy should not discriminate against parents who choose to stay at home and care for their children.
3. Federal policy should act to increase the range of child-care choices available to parents.
4. Federal assistance should be targeted to those most in need.

We believe that these are sound principles by which to guide subsequent federal family policy.

ACKNOWLEDGMENT

The authors work for the Assistant Secretary for Planning and Evaluation, U.S. Department of Health and Human Services. The opinions stated herein do not necessarily represent the official policy or position of the Department, or the Administration.

REFERENCES

Besharov, D. J., & Tramontozzi, P. N. (1990). *The costs of federal child care assistance* (Occasional Paper). Washington, DC: American Enterprise Institute, Studies of Social Welfare Policy.

Blau, D. M. (1990). *The quality of child care: An economic perspective*. Chapel Hill: The University of North Carolina at Chapel Hill.

Brush, L. (1987). Usage of different kinds of child care: An analysis of the SIPP data base. Report prepared for the Assistant Secretary for Planning and Evaluation, US Dept. Health & Human Services, Washington, D.C.

Committee on Ways and Means, U. S. House of Representatives. (1977). *Overview of entitlement programs: 1990 Green Book* (June 5, 1990). Washington, DC: U. S. Government Printing Office.

Connelly, R. (1990). The effect of child care costs on the labor force participation and AFDC recipiency of single mothers (Discussion Paper No. 920–90). University of Wisconsin, Institute for Research on Poverty. Madison, WI.

Data Resources/McGraw-Hill (1989). Differences in overall spending patterns and spending on child care by family type: An exploratory study using the consumer expenditure survey (Report prepared for the Assistant Secretary for Planning and Evaluation, U. S. Dept. of Health and Human Services) Washington, D. C.

Ditmore, J., & Prosser, W. R. (1973). A study of day care's effect on the labor force participation of low-income mothers (Working Paper). Washington, DC: Office of Planning, Research, and Evaluation, Office of Economic Opportunity.

Eisker, E. E., Hofferth, S. L., Phillips, D. A., & Farguhar, E. (1991). *Profiles of child care setting study: Early education and care in 1990*. Washington, DC. U.S. Government Printing Office.

Hofferth, S., Brayfield, A., Deich, S., & Holcomb, P. (1991). *National Child Care Survey 1990*. Washington, DC: The Urban Institute.

The House Wednesday Group. (1991). *Moving ahead: Initiatives for expanding opportunity in America*. Washington, DC: Congress of the United States.

Kisker, E., Hofferth, S., & Phillips, D. (1991). *A profile of child care settings: Early education and care in 1990*. Princeton, NJ: Mathematica Policy Research.

Kisker, E., Maynard, R., Gordon, A., & Strain, M. (1989). The child care challenge: What parents want and what is available in three metropolitan areas. Princeton, NJ: Mathematica Policy Research.

Low, S., & Spindler, P. (1968). Child care arrangements of working mothers in the United States. Washington, DC: U.S. Department of Health, Education, and Welfare, Children's Bureau and U.S. Department of Labor, Women's Bureau.

McGroder, S. M. (1991). Parental preferences for child care: What do policy-makers really know? (Technical Analysis Paper). Washington, DC: Office of the Assistant Secretary for Planning and Evaluation U.S. Dept HHS, Wash, D.C.

Michalopoulos, C., Robins, P. K., & Garfinkel, I. (1991). A structural model of labor supply and child care demand, (Discussion Paper No. 932–91) Madison, WI: University of Wisconsin, Institute for Research on Poverty.

Mott, F. L., & Baker, P. (1989). Evaluation of the 1989 child care supplement in the National Longitudinal Survey of Youth. Columbus, OH: Ohio State University, Center for Human Resource Research.

Prosser, W. R. (1972). Day care in the seventies: Some thoughts, Washington, DC: Office of Economic Opportunity.

Robins, P. K. (1990). Federal financing of child care: Alternative approaches and economic implications (IRP Reprint Series No. 628). Madison: University of Wisconsin.

Rodes, T. W., & Moore, J. C. (1975). *National Child Care Consumer Study*. Washington, DC: UNCO.

Sonenstein, F. (1989). *The child care preferences of parents with young children: How little is known*. Boston, MA: Brandeis University.

U.S. Bureau of the Census (1987). Who's minding the kids? Child care arrangements: Winter 1984–1985, *Current Population Reports*, Series P-20, No. 9. Washington DC: U.S. Government Printing Office.

Walker, J. R. (1990). Public policy and the supply of child care services (Paper No. 933–91). University of Wisconsin, Institute for Research on Poverty.

Are Parents Better Off Than They Were a Decade Ago? A Response to Prosser and McGroder

SANDRA L. HOFFERTH
The Urban Institute

CAN PARENTS FIND AFFORDABLE AND ACCEPTABLE CARE?

From a policy perspective, the first issue that Prosser and McGroder raise is a good one. Are parents who use child care better or worse off today than they were a decade ago? I conclude that parents are not having a much harder time finding care in 1990 than they did in 1975. In addition, they pay only slightly more (in real terms) for center-based care, although they may pay much more if they use an in-home provider who is not related to them. However, I do raise the issue as to whether the quality of the care children receive has improved.

Prosser and McGroder address the issue of whether families are better off than they were. They compile a very interesting set of data on federal and parental expenditures for child care, concluding that federal expenditures have increased along with parental and family expenditures since the mid-1970s. Because subsidy rates have increased slightly, families are, in fact, better off in terms of the assistance they receive from the government. Prosser and McGroder object to my suggesting that 20% to 25% is a high proportion of income to be spending on child care. Relative to high income families, who spend only about 4% to 5% on child care and to all families, who spend about 10% on child care, it is clearly an excessive burden. I want to clarify that this is not true for all low-income families, but only for those who pay for child care (about 40% of those low-income families with an employed mother). Many low-income families have benefitted greatly from federal child-care subsidies and pay little or nothing for child care.

I am very excited by the authors' observation that the proportion that pay for care may have declined. This is a very important insight to pursue in further research. It also fits with the notion that monetary subsidies have increased. The proportion of center-based programs that are subsidized is very high; this high level of subsidization is probably at least partially responsible for the increased demand for such programs. I agree with Prosser and McGroder that the quality of care is multifaceted. However, it is generally agreed that child–staff ratio and group size are important indicators of quality in the United States, and any increase in them is of concern. I want to reiterate that we do not know the extent to which the more educated staff that we now have can make up for these larger class sizes.

I am very excited about Prosser and McGroder's exploratory work on the market for child care, especially the discussion of the change in price, or lack of it, since the early 1980s. This raises a good question. In what units should child care be measured: in quality units, in subsidy units, or what? For example, if quality has declined and price has remained constant, then the true cost has gone up. That is, people are getting less for their money. What I have done is look at hourly expenditures, controlling for differences in cost of living. I have also examined individual family budget shares. I think that it is very useful to examine the proportion of expenditures that are subsidized and how that has changed over time.

I would like to point out that after Prosser and McGroder complete their analysis, their conclusion is not any different from mine. That is, there has been only a small rise in the proportion of income spent on child care (budget share), compared with a small rise in expenditures. The subsidy rates have also risen modestly (15%) since 1975.

Clearly multivariate work is needed to examine changes over time, controlling for a variety of other factors that could lead to further changes. Within such a context it would be worth examining whether the changes reported are statistically significant or not. At this point the populations are not exactly identical and tests of significance are probably not applicable.

ARE PARENTS GETTING WHAT THEY WANT AND CHILDREN WHAT THEY NEED?

The second issue that Prosser and McGroder raise is whether choices equal preferences. If so, then we can draw inferences about the future from present behavior. The issue is the relationship between actual choice and some hypothetical ideal choice or preference. This is probably the area in which there is the biggest disagreement in the field. There are two approaches: (a) Ask parents their preferences, or (b) see what parents do.

Prosser and McGroder take the first approach. They argue that parents may not be able to choose their first preference because they can't find something they can afford. Therefore, choices cannot indicate preferences. In order to address this question, in the NCCS (Hofferth, Brayfield, Deich, & Holcomb, 1991), we asked parents whether they wanted to change arrangements and what they would prefer. We also asked parents why they wanted to change. About one out of four wanted to change arrangements. When asked the reasons for wanted to change, the majority mentioned quality; few mentioned cost or convenience factors.

In many ways the child-care decision is no different from many other consumer decisions. Parents face a set budget that limits their purchase of goods and services. Similarly, consumers take their own preferences, characteristics of the alternatives, and budget constraints into account in making their decisions. We accept the decision parents make as what they prefer, given all the circumstances. Tradeoffs must always be made between different aspects of the alternatives available. The question, it seems, is whether the ultimate consequence of such decisions has wider impact than just on that individual family. For example, if a family buys a poor-quality television over a high-quality one, then it affects only their own television viewing. However, if they buy poor-quality child care for their child because they cannot afford anything else, and the child suffers long-term negative consequences as a result, then it is a problem for the rest of us as well as for that family. The extent to which parents have to trade off quality against cost is a very important issue.

My alternative is to examine the association between the characteristics of what people have available to them and their behavior. In recently completed work using the National Longitudinal Survey of Youth (NLSY), I examined the influence of price, characteristics of care (including quality), and parental characteristics on family choice of arrangements (Hofferth & Wissoker, in press). I feel that this is a more fruitful approach. However, such research will take years, not just the few months that the analysis presented here represents.

LATENT DEMAND FOR CHILD CARE

There is one additional issue to address, that of latent demand: Whether there are some parents who are not working at all because they cannot find child care. Prosser and McGroder suggest two ways to identify this latent demand:

1. Ask parents whether they would work or work more hours if they could find acceptable child care.

2. Examine the reasons parents give for leaving their jobs. Do they give child care as the reasons?

This issue has been a concern in this field for quite some time. Research consistently shows that a large proportion of parents—one out of four—say that child care constrains their employment. However, few have trouble finding child-care arrangements. In examining many surveys asking parental reasons for leaving their job, few (under 10%) cite a child-care problem as a reason for leaving a job.

How can both of these be true at the same time? One or all of the following may apply: (a) one may be a lower and the other an upper bound on constraint; (b) behavior is not simple: There are many reasons for everything, and child care may be only a small part of why a mother leaves a job; (c) the way questions are asked affects the responses elicited; and (d) hypothetical responses cannot be assumed to predict what parents would actually do in a given circumstance: Several major demonstrations such as the Seattle/Denver Income Maintenance Experiments (SIME/DIME) and the Mass Employment and Training (ET) have consistently shown that fewer parents than expected take advantage of child-care subsidies.

I simply do not agree that asking parents whether child care constrains their employment will yield valid or reliable indicators of what they would actually do under altered conditions. Furthermore, even if the responses predicted behavior in a given set of circumstances, they might not under another set of circumstances. For these reasons, in the NCCS we did not even ask the hypothetical question about perceived constraint. It is somewhat like the notion of satisfaction: Everyone is constrained, but they don't knows how they would behave if a given constraint were to be lifted.

Finally, I agree with Prosser and McGroder's assessment of the next few years' policy concern: the concern with child care for low-income families. My focus was on very long-term goals, which I think include parental leave and tax policies to assist families more generally.

CONCLUSION

In conclusion, I applaud Prosser and McGroder for having suggested a way of conceptualizing and measuring both parental and federal (state and local) expenditures on child care and children more broadly, and for having broadened the definition of *assistance with child-care expenses*. I especially thank them for raising the important issue for policy-makers, which is, after all, not whether we have reached some ideal, but whether parents and children are better off in terms of child care now than they were a decade ago.

REFERENCES

Hofferth, S., Brayfield, A., Deich, S., & Holcomb, P. (1991). National Child Care Survey 1990. Washington, DC: The Urban Institute.

Hofferth, S., & Wissoker, D. (1992). Quality, price and income in child care choice. *Journal of Human Resources, 27*(1), 70–111.

II

What Child-Care Practices and Arrangements Lead to Positive Outcomes for Children? Negative Outcomes for Children?

Consequences of Child Care for Children's Development

ALISON CLARKE-STEWART
University of California-Irvine

As Sandra Hofferth (this volume) has amply documented, for most American children today nonparental child care is a fact of life. From their earliest months until they are old enough to be on their own after school, more and more children are spending more and more time in the care of some adult other than their parents, in some kind of day care or early childhood program. As a result, questions that were once of academic interest have become the concern of a majority of parents and prospective parents in this country. Of particular concern are two broad questions: What effect does nonparental child care have on children's well-being and development, and what kinds of care are best — or worst?

Unfortunately, answers to these questions are not obvious. Experts asked by reporters about the effects of nonparental care on children's development must still rely on their own personal values and beliefs about what is best for mothers and for children in interpreting the results of scientific studies. Although a substantial number of studies have been undertaken since the early 1970s, which is when research in this area began, the findings of these studies have been neither completely consistent nor entirely reliable. The results therefore are open to interpretation. There are many discrepancies and confusions in the research literature in this area, and there are significant gaps in the available results. The studies themselves are easily criticized; they lack representativeness, random assignment, and rigor.

Rather than dwelling on these flaws and failures in the research literature, however, I have chosen to present in this chapter a broad overview of the results of these studies. I have integrated and summarized the results of the available investigations of the effects of child care in what I hope is a coherent and sensible way, but in a way that reflects my own interpretation of what the results mean. I have stressed possible links between child care and child development, although the empirical basis for these associations is not as strong as one would hope.

THE EFFECT OF ANY KIND OF DAY CARE

I begin with the question of whether day care — in any shape or form — is good for children's development. The answer to this question is perhaps clearest with respect to the intellectual development of preschool-aged children (2 to 4 years old) who attend day-care centers. (Effects on the social and emotional development of infants are less clear and are discussed in a later section.) Regarding the cognitive development of preschoolers, there is a substantial body of research that suggests that, within the limits of the day-care programs that have been studied, day care is not harmful to children, and may even help their development. Clearly this research does not include the most inadequate day care, but it is likely to reflect the majority of day-care programs available in this country. In the two dozen or so studies comparing the development of children who attended day-care centers, nursery schools, or early childhood programs in the preschool years with the development of children from comparable family backgrounds who did not (see reviews by Belsky, 1984; Clarke-Stewart & Fein, 1983; Hayes, Palmer, & Zaslow, 1990), only one or two showed that children in day-care programs did more poorly in overall intellectual development than children at home. These were studies of poor day care, with shockingly low adult–child ratios and poor caregiver training (e.g., Peaslee, 1976). The other studies, of better day care, all showed that children in day-care programs did at least as well — and some-times better — on tests of mental or intellectual development (e.g., Andersson, 1989; Burchinal, Lee, & Ramey, 1989; Cochran, 1977; Fowler, 1978; Garber & Heber, 1980; Golden et al., 1978; Kagan, Kearsley, & Zelazo, 1978; Ramey, Dorval, & Baker-Ward, 1983; H. B. Robinson & N. M. Robinson, 1971; Rubenstein & Howes, 1983; Scarr, Lande, & McCartney, 1989; Stukat, 1969, cited in Berfenstam & William-Olsson, 1973; Winnett, Fuchs, Moffatt, & Nerviano, 1977).

To be more specific, in the studies showing differences, children in day care scored higher on IQ tests, were more advanced in their eye–hand coordination, were more creative in the ways in which they explored and played with materials, knew more about the physical world, had more of the beginning arithmetic skills (like counting and measuring) before they went to school, could remember and recite back information — including their names and addresses — more accurately, and were able to use and understand more advanced language. In a study that I did in Chicago (Clarke-Stewart, 1984, 1987), for instance, 2- to 4-year-old children from a range of family backgrounds, who were attending a wide variety of nursery school and day-care center programs, were, on the average, 6 to 9 months advanced over children cared for at home by their mothers or babysitters or in day-care homes, on tests of these kinds of intellectual competence. Significant differences favoring center attendees have not been found in all studies, in all samples, or on all indices of intellectual competence, but when differences have been observed, they have consistently been in this direction.

This does not mean that children attending day-care programs are given a permanent head start toward a life of superior intelligence. Their advanced development, the research suggests, reflects a temporary gain in these children's abilities during the preschool years (see Clarke-Stewart & Fein, 1983). It seems to be a speeding up in the rate of early acquisition of these kinds of competent behavior rather than a permanent enhancement of their intellectual abilities. Generally, the gains last only as long as the children are in the day-care program. By the time they have gone through first grade, children who did not have experience in a preschool program have generally caught up to those who did (e.g., Fowler, 1978; Lally & Honig, 1977; Ramey, MacPhee, & Yeates, 1982). The gains are also not cumulative; they are not linked to the length of time children are in the day-care program nor to the age at which they started (see Clarke-Stewart & Fein, 1983). They show up by the time the children have been in day care for a year and then level off.

These gains are most evident in the school-related knowledge and abilities I have just described. Differences do not appear in all aspects of development (e.g., emotional adjustment, relations with parents, empathy and social sensitivity). They do, however, sometimes show up in children's social behavior. Preschool children who attend day-care programs are, according to the research, likely to be more self-confident, outgoing, assertive, and self-sufficient, more comfortable in new situations, less timid and fearful, more helpful and cooperative, and more verbally expressive (Cochran, 1977; Fowler, 1978; Kagan et al., 1978; Lally & Honig, 1977; Rubenstein, Howes, & Boyle, 1981; Schwarz, Krolick, & Strickland, 1973). They know more about social rules (Siegal & Storey, 1985) and gender roles (Clarke-Stewart, 1984), and are better liked by adults who meet them for the first time (Clarke-Stewart, 1984). Like the differences in intellectual competence, these differences in social competence do not appear in all studies of all day-care programs for all children (e.g., Golden et al., 1978; Lamb, Hwang, Broberg, & Bookstein, 1988), but when differences do appear, they are in this direction.

So, considering all this research, it looks as if day care — at least the day care that has been studied—is basically good for children; it promotes or at least does not hinder their cognitive and social development. There is another side to the story, however. The same studies also show that children in day care, in addition to having these positive qualities, are sometimes less polite, less agreeable, less compliant with their mothers' or caregivers' demands and requests, louder and more boisterous, more irritable and more rebellious, more likely to use profane language, and more aggressive than children who are not, or who have not been, in day care (e.g., Haskins, 1985; Rubenstein & Howes, 1983; Schwarz, Strickland, & Krolick, 1974; and see Clarke-Stewart & Fein, 1983).

These differences in behavior, although not inevitable, appear in tests and in natural observations, in the day-care center and on the playground, with adults and with other children, with strangers and with parents; they appear for both boys and girls, and for children from both model and mediocre day-care programs. They are more marked for children from lower income families, but they also appear in middle-class children.

One problem, obviously, is how to interpret these differences. Are day-care children more socially competent or less? They are helpful but also demanding, cooperative but also bossy, friendly but also aggressive, outgoing but also rude. My interpretation is that in the preschool years day-care children, as a group, are developmentally advanced in the social realm, just as they are in the intellectual realm, and that is why they are more knowledgeable, self-sufficient, and able to cooperate, but they are also more independent and determined to get their own way, and they do not always have the social skills to achieve this smoothly. That is why they are also more aggressive, irritable, and noncompliant.

Another problem in interpreting the differences observed in children's social and intellectual skills is determining whether the child care the children in these studies experienced is typical of child care found in the United States today. The studies were biased toward high-quality child care because many of them were studies of university based, "model" preschool programs and because even those studies that included community day care were limited to parents and child-care providers who were willing to be studied. Nevertheless, the evidence we have about the kinds of child care available today (from national child care surveys conducted by Mathematica Policy Research and the Urban Institute: Kisker, Hofferth, Phillips, & Farquhar, 1991; Hofferth, Brayfield, Deich, & Holcomb, 1991) show that, for preschool children today, the average class size (17), adult–child ratio (1:10), and likelihood of caregiver training (93% have some training) are in line with the class sizes, ratios, and training in the studies of day-care effects. Standards of acceptable practice set by the National Association for the Education of Young Children are met by more than two-thirds of the programs for preschool children in the United States today (Kisker et al., 1991). It seems likely, thus, that the results of the studies would apply to at least the top two-thirds of contemporary day-care programs.

A third problem lies in understanding the causes of the observed differences in development. Finding consistent differences between day-care and home-care children does not necessarily mean that day care alone has caused the differences. Only two studies, of low-income families, have used experimental designs in which children were randomly assigned to day care or home care (Garber & Heber, 1980; Ramey et al., 1983). In correlational studies of children whose parents have decided whether or not to use day care and have selected the day-care program or caregivers they will use, it seems that family characteristics also contribute to the observed differences in development.

A final problem in interpreting the results of research on day-care effects is that these are general findings for all children in all day-care programs compared with all children at home. These findings are based on differences between groups of children, not individuals. Do all day-care programs by their very nature have these effects, or are some programs better than others at enhancing children's intelligence or worse than others in promoting children's aggressiveness. What is it about day-care programs that enhances children's intellectual development or increases their aggressiveness?

CHILD CARE QUALITY

Consistent with common sense and casual observation, researchers have discovered that there are differences in children's development related to the kinds of day-care programs they are in. Although associations are not observed in every study or for every sample (e.g., Goelman & Pence, 1987; Kontos & Fiene, 1987; Lamb et al., 1988), several studies have revealed significant associations between children's cognitive and social development and indexes of global quality in the child-care setting (Howes & Olenick, 1986; McCartney, 1984; Ruopp, Travers, Glantz, & Coelen, 1979), associations that persist into elementary school (Howes, 1988; Vandell, Henderson, & Wilson, 1988). These results prompt us to ask whether these associations are really the result of a single critical factor, like adult–child ratio, for instance, or whether there are a number of critical features that determine day care "quality."

Distilling the results from all the studies linking children's development to different kinds of day-care programs, it is possible to identify four aspects of day-care programs that are most clearly and consistently related to children's behavior and development, four aspects that might be considered to be aspects of quality. These are the physical environment, the caregivers' behavior, the curriculum, and the number of children.

Physical Setting

Surprisingly, perhaps, the results of studies of children in day-care centers show that children's intellectual and social development is not related to the number of toys available or to the amount of physical space available, unless it is extremely crowded, which does have negative effects (Connolly & Smith, 1978; Smith & Connolly, 1980). What matters more is the *organization* of the space and the *quality* of the materials available. Children do better in centers that are neat, clean, safe, and orderly, that are organized into interest areas and oriented toward children's activities (Clarke-Stewart, 1987; Howes, 1983; Prescott & David, 1976). They do better in centers with toys and materials that are varied and educational (Clarke-Stewart, 1987; Connolly & Smith, 1978; Howes & Rubenstein, 1985). Children are more likely to do constructive, mentally challenging things with building materials, to have interesting and mature conversations in play using dramatic props, and to cooperate with peers in social games like checkers and pickup sticks (Sylva, Roy, & Painter, 1980), and having a variety of materials adds to the range of children's educational experiences. So the general conclusion to draw from the research on the physical environment might be that it is not quantity but quality that matters most, and simply adding more balls or games or space will not necessarily improve the program or enhance children's development, if the center already has some balls and some games and enough space. What is more, simply adding materials to preschool classrooms or having more varied materials does not lead to cognitive gains except in combination with teachers' behavior (Ruopp et al., 1979). This brings us to the second important aspect of the day-care program.

Caregivers' Behavior

Children are more likely to develop social and intellectual skills, the research suggests, when caregivers are stimulating, educational, and respectful, not custodial or demeaning (Carew, 1980; Clarke-Stewart, 1984, 1987; Clarke-Stewart & Gruber, 1984; Golden et al., 1978; McCartney, 1984; Phillips, Scarr, & McCartney, 1987). The children in our Chicago study who did best, for instance, had caregivers who were responsive, positive, accepting, and informative, who read to them, offered them choices, and gave them gentle suggestions, rather than simply hugging and holding or helping them, and rather than directing, controlling, restricting, or punishing them. The latter kinds of teacher behavior were associated with poorer development: Caregivers who initiated more physical contact, physical help, and physical control with the children they were in charge of had children who did more poorly in the assessments we made of their social and mental competence. If teachers were very busy, and there were many children demanding their attention, it seemed to make a difference just how much one-to-one conversation the teachers managed to have with the children, but if conversation was relatively frequent, it was the quality of the one-to-one conversation (its positive tone, responsive and accepting nature, informative content) that seemed to be more important than the sheer amount. Again, we see that once a floor of quantity has been achieved, it is quality of care that matters.

Researchers, of course, have also asked how these positive kinds of behavior are associated with the caregiver's background, her (they are almost exclusively female) age, education, training, and experience. Their studies show that caregivers who are most likely to behave in these positive ways are those with more experience as child-care professionals, those who have been in the day-care program longer, and those who have higher levels of training in child development (Arnett, 1987; Clarke-Stewart, 1987; Howes, 1983; Rosenthal, 1988; Ruopp et al., 1979). On all these dimensions, however, there is some suggestion that these relations are curvilinear. That is, past a certain point, having more experience, or stability, or training is no longer advantageous.

Teachers who have more professional experience, for instance, are likely to be more stimulating, responsive, accepting, and positive than teachers with less experience (Clarke-Stewart, Gruber, & Fitzgerald, 1992; Howes, 1983; Kontos & Fiene, 1987), but only up to a certain point. Teachers with more extensive experience in the field have been observed in other studies to provide less stimulating care than caregivers with less experience (e.g., Ruopp et al., 1979). Although there are still too few studies to reach a firm conclusion, extrapolating from available results suggests that the optimal length of experience might be about 10 years (Kontos & Fiene, 1987; Phillips et al., 1987; Ruopp et al., 1979). There are several possible explanations for this finding: The most likely are burnout (teachers just get worn down after years of challenging and demanding working conditions and constant giving of themselves for meager economic rewards), generational or age effects (the younger generation of teachers may be more stimulating than the older generation), selective attrition (the better teachers have risen to the top to become administrators or politicians), or simply inadequate information (i.e., we have not systematically studied the full range of caregivers' experience in a single comprehensive study). We need further research to sort out these possibilities and to establish what the experience curve might be.

Stability of the caregiver in a particular day-care setting, similarly, may be related to the quality of care in a curvilinear way. Staff turnover is clearly negatively related to day-care quality: The more staff changes the worse for the program—and the children. In the National Staffing study (Whitebook, Howes, & Phillips, 1990), centers rated higher on overall quality, centers in which children spent less time in aimless wandering and scored higher on a test of intelligence, had lower staff turnover. The question is whether if any given caregiver stays in the center longer, she will provide better care. When a caregiver stays in one center for three or four years, it makes sense that this is better than staying for only a year or two, and that, within this period, staying longer is better, but beyond this length of time, does staying longer improve the quality of care the caregiver provides? Available data, scant though they are, suggest not (Clarke-Stewart et al., 1992). Staff stability is an important aspect of day-care quality, not only because it is good for children to form relationships with their daily caregivers and vice versa, but also, I suspect, because such stability indicates that the center offers good working conditions, adequate wages, and high staff morale. In the National Staffing study, centers with lower turnover offered higher wages, and, in fact, the primary suggestion made by 90% of the teachers in that study for how to improve child-care quality was to pay better salaries for child-care work. What is important, therefore, is to provide working conditions and wages that encourage teachers to stay in a center for several years, rather than making misleading claims about the importance of caregiver stability.

In the National Staffing study, too, higher quality centers were found to have better educated and trained teachers. This association between training and quality of care has appeared in many earlier studies, and caregiver training is now generally considered to be a sine qua non of quality care (e.g., Arnett, 1987; Clarke-Stewart, 1987; Howes, 1983; D. G. Klinzing & D. R. Klinzing, 1974; Lazar, Darlington, Murray, Royce, & Snipper, 1982; Ruopp et al., 1979). Here again, however, the picture is not so simple. Although having no training in child development is clearly worse than having some, more training is not a guarantee of better care; taking 10 courses is not necessarily better than taking 6. It depends on the content, quality, and variety of the courses. As it is, with the training that is currently taken by child-care workers in America, there is some suggestion that, when teachers have taken more training in child development, they develop an academic orientation, which translates, in the day-care classroom, into an emphasis on school activities (reading, counting, and lesson-learning) to the exclusion of activities to promote children's social or emotional development. Formal training in child development may indeed be good background for providing a day-care environment that promotes children's intellectual development, but it is not necessarily so good for children's social development. In our study in Chicago (Clarke-Stewart, 1987), for example, the caregivers who had had more formal training in child development had children who were advanced intellectually but were significantly less competent in interactions with unfamiliar peers. Caregivers who had a moderate level of training had children who did well in both social and cognitive realms.

Curriculum

The same kind of complex, curvilinear associations appear when researchers examine the significance of the day-care program's curriculum, the third important component of day care. Having some kind of a curriculum — some lessons, some structure, some organized and supervised activities — is clearly better than having none (see Clarke-Stewart & Fein, 1983; and also Clarke-Stewart, 1987; McCartney, 1984), but having too much structure or too much regimentation is not beneficial (Miller & Dyer, 1975; Sylva et al., 1980). Children in day care need to express their needs and interests, and the day's activities cannot all be planned by the teacher. Children benefit from the opportunity and encouragement to explore and play and learn on their own. On the other hand, children who spend their time in day care just playing with other children and have no educational activities or teacher direction do not make the gains in intellectual or social development that have been observed in children who do have those experiences.

As for the type of curriculum — Montessori, Piagetian, Distar, behavioral — it seems that this is not critical for children's intellectual development; there are apparently many curricula available and in use today that promote children's acquisition of intellectual knowledge (Miller & Dyer, 1975; Royce, Darlington, & Murray, 1983; Schweinhart, Weikart, & Larner, 1986). The curriculum may matter more to children's social and motivational development. Children who are most likely to be cooperative, self-confident, assertive, and aggressive have teachers who, directly and indirectly, are most likely to encourage their self-direction and independence, cooperation and knowledge, self-expression and social interaction, intellectual development and academic skills, but who do not focus on teaching the children social skills (Miller & Dyer, 1975; Schweinhart et al., 1986). Day-care children who were observed to interact 13 times more aggressively than nonday-care children, for example, came from a model, university-based program, which was particularly focused on promoting the children's intellectual development (Haskins, 1985). Children who have developed social skills in day care or early childhood education programs, who have learned nonaggressive strategies for solving social problems, apparently do not pick them up incidentally by hanging around in a benign and permissive environment with other children, even if they are saying their ABC's or building with blocks together. These social skills come only from day-care programs in which special efforts are made to teach them. In the most satisfactory day care, it appears, children are offered a balanced menu of social and intellectual lessons.

Number of Children

Repeating the themes of "quality versus quantity" and "you *can* have too much of a good thing," the research on the number of children in day-care classes suggests that although the opportunity to interact with other children in day care is good — because other children offer advanced models of behavior, direct tutoring, and challenging play — having *more* interaction with other children typically is not so good. When children spend more of their time in the day-care center just watching, playing around with, fighting, and imitating other children (especially younger children), they tend to be less competent socially and intellectually (Clarke-Stewart, 1987; McCartney, 1984; Phillips et al., 1987).

Often the reason children spend their time in day care just hanging around with the other kids, is that the class is large or that the ratio of adults to children is low. We are all well aware of the importance of class size and adult–child ratio as indexes of day-care quality (Holloway & Reichhart-Erickson, 1988; Howes, 1983; Howes & Rubenstein, 1985; Ruopp et al., 1979; Smith & Connolly, 1980; Sylva et al., 1980). Once again, the relation between class size or adult–child ratio and children's behavior is not a simple one though. First, on some measures of competence, children in larger classes have been observed to do better. In our study in Chicago, for instance, children in larger classes were more knowledgeable about social rules and emotional expressions and less avoidant of an unfamiliar peer; children with a lower adult–child ratio, on the other hand, were more socially competent with unfamiliar adults and peers (Clarke-Stewart, 1987; Clarke-Stewart & Gruber, 1984). Second, the extent of the negative influence of the size of the class or the ratio of adults to children on children's development depends on the range of class sizes and ratios, the absolute level of class sizes and ratios, and the age of the children being considered. Significant associations with class size and adult–child ratio have been found in studies that have included a larger range of sizes, class sizes at the high end of the range, and younger children (Howes, 1983; 1987; Howes & Rubenstein, 1985; Howes, Rodning, Galluzzo, & Myers, 1988; Phillips et al., 1987; Ruopp et al., 1979), but not in studies that have included a smaller range, smaller classes, or older children (e.g., Clarke-Stewart, 1987; Kontos & Fiene, 1987; McCartney, 1984). Extrapolating from these studies, it seems likely that children will be more affected by differences in class size and adult–child ratios when the number of children in the class is very large (for 3- to 4-year-olds, larger than 20) or the adult–child ratio is very low (lower than 1:10), or when the age of the children is very young (younger than 3 years), than they will be by differences in class size or adult–child ratio within these limits.

Child-Care Quality in Brief

In sum then, these four aspects of day care — the physical setting, the caregivers' behavior, the curriculum, and the number of children — are linked to children's behavior and development in ways that are clear and sensible, but not simple. One way in which the relation is not simple is that on these dimensions, more is not necessarily better (whether it be more training, more experience, more time in the center for the caregiver, more toys or more space, more structure or more academic activities, more direction or more physical contact from the caregiver, more other children to play with or more time to play with them). Another way in which the relation is not simple is that, on these dimensions, quality seems to matter more than quantity. Beyond the minimal acceptable standards of quantity, it is the quality of the program that matters the organization of the physical space, the responsiveness of the caregivers' behavior, the content of the curriculum, and the type of interactions with peers — not the quantity — more space, more toys, more interaction with the caregiver or other children, more lessons on the ABC's.

Type of Day Care

So far, I have been discussing quality in center day care, because most research is about centers, but given the current day-care scene, it is also important to ask whether home day care has the same effects and whether these same indices of quality predict child development outcomes in home day care as well as in centers. There is a little research that speaks to these questions. In day-care homes, of course, unlike centers, quality is not usually defined by the presence of a curriculum, but the other three dimensions that were important in centers do appear to be linked to good care in homes as well. Children do better when the physical environment in the day-care home is organized to encourage their activities, when the home-care provider has a professional attitude and some training or education; and when there is a moderate number of children (more than 2, fewer than 10; Clarke-Stewart, 1987; Fosburg et al., 1980; Howes, 1983; Howes & Rubenstein, 1985; Stith & Davis, 1984).

As to which type of care is better, center or home, most people in the field think that either can offer excellent care. In our Chicago study and in other research, however, children's development and observed experiences with a sitter or in a day-care home were not different from those of children at home with their own mothers (Andersson, 1989; Clarke-Stewart, 1987; Cochran, 1977; Golden et al., 1978). They did not exhibit the advanced competence of the children in day-care centers and nursery schools. This may be because, in the real world of child care in America, or at least in the centers and homes that have been the subjects of study, centers, on the average, offer care and stimulation of higher quality than do homes, on the average. Differences are less when the day-care homes are of high quality. For example, in one study, although the competence of children in unregulated day-care homes was inferior to that of children in centers, the competence of children in regulated homes was equivalent (Goelman & Pence, 1987). More telling, when care in day-care homes was enriched by the experimental addition of a structured educational curriculum, the intellectual competence of the children was observed to improve to the level of children in day-care centers (Goodman &

Andrews, 1981). Although activities in centers are typically more educational than those in homes, then, this is probably not a necessary difference between the two environments.

Day Care for Infants

So far, we have focused our discussion on the effects of day care on preschool-aged children. What about infants who are placed in day care in the first year of life? Since the mid-1980s there has been a heated debate about whether day care is good for infants or places them at risk for developing emotional insecurity and causes them to become socially maladjusted. The major source of the debate is research assessing infants' relationships with their mothers. The infant–mother relationship is, of course, central in the infant's psychological development. It is also vulnerable when infants are separated from their mothers for 8 to 10 hours a day. Although research has consistently shown that infants of working mothers do form relationships with their mothers and prefer their mothers to their substitute caregivers (see review by Clarke-Stewart & Fein, 1983), the question is whether the quality of their relationships is as good and as emotionally secure as the relationships of infants who are being raised exclusively at home.

As a first step in answering this question, one can look at data from all studies of infants in day care that have included the current standard assessment of children's relationships with their mother. Combining 16 studies that have used this assessment, I found (Clarke-Stewart, 1989), reveals that the infants who are in day care full time, compared with infants who are in day care part time or not at all, are indeed more likely to be classified as having an insecure relationship with their mothers. The problem, again, is how to interpret this difference. Does the standard assessment that was used really reflect emotional insecurity in these children? And if it does, is the difference large enough that we need to be concerned about it? It is because the difference is open to interpretation that controversy about infant day care exists.

To appreciate the first problem, one must consider the assessment on which the judgment that these babies have insecure relationships with their mothers is based. The standard assessment of infants' relationships with their mothers (the Strange Situation; Ainsworth, Blehar, Waters, & Wall, 1978) involves the following scenario: The infant plays with toys in an unfamiliar room; he is left by his mother alone in the room with an unfamiliar woman; he plays with and is comforted by that woman in his mother's absence; his mother returns and picks him up. The child's relationship is assessed by observing how he or she responds at this final step when the mother returns to the room. If the child goes to or greets the mother, this is a sign of a secure relationship. If he avoids or ignores her, this is the sign of an insecure relationship.

Unfortunately, there is a problem with using this assessment for day-care infants, because the scenario sounds similar to the kind of experience that infants in day care go through regularly. Could it be that infants who have had this kind of experience repeatly are less likely therefore to seek physical closeness with their mothers, which is the basis for saying their relationship with their mother is insecure? When other methods of assessing infants' relationships with their mothers are used, it turns out, the differences are not as marked (see Clarke-Stewart, 1989). What is more, one must question whether, even if babies did have less secure relationships with their mothers, this would mean they were emotionally disturbed. On other measures of emotional adjustment, children who were in day care as infants have been observed to do as well as children who were not, suggesting that day-care infants are not more emotionally disturbed overall.

One must also question whether, even if the observed difference in these infants' relationships with their mothers does indicate a degree of emotional insecurity, the difference is large enough that we should be concerned about it. Among the approximately 1,200 children in the 16 studies tabulated in Clarke-Stewart (1989), 36% of those who were in day care full time were classified as insecurely attached to their mothers, and 29% of the children who were not in day care full time were insecurely attached. Is this difference between 36% and 29% large enough to be of concern? This is a difference that turns out to be within the normal range when one looks at research from around the world, and it is a difference that is found only in infants from low-risk, middle-class families. For infants from high-risk families, those who are in day care are more likely to have secure relationships with their mothers not less. It is also a difference whose meaning is open to interpretation. The significance of the difference, I think, lies not in demonstrating that day care is harmful to infants but in alerting us to possible problems that day care *may* create for infants.

Another potential problem with infant day care that research alerts us to is in the intellectual domain. Recent evidence from the National Longitudinal Study of Youth (Desai, Chase-Lansdale, & Michael, 1989) suggests that boys from high-income families in full-time infant care may be at risk for lower intellectual development. There were no negative effects for girls or for children from low-income families (confirming earlier research that showed that children who were in day care as infants were advanced in development in the same ways as children who started day care at 2 or 3 or 4 years of age; Ramey et al., 1982).

The data so far collected on infants in day care suggest that we need to be cautious as we try out different forms and programs of day care for infants and as we evaluate the effects of these forms and programs of day care on infants. We need to put our efforts into trying to discover under what circumstances infants in day care are likely to suffer. It would not be surprising to discover that some day care for babies is good and some is bad, just as for older children. Perhaps for infants, also, some day care is good and too much day care is bad. Perhaps day care is good for some infants but not for others. We need to identify the conditions in infant day care that, in combination with the infant's home circumstances and individual constitution, are likely to lead to negative or positive outcomes — conditions like the kind of training and personal qualities that prepare a person to be a good caregiver, or the maximum number of infants that a caregiver can adequately care for at one time. Although it is clear that no adult, regardless of training, can provide adequate care and stimulation for 8 infants, let alone evacuate them in an emergency, for instance, it is not clear whether the minimum acceptable adult–infant ratio is 1:5 or 1:4 or 1:3, or 3:1.

CAUTIONS AND CONCLUSIONS

I close with some cautions and some conclusions. The cautions stem from the fact that the research and the results on which this discussion was based are limited in significant ways. The research was, for the most part, not experimental; the samples, not nationally representative. The correlations and group differences reported, even when statistically significant, were disappointingly modest in size and inconsistent from sample to sample. The differences that were robust were short-lived. Perhaps most troublesome of all, the contribution of self-selection to the correlations and group differences observed could not be adequately evaluated because few investigators assessed preexisting differences among children and their families. Although the few investigations that used either an experimental design (see Bryant & Ramey, 1986) or regression analyses (Clarke-Stewart, 1984; Howes & Stewart, 1987; Owen & Henderson, 1989) do support the suggestion that child care makes a contribution to children's development beyond that of family characteristics, the fact that family background is confounded with day-care quality in the vast majority of studies suggests that even the modest associations that have been discovered overestimate the effects of child-care quality. These limitations must be kept in mind before any extrapolation to policy recommendations should be attempted.

In the not-so-distant future, we may learn more about the effects of child care on children's development from several large-scale studies that have just begun. In the National Institute of Child Health and Human Development (NICHD) Study of Early Child Care, children are being identified at birth and observed throughout their first three years, at home and in any regular child-care arrangement in which they spend at least 10 hours per week. Their experiences at home and in child care will be related to their cognitive, social, and emotional development, assessed using a variety of standard and original instruments. Some 1,200 infants, from a wide range of family backgrounds, in 10 different sites across the country, will be studied. In the Child and Family Study being conducted by ChildTrends and the Manpower Demonstration Research Corporation, the effects of one year of child care on children whose welfare mothers are randomly assigned to the JOBS (Job Opportunity and Basic Skills Training) program are being studied. The cognitive, physical, emotional, and social development of 2,500 3- to 5-year-olds will be studied over a 5-year follow-up period. In a third study, the Expanded Child Care Options (ECCO) demonstration project, funded by the Rockefeller Foundation, the development of 1,800 children will be assessed, beginning in early childhood and extending into young adulthood, to compare the effects of basic child care (one year of child care), extended child care (lasting until first grade), and extended enhanced child care (high-quality care lasting until first grade). Welfare mothers with a child under 3 years will be randomly assigned to one of these conditions. Because of their scope and design, these studies promise to yield important data on child-care effects.

Until these studies are completed, keeping in mind the cautions regarding existing data, it is possible to make some general conclusions on the basis of this simple and interpretive review of the available research. Four conclusions seem most reasonable:

1. Day care is potentially beneficial to preschool children's development, if it is of high quality.

2. High quality is most clearly defined by the following: a well-organized and stimulating physical environment, a responsive and trained caregiver, a balanced curriculum, and relatively small classes.

3. Because of the finding that the relation between these dimensions of quality and child development outcomes tends to be curvilinear, it is probably more important to put our efforts into ensuring that all day-care programs meet minimal acceptable standards than into trying to improve the quality of already adequate care. For example, at present, state regulations of adult–child ratios for 3-year-olds vary from 1:7 to 1:15 (Kisker et al., 1990). It would probably make more sense to require that adult–child ratios of 1:15 be increased to 1:10 — which happens to be the ratio recommended by the National Association for the Education of Young Children and the average ratio actually observed for preschoolers in the national survey of child child settings (Kisker et al., 1991) — than to require that 1:10 ratios be increased to 1:7. We should probably also require a moderate amount of training for all

caregivers rather than stressing high levels of training for a few. Currently, only 27 states require any preservice training for day-care center caregivers and less than half that number require preservice training for day-care home providers (Kisker et al., 1991).

4. We are on shakier ground in making recommendations about optimal or even adequate care for infants and toddlers, but we have every reason to believe that doing so for them is even more important than doing so for preschoolers. We should proceed with caution as we provide and study day care for infants as we enter the 21st century.

REFERENCES

Ainsworth, M. D. S., Blehar, M., Waters, E., & Wall, S. (1978). *Patterns of attachment: Observations in the Strange Situation and at home.* Hillsdale, N.J.: Erlbaum.

Andersson, B.-E. (1989). Effects of public day care: A longitudinal study. *Child Development, 60,* 857–866.

Arnett, J. (1987, April). *Training for caregivers in day care centers.* Paper presented at the biennial meeting of the Society for Research in Child Development, Baltimore, MD.

Belsky, J. (1984). Two waves of day care research: Developmental effects and conditions of quality. In R. C. Ainslie (Ed.), *The child and the day care setting* (pp. 1–34). New York: Praeger.

Berfenstam, R., & William-Olsson, I. (1973). *Early child care in Sweden.* London: Gordon & Breach.

Bryant, D. M., & Ramey, C. T. (1986). An analysis of the effectiveness of early intervention programs for high risk children. In M. Guralnick & C. Bennett (Eds.), *Effectiveness of early intervention* (pp. 33–78). New York: Academic Press.

Burchinal, M., Lee, M., & Ramey, C. (1989). Type of day care and preschool intellectual development in disadvantaged children. *Child Development, 60,* 128–137.

Carew, J. (1980). Experience and the development of intelligence in young children. *Monographs of the Society for Research in Child Development, 45*(6–7, Serial No. 187).

Clarke-Stewart, K. A. (1984). Day care: A new context for research and development. In M. Perlmutter (Ed.), *The Minnesota symposium on child psychology* (Vol. 17, pp. 61–100). Hillsdale, NJ: Lawrence Erlbaum Associates.

Clarke-Stewart, K. A. (1987). Predicting child development from child care forms and features: The Chicago Study. In D. A. Phillips (Ed.), *Quality in child care: What does research tell us?* (pp. 21–42). Washington, DC: National Association for the Education of Young Children.

Clarke-Stewart, K. A. (1989). Infant day care: Maligned or malignant? *American Psychologist, 44,* 266–273.

Clarke-Stewart, K. A., & Fein, G. G. (1983). Early childhood programs. In P. H. Mussen, M. Haith, & J. Campos (Eds.), *Handbook of child psychology* (Vol. 2, pp. 917–1000). New York: Wiley.

Clarke-Stewart, K. A., & Gruber, C. P. (1984). Day care forms and features. In R. C. Ainslie (Ed.), *The child and the day care setting* (pp. 35–62). New York: Praeger Special Studies.

Clarke-Stewart, K. A., Gruber, C. P., & Fitzgerald, L. M. (1992). *Predicting children's development from their experiences at home and in day care.* Unpublished manuscript, University of California-Irvine.

Cochran, M. M. (1977). *Group day care and family childrearing patterns in Sweden.* Unpublished report to the Foundation for Child Development, Cornell University, Ithaca, NY.

Connolly, K. J., & Smith, P. K. (1978). Experimental studies of the preschool environment. *International Journal of Early Childhood, 10,* 86–95.

Desai, S., Chase-Lansdale, P. L., & Michael, R. T. (1989). Mother or market? Effects of maternal employment on the intellectual ability of four-year-old children. *Demography, 26,* 545–561.

Fosburg, S., Hawkins, P. D., Singer, J. D., Goodson, B. D., Smith, J. M., & Brush, L. R. (1980). *National Day Care Home Study.* Cambridge, MA: Abt Associates.

Fowler, W. (1978). *Day care and its effects on early development: A study of group and home care in multi-ethnic, working-class families.* Toronto: Ontario Institute for Studies in Education.

Garber, H., & Heber, R. (1980, April). *Modification of predicted cognitive development in high-risk children through early intervention.* Paper presented at the annual meeting of the American Educational Research Association, Boston, MA.

Goelman, H., & Pence, A. R. (1987). Effects of child care, family, and individual characteristics on children's language development: The Victoria day care research project. In D. A. Phillips (Ed.), *Quality in child care: What does research tell us?* (pp. 89–104). Washington, DC: National Association for the Education of Young Children.

Golden, M., Rosenbluth, L., Grossi, M. T., Policare, H. J., Freeman, H., & Brownlee, E. M. (1978). *The New York City Infant Day Care Study.* New York: Medical and Health Research Association of New York City.

Goodman, N., & Andrews, J. (1981). Cognitive development of children in family and group day care. *American Journal of Orthopsychiatry, 51,* 271–284.

Haskins, R. (1985). Public school aggression among children with varying day care experience. *Child Development, 56,* 689–703.

Hayes, C. D., Palmer, J. L., & Zaslow, M. J. (Eds.). (1990). *Who cares for America's children?* Washington, DC: National Academy of Sciences.

Hofferth, S. L., Brayfield, A., Deich, S., & Holcomb, P. (1991). *National Child Care Survey 1990.* Washington, DC: The Urban Institute.

Holloway, S. D., & Reichhart-Erickson, M. (1988). The relationship of day care quality to children's free play behavior and social problem solving skills. *Early Childhood Research Quarterly, 3,* 39–54.

Howes, C. (1983). Caregiver behavior in centers and family day care. *Journal of Applied Developmental Psychology, 4,* 99–107.

Howes, C. (1987). Quality indicators in infant and toddler child care: The Los Angeles Study. In D. A. Phillips (Ed.), *Quality in child care: What does research tell us?* (pp. 81–88). Washington, DC: National Association for the Education of Young Children.

Howes, C. (1988). Relations between early child care and schooling. *Developmental Psychology, 24,* 53-57.

Howes, C., & Olenick, M. (1986). Family and child influences on toddlers' compliance. *Child Development, 57,* 202-216.

Howes, C., & Rubenstein, J. (1985). Determinants of toddlers' experiences in day care: Age of entry and quality of setting. *Child Care Quarterly, 14,* 140-151.

Howes, C., Rodning, C., Galluzzo, D. C., & Myers, L. (1988). Attachment and child care: Relationships with mother and caregiver. *Early Childhood Research Quarterly, 3,* 403-416.

Howes, C., & Stewart, P. (1987). Child's play with adults, toys, and peers: An examination of family and child care influences. *Developmental Psychology, 23,* 423-430.

Kagan, J., Kearsley, R. B., & Zelazo, P. R. (1978). *Infancy: Its place in human development.* Cambridge: Harvard University Press.

Kisker, E. E., Hofferth, S. L., Phillips, D. A., Farquhar, E. (1991). *A profile of child care settings: Early education and care in 1990* (Report submitted to U.S. Department of Education, Contract No. LC88090001) Princeton, NJ: Mathematica Policy Research.

Klinzing, D. G., & Klinzing, D. R. (1974). An examination of the verbal behavior, knowledge, and attitudes of day care teachers. *Education, 95,* 65-71.

Kontos, S., & Fiene, R. (1987). Child care quality, compliance with regulations, and children's development: The Pennsylvania Study. In D. A. Phillips (Ed.), *Quality in child care: What does research tell us?* (pp. 57-80). Washington, DC: National Association for the Education of Young Children.

Lally, J. R., & Honig, A. S. (1977). *The family development research program* (Final Report, No. OCD-CB-100). Syracuse, NY: University of Syracuse.

Lamb, M. E., Hwang, C.-P., Broberg, A., & Bookstein, F. L. (1988). The effects of out-of-home care on the development of social competence in Sweden: A longitudinal study. *Early Childhood Research Quarterly, 3,* 379-402.

Lazar, I., Darlington, R. B., Murray, H., Royce, J., & Snipper, A. (1982). Lasting effects of early education: A report of the Consortium for Longitudinal Studies. *Monographs of the Society for Research in Child Development, 47*(2-3), Serial No. 195).

McCartney, K. (1984). Effect of quality of day care environment on children's language development. *Developmental Psychology, 20,* 244-260.

Miller, L. B., & Dyer, J. L. (1975). Four preschool programs: Their dimensions and effects. *Monographs of the Society for Research in Child Development, 40*(5-6, Serial No. 162).

Owen, M. T., & Henderson, V. K. (1989, April). *Relations between child care qualities and child behavior at age 4: Do parent–child interactions play a role?* Paper presented at the meeting of the Society for Research in Child Development, Kansas City, MO.

Peaslee, M. V. (1976). *The development of competency in 2-year-old infants in day care and home reared environments.* Unpublished doctoral dissertation, Florida State University, Tallahassee.

Phillips, D. A., Scarr, S. & McCartney, K. (1987). Dimensions and effects of child care quality: The Bermuda Study. In D. A. Phillips (Ed.), *Quality in child care: What does research tell us?* (pp. 43-56). Washington, DC: National Association for the Education of Young Children.

Prescott, E., & David, T. G. (1976). *Concept paper on the effects of the physical environment on day care.* Unpublished manuscript, Pacific Oaks College, Pasadena, CA.

Ramey, C. T., Dorval, B., & Baker-Ward, L. (1983). Group day care and socially disadvantaged families: Effects on the child and the family. In S. Kilmer (Ed.), *Advances in early education and day care* (Vol. 3, pp. 69–106). Greenwich, CT: JAI Press.

Ramey, C. T., MacPhee, D., & Yeates, K. O. (1982). Preventing developmental retardation: A general systems model. In L. Bond & J. Joffe (Eds.), *Facilitating infant and early childhood development.* Hanover, NH: University Press of New England.

Robinson, H. B., & Robinson, N. M. (1971). Longitudinal development of very young children in a comprehensive day care program. *Child Development, 42,* 1673–1683.

Rosenthal, M. K. (1988). *Social policy and its effects on the daily experiences of infants and toddlers in family day care in Israel.* Unpublished manuscript. The Hebrew University, Jerusalem, Israel.

Royce, J. M., Darlington, R. B., & Murray, H. W. (1983). Pooled analyses: Findings across studies. In Consortium for Longitudinal Studies, *As the twig is bent: Lasting effects of preschool programs* (pp. 411–459). Hillsdale, NJ: Lawrence Erlbaum Associates.

Rubenstein, J. L., & Howes, C. (1983). Social-emotional development of toddlers in day care: The role of peers and of individual differences. In S. Kilmer (Ed.), *Advances in early education and day care* (Vol. 3, pp. 13–45). Greenwich, CT: JAI Press.

Rubenstein, J. L., Howes, C., & Boyle, P. (1981). A two-year follow-up of infants in community based infant day care. *Journal of Child Psychology and Psychiatry, 22,* 209–218.

Ruopp, R., Travers, J., Glantz, F., & Coelen, C. (1979). *Children at the center.* Cambridge, MA: Abt Associates.

Scarr, S., Lande, J., & McCartney, K. (1989). Child care and the family: Complements and interactions. In J. Lande, S. Scarr, & N. Gunzenhauser (Eds.), *Caring for children: Challenge to America* (pp. 38–62). Hillsdale, NJ: Lawrence Erlbaum Associates.

Schwarz, J. C., Krolick, G., & Strickland, R. G. (1973). Effects of early day care experience on adjustment to a new environment. *American Journal of Orthopsychiatry, 43,* 340–346.

Schwarz, J. C., Strickland, R. G., & Krolick, G. (1974). Infant day care: Behavioral effects at preschool age. *Developmental Psychology, 10,* 502–506.

Schweinhart, L. J., Weikart, D. P., & Larner, M. B. (1986). Consequences of three preschool curriculum models through age 15. *Early Childhood Research Quarterly, 1,* 15–45.

Siegal, M., & Storey, R. M. (1985). Day care and children's conceptions of moral and social rules. *Child Development, 56,* 1001–1008.

Smith, P. K., & Connolly, K. J. (1980). *The ecology of preschool behaviour.* Cambridge, England: Cambridge University Press.

Stith, S. M., & Davis, A. J. (1984). Employed mothers and family day care: A comparative analysis of infant care. *Child Development, 55,* 1340–1348.

Sylva, K., Roy, C., & Painter, M. (1980). *Child watching at playgroup and nursery school.* London: Grant McIntyre.

Vandell, D. L., Henderson, B. K., & Wilson, K. S. (1988). A longitudinal study of children with day care experiences of varying quality. *Child Development, 59,* 1286–1292.

Whitebook, M., Howes, C., & Phillips, D. (1990). *Who cares? Child care teachers and the quality of care in America.* Berkeley: Child Care Employee Project.

Winnett, R. A., Fuchs, W. L., Moffatt, S., & Nerviano, V. J. (1977). A cross-sectional study of children and their families in different child care environments. *Journal of Community Psychology, 5,* 149–159.

Consequences of Child Care for Children's Development: A Deconstructionist View

JAY BELSKY

Pennsylvania State University

In her analysis of the effects of day care on child development, Professor Clarke-Stewart underscores the fact that her conclusions reflect her interpretation of the available evidence. What this means, of course, is that other interpretations of the very same evidence are possible. Those familiar with my previous writings on the topic of the so-called "effects" of day care, especially infant day care as we know it and have it in this country today, will not be surprised to learn that my reading of the evidence is different from Clarke-Stewart's. Before proceeding to identify where I take issue with her, I must say explicitly that I, too, believe that honest differences of opinion can — and perhaps even should — exist between well-meaning and open-minded developmentalists about how the available data can be interpreted. If there is one thing that is a serious threat to both science and social policy concerned with child care, it is the kind of hegemony of opinion that emerges when only politically correct points of view are tolerated.

Having noted this point of agreement, that we both recognize the legitimacy of varied opinions regarding what conclusions can be drawn from the available evidence, I now deconstruct Clarke-Stewart's analysis, in order to offer a dramatically different interpretation of much of the very same evidence. One of my major goals in critiquing this analysis is to provide not only a different point of view but, in so doing, to demonstrate how the very orchestration of the evidence leads to very different interpretations of it. After documenting this point, I show that dramatically different political rhetoric regarding child-care policy emanates from different organization of the evidence.

PUTTING RESEARCH ON DAY-CARE "EFFECTS" IN CONTEXT

Central to my interpretation of research on the developmental correlates of day care, especially full- and near-full-time nonparental care initiated in the first year of life, is the context in which day care is experienced in America. Nothing that I have to say can be appreciated fully, I believe, without embedding it in the contemporary ecology of day care, maternal employment, and family life. Central to this ecology is the fact that patterns of maternal employment changed dramatically during the 1980s, with more and more mothers returning to the work place when their children were still babies. Thus, by 1985, the rate of employment for women with children under 6 — 49% — was virtually identical to that for women who had not yet celebrated their child's first birthday — 48% (Hofferth & Phillips, 1987). The important point to be made, ultimately, is that the issue of infant day care is of special importance in the changing ecology of maternal employment and day care in the United States, not only because it is the arena in which opinion is divided, but because increasing numbers of American children who will experience routine nonparental care in their preschool years will initiate that care in their first year of life.

On the basis of the results of the recently completed National Child Care Staffing Study (Whitebrook, Phillips, & Howes, 1990), there would seem to be grounds to conclude that the quality of care available to infants, as well as to preschoolers, is quite limited. Multiple assessments of 227 infant and preschool centers in five major metropolitan cities led its child-care–advocate authors to note that "the quality of services provided by most centers was rated as *barely adequate* [italics added]" (Whitebrook et al., 1990, p. 4). It is important to note that because of the refusal of some centers to participate, the 227 centers subject to intensive scrutiny "consist(ed) of higher quality centers than in the eligible population as a whole" (p. 7). Thus, there is reason to believe that the rating of *barely adequate* may be an inflated estimate of the quality of center-based services in America. What, then, is the state of less visible, more informal, underground arrangements, which account for 90% of the care available to infants (Dawson & Cain, 1990)? Although it is true that no one really knows, there is every reason to concur with the observation made by Whitebrook et al., that their investigation "raises serious concerns about the quality of services that many American children receive" (p. 19).

The quality of care and the increasingly early age at which more and more American children are beginning routine nonparental care is only part of the picture of day care in context. We cannot lose sight of the fact that the United States remains in the company of only South Africa in the Western industrialized world in being without a national parental leave policy. We also must acknowledge that our country lacks any family-oriented, flexible employment policy that would enable a mother or father to change a full-time job into a part-time job—with benefits maintained—so that parents could rely on less nonparental care in their child's first year (or even years) of life before returning to full-time employment. Finally, we need to recognize that the value of the personal tax exemption per dependent child has withered tremendously since the 1950s. One reason, perhaps, why fewer infants and even young children experienced extensive nonparental care when I was a child (in the 1950s) was because the tax deduction per dependent child was worth more than three times what it is today (Rauch, 1989). Thus, not only do we have a society in which increasing numbers of children are being reared by persons other than their parents, beginning at earlier and earlier ages, in part, perhaps because we lack tax, employment, and leave policies that would enable them to do otherwise, but there is good reason to believe that the nonparental care relied upon by all too many of these families is seriously lacking in quality. Now that this context of care has been articulated, I turn to my alternative reading of the literature on infant day care.

EFFECTS OF EARLY AND EXTENSIVE NONPARENTAL CARE

The first thing to note in any discussion of the effects of day care—infant or otherwise—is that the data do not permit unqualified assessment of causal processes. What we are dealing with, given the current state of the evidence, is correlational data in which confounding selection factors have not been fully taken into account, if they have been considered at all. Here, of course, I am simply reiterating and thus concurring with a point made by Clarke-Stewart. As I deconstruct and re-arrange some of Clarke-Stewart's presentation, I discuss attachment data, then data pertaining to aggression and noncompliance, and finally return to the issue of quality as it relates to timing of entry into nonparental care.

Basic to my deconstruction of Clarke-Stewart's analysis is the view that her interpretation of the evidence rests on her own organization of the research. Only by separating the attachment data from that pertaining to noncompliance and aggression can she sustain her arguments that (a) the linkage between attachment insecurity and early and extensive nonparental care is an artifact of a separation-based methodology; (b) group differences in rates of insecurity are almost so small as to be meaningless; (c) aggression and noncompliance reflect assertive independence; and, thus, (d) most day care promotes social competence.

Attachment

On the basis of her analysis of 16 studies involving some 1,200 cases, Clarke-Stewart is led to conclude, on the one hand, that the relation between attachment insecurity and infant day care is quite small and, on the other, that this almost meaningless difference between groups that vary in timing and extent of nonparental care may well be the product of a methodological artifact. An earlier analysis of a smaller set of studies that I carried out, as well as a data set that Professor Clarke-Stewart continues to disregard, lead me to take issue with both of these conclusions.

In 1988, a colleague and I published a report pertaining to infant day care and attachment in which I compiled the results of five studies of nonimpoverished children (Belsky & Rovine, 1988). Using a total sample size of 491 cases, rate of insecurity for children with 20 or more hours of nonparental care per week in their first year was found to be 43%, whereas that for children with less or no nonmaternal care was found to be 26%. The magnitude of difference here is greater than that which Clarke-Stewart discerned: She reported a lower rate of insecurity among infants exposed to 20 or more hours per week of nonparental care (36%) and a higher rate of insecurity among those exposed to less than 20 hours per week of nonparental care (29%). Recently, Lamb, Sternberg, and Prodromidis (1990) compiled data on 701 cases from 16 different studies and produced a 42% rate of insecurity for children who experienced more than 20 hours of nonparental care in their first year. In contrast, only 23% of those who experienced less care, or none at all, in their first year were classified as insecure.

In the course of analyzing data from my own investigation and that of the other four carefully selected studies that I reviewed, two additional findings emerged that I found particularly noteworthy. Both of them lead me to question the results of Clarke-Stewart's analysis. First, rate of insecurity was elevated only in the case of children experiencing early and extensive nonparental care, not nonmaternal care. In other words, no developmental risk was associated with father care. Second, there was statistically significant evidence that the timing of family participation in research affects the results obtained. When families were enrolled in the research process after the child's first year, no association between infant day care and attachment insecurity was discerned, yet when families were enrolled before they knew how day care and family relationships were developing, rates of insecurity were found to be significantly higher among children exposed to more than 20 hours per week of nonparental care in their first year (Chase-Lansdale & Owen, 1987; Belsky & Rovine, 1988).

These data strongly suggest that not all data are created equal and, thus, that research designs have to be scrutinized carefully when one is evaluating day-care findings. In fact, studies that enroll families into the research process well into the child's first year, especially if they are billed as studies of the effects of maternal employment and day care—as they often are—may systematically, though inadvertently, chase away many of the families responsible for the association between insecurity and infant day care, which emerges in studies that enroll families so much earlier in the child's life. In sum, what the evidence indicate to me is that not only do we have to distinguish nonparental from nonmaternal care, but we need to be alert to the very real possibility that some ways in which day care and maternal employment research is carried out may affect the results obtained.

It is as a direct result of these empirically based lessons that I have serious problems with Clarke-Stewart's (1989) analysis of 16 studies yielding an insecurity rate of just 36%. In her analysis of quality of care, Clarke-Stewart insightfully observed that more is not always better. Simply because her analysis included more studies and more subjects does not make her estimate more accurate. It has been almost three years since Clarke-Stewart published her analysis and more than that since some of the data became available to her, yet it remains the case that almost 25% of the data she compiled has still not been published by those who so readily shared it with her, so there is no way of obtaining critical information about the timing of sample recruitment and the utilization of father care versus nonparental care. Thus, her seemingly authoritative, yet quite indiscriminate tabulation of the evidence may well obfuscate as much as it illuminates. There is simply no way of knowing what to make of the 36% versus 29% rates of insecurity, respectively, of infants with and without early and extensive nonmaternal care experience, a difference which seems to me to be minimized by Clarke-Stewart.

In any event, the sad truth is that whatever meaning one breathes into these or other figures, no one has any idea how big a difference has to be in order to be individually or societally important. With 50% of mothers employed in the first year of their infants' lives, and one estimate being that 75% of them are working full time (Hofferth & Phillips, 1987), it is simply too convenient to minimize the magnitude of the association between early and extensive nonparental care—as we know it and have it in this country—and attachment insecurity. This would seem to be especially true in light of data on aggression and noncompliance, but here I am getting ahead of myself.

I turn now to what I regard as a further effort by Clarke-Stewart to minimize the meaning of the association between early and extensive nonparental care and attachment insecurity. Clarke-Stewart raises the spectre that the elevated rates of insecurity in the case of infants with early and extensive nonparental care experience may be an artifact of the separation-based measurement procedure used for assessing attachment. What she has failed to acknowledge, however, is that her very own review of studies of differential stress in the Strange Situation, as a function of day care experience, yields no consistent evidence that infants with repeated exposure to nonparental care are less stressed by this experimental procedure (Clarke-Stewart & Fein, 1983). Moreover, a study I recently completed — in direct response to criticism advanced by Clarke-Stewart (and others) — yields evidence dramatically inconsistent with her analysis of *possible* problems with using the Strange Situation to study the effects of day care. Rather than finding that insecure infants with early and extensive day-care experience were less stressed and more independent in the Strange Situation than insecure infants without such child-care history, we found (Belsky & Braungart, 1991) exactly the opposite. Thus, concerns that children who are independent may be mistakenly classified as insecure remain unsubstantiated, however logically possible and ideologically attractive they may be.

Not only is it disconcerting to see these data ignored as a case is made against the Strange Situation, but it is especially disconcerting to see patently inaccurate statements made about this widely employed methodology. For instance, it is not the case that the child's failure to seek physical closeness with the mother is, as Clarke-Stewart asserts, the basis for saying their relationship is insecure, any more than it is the case, as others have misleadingly argued, that crying determines whether a child is classified as secure or insecure. What is critical in the scoring of insecurity is the psychological contact the child does or does not establish with the parent: It may take the form of a smile and a vocalization across a distance or the seeking and finding of comfort in close, physical contact.

Perhaps the best evidence of the utility and, in fact, the sensitivity of the Strange Situation procedure is its well-chronicled ability to distinguish among children with varying rearing experiences. Consider in this regard what research shows about rates of insecurity among maltreated children, children with depressed mothers, children with early and extensive nonparental care experience, and children without any infant day-care experience. An analysis of eight independent studies of child abuse and neglect reveals a 65% rate of insecurity among maltreated infants (Youngblade & Belsky, 1989), and studies of depressed mothers yield insecurity rates hovering near 50% (47% in Radke-Yarrow, Cummings, Kuczynski, & Chapman, 1985; 48% in Teti, Gelfand, Messinger, & Isabella, 1991). When children with early and extensive nonparental care are the focus, the simple averaging of Clarke-Stewart's (1989) 16-study figure (36%), Lamb et al.'s (1990) 16-study figure (42%), and my own (Belsky & Rovine, 1988) 5-study figure (43%) yields an insecurity rate of 40%. Finally, these three multi-study analyses yield an average rate of insecurity of 26% in children with less than 20 hours per week of nonmaternal care in their first year of life. In other words, as we move from samples with little or no infant day-care experience, to those with extensive infant day-care experience, to those with depressed mothers, to those of children who are abused and neglected, rates of insecurity, as discerned using the much-maligned Strange Situation procedure, increase from about 25% to about 40% to more than 60%! Thus, rather than arguing, as Clarke-Stewart seems to, that the Strange Situation is a problematic methodology for studying the developmental correlates of early and extensive nonparental care, it is my contention that this is the best methodology we currently have available for examining how variation in rearing experience relates to infant socioemotional development.

Beyond Attachment

When summarizing evidence on the effects of day care, Clarke-Stewart maintains a now rather well-established tradition of failing to evaluate the data in developmental context. Studies are considered in terms of the overriding question they were originally designed to address rather than in terms of commonality in the child-care experiences of the subjects studied. As a result, she discusses first the early studies that looked at "the effect of any kind of day care"; these discerned, among other things, an association between child-care experience and elevated levels of aggression and noncompliance. Only much later in her chapter does she consider studies of infant day care that discerned an association between elevated rates of insecurity and early and extensive day care. One consequence of this approach is that it allows her to minimize the attachment data and interpret the social development data in terms of enhanced social competence. Although I would be among the first to defend Clarke-Stewart's right to her own orchestration and, thereby, her own interpretation of the evidence, I am also among the first, and perhaps the only, to take a different approach, which leads to dramatically different conclusions.

The minute one realizes that the overwhelming majority of studies that have found linkages between day-care experience and heightened aggression and noncompliance are studies of children whose full- or near full-time care began in their first year of life, one is forced to regard all of the data differently. A pattern clearly emerges in which early and extensive nonparental care, at least as it is routinely experienced in this country, is systematically associated with elevated rates of insecure attachment in infancy and with increased levels of aggression and noncompliance in the preschool and early elementary school years. This should not be taken to mean that we are talking about psychopathology, that these findings have been discerned in each and every study, or that every child is affected. Nevertheless, these results have emerged with sufficient frequency that it is very hard for me to reconcile these data with Clarke-Stewart's conclusion that maturation is being facilitated because day care promotes social competence.

How can this interpretation be maintained, much less entertained, when at least one study she cites chronicles greater hitting, kicking, and pushing in the first three years of public school, as well as greater difficulties avoiding conflicts, among children whose center-based day care was initiated in their first year of life (Haskins, 1985)? How is one to account for the very recent and unmentioned data of Vandell and Corasaniti (1990) on third graders from middle-class Dallas elementary schools, which showed that children who began nonmaternal care on a full-time basis in their first year of life and continued in such care through their preschool years were rated — in comparison to all other children — as less compliant by both teachers and parents and as less likable by agemates, and received poorer conduct grades and performed more poorly on achievement tests?

Quality of Care

One way to account for these data is to draw attention to the probable limited quality of care that these children received, given child-care regulations in the state of Texas. This interpretation, rather than one that considers aggression and noncompliance as evidence of assertiveness and thus of social competence, is quite consistent with recent research in the United States and Sweden. In a nation with a dramatically different social ecology, in which parents are offered extensive paid parental leave and then have the opportunity to place their children in centers with reasonably well-paid and well-trained caregivers, Andersson (1989) discerned absolutely no detrimental effects of extensive nonparental care in the first year. In our country, which is quite different from Sweden, Howes (1990) found, in another recent study not mentioned by Clarke-Stewart, that the detrimental consequences of poor quality day-care are most pronounced when such care is initiated in the first year of life. Children exposed to such care, when compared to agemates who began poor quality care in their second year, or whose good quality care began in their first or second year, were the ones who were least compliant as toddlers, who were regarded by teachers as most difficult as preschoolers, and who as kindergartners were least considerate of their classmates and least task-oriented.

Unfortunately, what Howes' (1990) study could not tell us is whether this subset of her sample, whose poor quality care was initiated in their first year, was experiencing care that was the rule or the exception. Even more unfortunate, though, are the aforementioned findings from National Child Care Staffing Study which lead me to suspect that it was the rule. Consider the fact, then, that it is infant day care that has been associated with attachment insecurity, aggression, and noncompliance; that more and more children are beginning their nonparental care in their first year of life; that it is likely to be poor quality of care that is most problematic; and that it is care of limited quality that is probably widely relied on by families that live in a society that has no parental leave policy, and has few flexible employment policies. On the basis of this developmental and social ecology of day care in America, I conclude that we have a nation at risk.

CONCLUSION

Needless to say, this is a provocative conclusion, but what I am struck by more than anything, having gone through what I refer to as *the day care wars* these last five years, is how conservative child developmentalists have been in considering so much of the day-care evidence. The recent National Research Council Report on day care (Hayes, Palmer, & Zaslow, 1990) is a case in point. Consider the structure of its logical argument: (a) many children are in day care; (b) good day care is good for children; and, thus, (c) programs to support quality of care are required. To me this is thoughtful, but weak, political rhetoric.

Just imagine how much interest there would be in American education today had a report been issued early in the last decade saying: (a) that most children are in schools; (b) that good schools are good for children; and, thus, (c) that we need good schools. I submit that the power of the report, *A Nation at Risk* lay in its logical structure and, thus, its political rhetoric. The argument was structured not as progressive day-care advocates structure their arguments, but rather, as follows: (a) bad schooling is bad for children; (b) there are too many bad schools, providing inferior education; (c) therefore, the nation is at risk; (d) in consequence, something must be done.

I now apply that same logic to day care:

1. Poor day care is bad for children, especially in the early years of life;
2. ever-increasing numbers of America's supposedly most valuable re-source — its children — are experiencing extensive nonparental care in their early years of life;
3. recent evidence indicates that the quality of care available to all too many children is quite limited;
4. the nation is still at risk; and
5. therefore, something must be done.

Why has this argument not been made? Why have my motives been questioned and the "messenger" been shot at when I have called attention to disconcerting evidence linking attachment insecurity, aggression, and non-compliance with early and extensive infant day care that some are all too willing to minimize, explain away, or disregard entirely? As far as I can tell, there are three reasons, one acceptable and the other two not. The first, and respectable one, is scientific: A more conservative reading of the data is called for because the findings are mixed and the interpretations given to them — actually all interpretations — are suspect.

A second, and totally unacceptable reason why so many are unwilling to acknowledge, much less speak about or have others speak about, the bad news regarding day care is fear of what the New Right, which by this time is the Old Right, will do with it. They will say we should have no day care. Perhaps they may, but after all, it is a free country and diversity of opinion, I thought, was to be tolerated if not welcomed. If, as justifiable scientific criticism holds, the data are mixed, then multiple interpretations are called for; why should only some interpretations of mixed data be tolerated and not others?

In fact, not only can the New Right's interpretation of the meaning of the evidence be countered by highlighting the ecological context of day-care effects and the national economy's dependence on female labor, but some aspects of the conservative viewpoint should also be embraced, so that a bipartisan and multidimensional child-care policy can emerge. Here I am referring to the conservatives' persistent and astute observation that the tax structure no longer supports families with children the way it did when I was growing up. Perhaps if the personal exemption per dependent child was worth to American families in the 1990s what it was worth to families in the 1950s the child-care crisis would not be so huge, because fewer mothers would be obligated to work.

The third reason, I believe, why the disconcerting evidence has been minimized is out of an understandable, but unacceptable, humanistic fear: With so many mothers forced to work, messages to the public about developmental risks will create anxiety. Again and again, I have heard, in reviews I and others have received by journal referees, and by laymen, that because the kind of analysis I have offered will make mothers feel guilty, we should not offer it.

I contend that a sad day has come to science when only some interpretations are regarded as permissible because others will make someone feel guilty. The way to support working women is not to deny them their guilt and anxiety, but to make their difficulties worthwhile. I have no doubt that if this generation of cultural pioneers felt confident — and were made to feel confident — that their stress would bring an easier life for their children and grandchildren, that their daughters would face better times when it came to integrating work and family, then they would wear their guilt on their sleeves. It has never been easy to cut new ground, especially new cultural ground.

For better or for worse, in America we do not stand up and take notice until pain and suffering are apparent. Look at the Three-Mile Island accident; look at the savings and loan debacle; look at the recent invasion of

Kuwait and the Desert Storm operation. As much as we would like to have a society that engages in prevention rather than remediation, the sad truth is that unless something is broken, we do not fix it. I contend that our child care system — or better yet, our nonsystem — is broken and needs to be fixed. I argue further that evidence pertaining to poor quality child care, attachment insecurity, noncompliance, and aggression reflect this ecological reality and, therefore, should not be minimized or avoided. Moreover, I contend that there are many solutions; the task at hand is to develop conservative and liberal policies that satisfy different constituencies rather than asserting, as so many ideologues on both sides of the day-care debate have, that parental leave and tax policies are anti-feminist, because they may promote traditional family practices, or that Alliance for Better Child Care legislative initiatives are anti-family because they reward women for abandoning the care of their children to strangers.

Unless we get smart and stop fearing conservatives or worrying about mothers feeling guilty, we, as policy-oriented scientists, will be less rather than more influential. After all, no one was concerned about the guilt that school teachers and principals would feel when *A Nation at Risk* was written, and look at all the attention that public education has received in the past few years. Perhaps one day real resources will be devoted to day care, as it has been to public education, if we stopped avoiding the bad news.

REFERENCES

Andersson, B.-E. (1989). The importance of public day care for preschool children's later development. *Child Development, 60,* 857–866.

Belsky, J., & Braungart, J. (1991). Are insecure-avoidant infants with extensive day care experience less stressed by and more independent in the Strange Situation? *Child Development, 62,* 567–571.

Belsky, J., & Rovine, M. (1988). Nonmaternal care in the first year of life and security of infant–parent attachment. *Child Development, 59,* 157–167.

Chase-Lansdale, L., & Owen, M. (1987). Maternal employment in a family context: Effects on infant–mother and infant–father attachment. *Child Development, 58,* 1505–1512.

Clarke-Stewart, K. A., & Fein, G. (1983). Early childhood programs. In M. M. Maith & J. J. Campos (Eds.), *Handbook of Child Psychology: Vol. 2. Infancy and developmental psychobiology* (pp. 917–1000). New York: Wiley.

Clarke-Stewart, K. A. (1989). Infant day care: Maligned or malignant. *American Psychologist, 44,* 266–273.

Dawson, D., & Cain, V. (1990). *Child care arrangements: Health of our nation's children: United States, 1988.* Unpublished data from Report No. 187. Hyattsville, MD: National Center for Health Statistics.

Haskins, R. (1985). Public school aggression among children with varying day-care experience. *Child Development, 56,* 689–703.

Hayes, C., Palmer, J., & Zaslow, M. (Eds.). (1990). *Who cares for America's children: Child care policy for the 1990s.* Washington, DC: National Academy Press.

Hofferth, S., & Phillips, D. A. (1987). Child care in the United States: 1970 to 1995. *Journal of Marriage and the Family, 49,* 559–571.

Howes, C. (1990). Can the age of entry and the quality of infant child care predict adjustment in kindergarten? *Developmental Psychology, 26,* 252–303.

Lamb, M., Sternberg, K., & Prodromidis, M. (1990). *Nonmaternal care and the security of infant–mother attachment: A re-analysis of the data.* Unpublished manuscript, National Institute of Child Health and Human Development, Bethesda, MD.

Radke-Yarrow, M., Cummings, E., Kuczynski, L., & Chapman, M. (1985). Patterns of attachment in two- and three-year-olds in normal families with parental depression. *Child Development, 56,* 884–893.

Rauch, J. (1989, August). Kids as capital. *Atlantic Monthly,* pp. 56–61.

Teti, D., Gelfand, D., Messinger, D., & Isabella, R. (1991, April). *Security of infant attachment and maternal functioning among depressed and nondepressed mothers and infants.* Paper presented at the biennial meeting of the Society for Research in Child Development, Seattle, WA.

Vandell, D., & Corasiniti, M. (1990). Child care and family. *New Directions for Child Development and Maternal Employment, 49,* 23–38.

Whitebrook, M., Howes, C., & Phillips, D. (1990). *Who cares?* (executive summary of the National Child Care Staffing Study). Available from Child Care Employee Project, Berkeley, CA.

Youngblade, L., & Belsky, J. (1989). Child maltreatment, infant–peer attachment security, and dysfunctional peer relationships in toddlerhood. *Topics in Early Childhood Education, 9,* 1–15.

Child Development and Its Implications for Day Care

BARBARA T. BOWMAN
Erikson Institute

I find little to quarrel with in Clarke-Stewart's conclusions, so I focus here on the quality of research being done on day care and our interpretations of it.

I have two concerns. The first is the suggestion that the research reviewed reflects day-care effects on development. Clarke-Stewart's paper is entitled "Consequences of Child Care for Children's Development," but I think it would be better entitled "Consequences of Child Care for Children's Learning." I think it is important to make a distinction between development and learning. Whereas development may be reflected in learned behavior, all learning is not synonymous with development. Within each developmental phase there are numerous different cultural forms of learning that result in developmental achievement.

To give a simple example: Learning a primary language is a developmental milestone for young children. Linguistic interactions act as triggers for the developmental achievement of learning language, and language knowledge and skill reflect development. Linguistic interactions also determine the particular language children learn. Some children learn Spanish, some standard English, and some non-standard dialects, such as Black English or Creole. The actual language learned is unimportant from a developmental point of view because they are developmental equivalents.

Developmental learning refers to the changes that occur in children's minds as a result of the interaction of their biological potential with experience, reflected in achievements like learning language, learning categorizing systems, establishing interpersonal relationships, abstracting relationships between objects and events, thinking, planning, and using symbols. These achievements signal developmental competence.

Children also learn cultural forms of behavior from family and community. These include learning a specific vocabulary, learning to categorize particular things, and learning particular relationships with others, like how to act toward unfamiliar adults. Although the major developmental changes in young children are remarkably alike across culture groups, the specific knowledge and skills learned may appear quite different.

I find it is useful to think of these two aspects of learning — developmental structures and cultural forms — as two sides of the same coin. Development is dependent on some form of cultural learning, but it is not dependent on the same form. Learning that reflects children's developmental status is of great significance, whereas, the specific cultural forms children have learned is of less developmental significance. Children who have mastered one cultural form can master other, similar ones. Thus, children who can speak one language have the developmental capability, if not the motivation, to learn others.

Making this distinction between learning that represents developmental achievement and learning that is an alternative cultural form is difficult, but worthwhile. Unless we can distinguish between the two, we are unsure if observed differences are significant to development or are just different pathways for achieving developmental potential. Developmentally normal children from some minority groups, whose experiences in life are different from those of the mainstream, are regularly diagnosed as developmentally delayed. These diagnoses result from beliefs and practices in research, public policy, and clinical practice that ignore this relationship between learned behavior and development.

Behavior that reflects similar developmental competence is regularly disregarded when it is not encoded in the forms we expect. It is unfortunate that much of the research on children's behavior suffers from this kind of cultural myopia. Measures of program effects rely primarily on standard instruments, which assess only one kind of response to a developmental challenge. Despite the fact that most researchers are well aware that standardized measures in common usage are culturally biased, we continue to equate development with the cultural content specific to a particular class and caste. As Cole (1985) has pointed out: "With a few exceptions, textbooks on cognitive and developmental psychology are written as if data on condition and cognitive development were separable from an understanding of the cultural circumstances in which people grow up" (p. 146).

The problem of selecting behavioral markers that are surrogates for developmental achievement across cultural and family differences is a difficult one. Clearly, some behavior does reflect developmental competence. In small, tightly knit, homogeneous communities, locating behavioral markers for development may be relatively easy, but in large, multicultural settings like the United States, it is much more difficult. Children who have not learned the forms of behavior expected in a particular social or physical environment, may be judged as developmentally delayed unless other, comparable, learning is elicited. Research on child care has rarely made an effort to assess the extent to which "quality" markers are tied to significant developmental consequences as opposed to White, middle-class cultural preferences.

The importance of assessing children's developmental status in planning and evaluating program effects is obvious. Programs that address developmental delay and deviance are quite different and their outcomes less assured than those designed to add new cultural expressions to the repertoire of developmentally adequate children. Let me hasten to add, however, that modifying and/or extending developmentally adequate, culturally embedded behavior may be difficult if the conditions of everyday life stay the same for children and families.

My second and related concern is the failure to critically examine research questions and conclusions in the context of their meanings in the lives of real people. As educators and researchers we must go beyond asking whether a child does or does not show a particular bit of learned behavior; we must also understand what that behavior means in the society in which we live.

Clarke-Stewart appropriately points out that science is embedded in community values. Why do we select the subjects we study and the questions we ask? Researchers often claim that their conclusions are data driven and that such findings should provide guidance for public policy and program design. We must remember, however, that every pernicious social movement in the last century was buttressed by scientific research (Gould, 1981). Critical scholars remind us that events, research, and policies do not just happen but reflect powerful influences at work that shape people's thinking and their institutions. Freud's perspective on human development was shaped by the social role of women in the times in which he lived and led him, incorrectly, to make the symptoms of hysteria a central part of his thinking on development (Stern, 1991). Today's fascination with day care and attachment may say more about the conservative longings in the country than about developmental consequences.

The pace of social change has increased rapidly since the 1960s, and family life has been jolted by new demands. As a consequence, the context of child rearing in America has changed radically. With over 60% of mothers working and over half of all women with a child under 1 year in the work force (Wellesley College, 1991), family life has had to adapt to circumstances that challenge deeply held beliefs about the proper way to raise children. It has awakened the need in many Americans to hold more tightly to past cultural forms, even though these may be idealized. The stay-at-home mother, the biologically related two-parent family, and "natural maternal drives" have come into head-on confrontation with women's achievement, personal happiness, and male nurturance. It is little wonder that families and communities are concerned, that these changes and conflicts create anxiety, and that many people long to return to more familiar social patterns of child rearing. This might explain why, despite considerable evidence, throughout the world and over time, that a number of different ways of raising children leads to different but developmentally equivalent outcomes, many people continue to make developmentally invidious comparisons between day-care children and home-reared children. By using home-reared children as the standard against which day care is measured, we confound development with cultural preference. By failing to distinguish the value base on which studies are conducted, we give the imprimatur of science to our belief.

Attachment research is currently the most prominent dimension along which comparisons between home- and day-care children are made, and it has drawn enormous interest. Legitimate questions exist, however, about whether the particular behavior measured by the procedure used is essential to activate the human potential for love, caring, interpersonal enjoyment, and satisfaction, or whether it is one of a number of possible manifestations of adequate interpersonal relationships (for effective functioning in a given society). Are anxiously attached children who are in day care reflecting a constriction in their relationship-making or self-imaging capacity? Do they simply have another way of organizing their self/other relationships, a different way but one well within some standard for normal development?

A recent article demonstrates how slippery the connection is between research findings and conclusions regarding family life. Bronfenbrenner (1991) concluded, in a recent review of the research literature, that "human development occurs in the context of an escalating psychological ping pong game between two people who are crazy about each other" (p. 3). Does this mean that development requires interaction only between the same two people, or can developmental support be provided by two, three, four, or ten different, but responsive, adults? Does the emotional attachment have to escalate with the same person, or can different persons provide for different or changing needs? Is the two-person paradigm essential to development, or is it simply the format considered best suited to the cultural preferences of (at least some) Americans in 1991? As Clarke-Stewart has pointed out, the interpretation of research is inevitably colored by personal beliefs and experiences.

There is little question that for many, attachment research is used in support of stay-at-home mothers, a social arrangement that fits well with traditional middle-class values and beliefs about family life. The effects of hunger are more easily assessed and more damaging to human development, yet considerably more public interest is aroused regarding support of unpaid maternal leave than in response to other, more severe, threats to human development.

It is useful to look at the beneficiaries of so-called pro-family social policies to see why the current wave of attachment research has found such a ready audience. It is also instructive to note that adolescent mothers are all but forced to remain in school (and away from their babies), and welfare mothers are being encouraged to enroll in employment programs at the same time that middle-class mothers are being encouraged to retire from the work force and care for their own infants and employers are being asked to subsidize parental leave. Why?

For some, the research and the family life implications drawn, are a source of anxiety and tension. For them it seems that mothers, again, have been singled out as the primary subverters of children's health. (One is reminded of the early research on autism, which blamed aberrant mother-care for the devastating symptoms in their children.) For them, attachment research is just further evidence of the extent to which the society will go to subjugate women.

For other mothers who leave their infants in day care in violation of the belief in the idealized family, the popularization of attachment research is stressful, the very condition most apt to lead to inadequate attachment and bonding. So, while some parents are consumed with guilt for abandoning their infants, other parents respond by denying the importance of mother-care for children entirely and fail to do the things they can do to stabilize this important relationship.

These are just a few examples of how difficult it is to make sense of this research, particularly in a society in which people live their lives in different ways, where people's behaviors, beliefs, and attitudes about the meaning of life itself are so different. However, the failure to consider research in social, economic, and political contexts may lead to serious distortions in its meaning and to compromising the effectiveness of interventions. We must be careful how we use research to justify values. Those of us who favor more social and economic support for families must avoid misusing research trying to "prove" we are right. It is also the obligation of the research community to make sure that everyone understands what they have really found.

REFERENCES

Bronfenbrenner, U. (1991). What do families do? *Family Affairs, 4,* 2–4.

Cole, M. (1985). The zone of proximal development: Where culture and cognition create each other. In J. Wertsch (Ed.), *Culture, communication and cognition: Vygotskian perspectives.* New York: Cambridge University Press.

Gould, S. J. (1981). *The mis-measure of man.* New York: W. W. Norton.

Stern, D. (1991). Symposium, Society for research on child development.

Wellesley College. (1991). Evaluating the effects of maternal employment on in-fant–mother attachment (Report xxx). Wellesley, MA: Wellesley College, Center for Research on Women.

Is Anything More Important Than Day-Care Quality?

RON HASKINS
Committee on Ways and Means
U.S. House of Representatives

One of the nation's major social problems is non-working women who are heads of families, particularly those who have a history of welfare dependency. In recent years, Congress has embarked on a series of initiatives designed to address the dependency issue, primarily by adopting policies designed to increase work by welfare mothers who head families. If these mothers are to work, however, their children must be cared for. Thus, the supply and price of day care are critical to the strategy of reducing dependency by increasing employment.

Although the media often carry stories about shortages and high prices of day care, scientific evidence and expert opinion seem now to support the conclusion that neither supply nor price is much of a problem for most American families seeking day care (Haskins, 1988; Hofferth, this volume). Some families may not be able to find precisely the type of care they want at the price they want to pay, but then not every family can find an inexpensive four-bedroom home in a nice neighborhood either.

By contrast, there is some alarm about day-care quality. Although Clarke-Stewart's chapter in this volume, like her other writing on day-care quality (e.g., 1987), is illuminating and temperate, a number of the researchers conducting studies of day-care quality have concluded that low-quality care has a negative impact on children's development. The National Research Council (1990) of the National Academy of Sciences even went so far as to conclude, based on a 2-year study, that the quality problem was serious enough to require federal regulation of day care.

My purpose here is to argue that the evidence on the effects of day-care quality does not support grandiose claims about its long-term impact on children's development. Further, there is virtually no evidence about how much low-quality day care is on the market, and therefore little basis for arguing that the government should adopt stronger regulations than currently exist.

If the federal policy-making context were such that day care was the only, or even the most important, issue on the social policy agenda, then fastidious attention to the possible effects of quality on children's development might make sense. But day care is not a major issue for politicians. Even more to the point, strong federal regulations to improve quality would, in all likelihood, increase price and constrict supply (Clifford & Russell, 1989). Thus, strict day-care regulation runs afoul of the objective of helping poor single mothers enter the labor force.

REDUCING DEPENDENCY:
A POLICY WITH SOME MOMENTUM

Two Approaches to Attacking Poverty

We begin by reviewing the "new" welfare politics (Mead, 1991) in which day care and day-care regulation are beginning to play an important role. Virtually everyone agrees that poverty is a serious national problem and that reducing poverty is a legitimate purpose of government policy. The arguments start the moment we begin to spin our theories regarding the methods by which government policy should address poverty.

The history of welfare policy in the United States is characterized by ongoing tension between society's desire to protect citizens (especially children) from the impact of poverty and society's desire to avoid creating a class of dependent citizens. Like England (Himmelfarb, 1983), the United States has experienced periods in which government emphasized one or the other side of the welfare–dependency balance. Beginning with the Social Security Act of 1935, federal social policy shifted strongly in the direction of providing, even guaranteeing, benefits for the poor. Both Republican and Democratic presidents supported and expanded these welfare programs. In fact, some of the most remarkable growth in welfare spending occurred under Republican Presidents Nixon and Ford.

In any case, by the mid-1970s the nation guaranteed cash and medical care to needy families with children (although the definition of *need* was often left to states) and food to virtually all poor citizens. In addition to these guaranteed benefits, the federal government evolved a complicated system of 150 or so programs that provide cash, housing, health care, day care, social services, and other in-kind benefits. By 1991, the federal government was spending about $200 billion on programs for poor and low-income families, and over 20% of the American population received at least some means-tested benefits.

From Welfare Expansion to Dependency Reduction

Several events during the 1980s conspired to shift the focus of American welfare policy from simply providing benefits to fighting the dependency that more and more observers believed was the inevitable companion of welfare benefits (American Enterprise Institute, 1987; Mead, 1991). In one of the most provocative and maligned books of the decade, Charles Murray (1984) held, in *Losing Ground,* that the array of welfare programs had the unintended effect of making families dependent on public largesse. According to Murray, America lost the war on poverty by declaring it with a host of new welfare benefits in the 1960s. Murray's solution was to terminate welfare programs and thereby force people to provide for themselves. Although there was outraged reaction to both this conclusion and the analysis on which it rested (e.g., Greenstein, 1985; Kuttner, 1984), *Losing Ground* unquestionably stimulated attention to the dependency problem.

At about the same time, Bane and Ellwood (1983) and O'Neill, Wolf, Bassi, and Hannan (1984) published studies of the length of time families stayed on welfare. Length of welfare spells is critical to the dependency issue because, by definition, if people stay on welfare for long periods of time they are dependent. Both studies were based on longitudinal data sets; both produced evidence that the majority of families that enter welfare are off the rolls within about 2 years (although many return to the rolls later). However, both also produced the surprising finding that, at any given moment, a majority of mothers on welfare would eventually be on the rolls for very long periods. Bane and Ellwood, for example, concluded that 65% of mothers on welfare at a given moment would eventually be on the rolls for 8 years or more.

Murray highlighted the importance of dependency; Bane, Ellwood, and O'Neill showed that dependency was real and frequent. As if to compensate for these somewhat dour messages, the 1980s also produced excellent research showing that job training and employment programs could help mothers find jobs and leave welfare. Based on large and representative samples, random assignment to treatment and control groups, and longitudinal designs, these studies provided solid evidence that welfare mothers who participate in work experience or job search programs are more likely to find a job, to be employed up to 3 years later, earn more and collect less money from welfare than welfare mothers in control groups who did not participate in these programs (Gueron & Pauly, 1991).

Congressional Action on Dependency

These three lines of social science research had a substantial impact on the U.S. Congress as welfare reform legislation was being written between 1986 and 1988 (Haskins, 1991). Furthermore, they contributed to a growing agreement among scholars and policymakers that dependency was a critical welfare issue and that work was its natural antidote. Hence, the Family Support Act of 1988, among other things, gave states about $700 million per year to conduct employment and training programs for welfare mothers, offered open-ended funding for day care while mothers were enrolled in education or training, and provided open-ended funding for day care and health insurance of mothers who took jobs and left welfare.

In essence, this bill said to welfare mothers: We are going to help you escape from public assistance by providing job search and work experience, by providing education and job training, by trying to force your children's father to pay child support, and by paying for child care. Furthermore, if you find a job and leave welfare, we will continue to pay for your medical insurance and help pay for your day care for 1 year. Nice stuff — and widely hailed as the most significant welfare reform since the Aid to Families with Dependent Children (AFDC) program was created in 1935.

The welfare reform debate showed that both Republicans and Democrats were greatly concerned about dependency. Both the debate and the Act itself seemed to tilt the benefits–dependency balance somewhat in the direction of concern for dependency. This judgment is supported by even more dramatic, if less publicized, action taken by Congress in 1990. Despite the highly partisan and bitter struggle over spending and taxes that characterized the 1990 budget debate, Congress voted to spend more than $18 billion over the next 5 years on the Earned Income Tax Credit (EITC) and another $5 billion on two new day-care programs. On top of the rather generous EITC that was originally enacted by Congress in 1975 and expanded in 1986, the total value of the EITC to a working family in the maximum income range will be nearly $3,000 by 1994. The total cost of the EITC between 1991 and 1995 will be $53 billion. Even in Washington, this is serious money.

The EITC enjoys solid bipartisan support for good reason:

- The EITC is refundable: Even families whose incomes are so low that they don't pay income taxes (for a three-person family, roughly under $15,000) nonetheless receive the credit.
- The credit addresses the dependency issue because it encourages work:

Low-income families receive wage supplements of up to 25%, but receive nothing at all if they don't work.

- The credit is well-targeted because only families with dependents and with earnings below about $21,000 in 1991 receive money.

In short, the EITC conveys a simple message to poor and low-income families from taxpayers: If you work but don't earn much, we'll help. Of course, the message through the welfare system is equally clear: If you don't work, we'll still help. Passage of the Family Support Act and the EITC expansions seem to show that the welfare message is in decline and the work message is ascendant.

DAY-CARE REGULATIONS AND WELFARE DEPENDENCY

Regulation of day care, however, presents a potential threat to the new emphasis on dependency reduction through work. To understand why, consider the types of care most often used by working mothers. As shown by the U.S. Bureau of the Census (1990, 16; see Table 1), in 1987 working mothers with children under age 5 were more likely to use relative care than any other type of care. Nearly half the child care for preschool children was provided by relatives. Even more important for my purposes, poorer families were more likely than wealthier families to use relative care. Whereas only

TABLE 1

Percentage of Families With Varying Incomes That Use Various Types of Day Dare

| Type of Care | Family Income | | | |
	All Families	Less Than Poverty	Less Than $15,000	More Than $45,000
Relatives	45.9	60.1	54.2	32.9
Father	(15.3)	(13.1)	(11.7)	(9.1)
Other Relative in Child's Home	(8.4)	(18.9)	(13.9)	(8.0)
Other Relative in Own Home	(13.3)	(16.3)	(18.0)	(10.2)
Mother While Working	(8.9)	(11.8)	(10.6)	(5.6)
Center/Nursery	25.4	15.9	15.9	35.0
Family Day Care	22.3	15.0	22.9	23.5
Nonrelative in Child's Home	6.2	9.0	7.0	8.7

Note. From U.S. Bureau of the Census, 1990, p. 16.

33% of families earning over $45,000 used relative care, more than half of the families earning under $15,000 and over 60% of families in poverty used relative care. Brush (1987) analyzed these Census Bureau data in greater detail and came to the same conclusion for mothers receiving AFDC: Between 50% and 60% of AFDC mothers who work use care by relatives.

Relative care is inexpensive. As Brush (1987, Table 4) showed, 60% of the working mothers on AFDC with preschool children do not pay for care at all. The 40% who do pay for care enjoy low payments averaging about $26 per week (in 1991 dollars). Surprisingly, former AFDC mothers who left welfare and were working in 1987 were only somewhat less likely to have free care — 50% versus the 60% for mothers still on welfare. On the other hand, they paid considerably more than mothers on AFDC, $46 versus $26 per week, perhaps because they worked longer hours.

Unfortunately, Census Bureau data on child care are collected in such a way that cost of care cannot be computed by type of arrangement. Even so, Martin O'Connell (personal communication, August 7, 1991), who directs the Census Bureau studies on day care, analyzed preliminary 1988 data on this issue. These data show that only 28% of families with preschool children using grandparent care in the child's home and only 70% of families using care by a relative other than a grandparent in the child's home actually pay for care. By contrast, nearly 100% of families using care by a nonrelative in either the child's home or the nonrelative's home pay for care. Similarly, 95% of families using center care and nearly 90% using nursery school care (which includes Head Start) pay for care. Thus, low-income families are likely to use the kind of care that requires either no payment or low payment.

Steiner (1971) was one of the first to recognize the crucial role of low day-care fees in helping welfare mothers enter the workforce. Carefully examining the case for trying to help AFDC mothers work, Steiner concluded that success depended in large measure on "finding some cheaper substitute for traditional day-care centers" (p. 71). His conclusion is still valid today.

Here is why. Let us assume that the average AFDC mother can find and qualify for a job paying $5.50 per hour, or about $11,500 per year (see Gueron & Pauly, 1991). If this mother is paying for care at the average cost (U. S. Bureau of the Census, 1990; costs inflated to 1991 prices), she will devote about $2,700 or nearly 25% of her gross income to day care. At this cost, it seems difficult to disagree with Steiner's conclusion that attacking welfare dependency through work may not save much public money.

Today's cost picture might be even worse than the one portrayed in the 1970s by Steiner. According to Clifford and Russell (1989), day care that provides adequate compensation for staff but does not improve facilities, curriculum, or staff–child ratios beyond those widely prevalent now would cost about $4,600 per year, about 70% higher than the Census Bureau's estimate of current actual payments. This amount would reduce the former welfare mothers' income by 40% rather than the mere 25% resulting from current average costs.

Fortunately, the real world offers a way around these discouraging computations. As we have seen, not every mother with a preschool child pays the average cost of $2,700 per year for day care, let alone the $4,600 cost of higher quality care. In fact, if we include children of all ages, only 30% of all working mothers and only 20% of those living in poor families pay anything at all for care. Moreover, of those with preschool or school-age children who do pay for care, the average cost is only $1,737 (1986 costs inflated to 1991 dollars). On average, then, working mothers below the poverty level, including the 20% who pay for care and the 80% who do not, pay only about $340 per year for child care.

This figure is shocking. It would be higher for mothers with preschool children, even higher for mothers with more than one child, and higher still for mothers who live in cities and work full-time. So double it; even triple it. The point is still that if poor and low-income mothers move into the labor force, and if they use the same types of day care at the same prices as poor and low-income families now use, the costs will be much lower than Steiner and most other observers who have looked into the issue would anticipate. If work by low-income mothers is to be profitable, both in saving public dollars through reduced welfare spending and in boosting incomes for families on welfare, we must let parents make their own arrangements and protect the current operation of the day-care market. This is the heart of my argument: Strong federal day-care regulations would raise the cost of care and make it more difficult for low-income families, especially single mothers, to achieve independence through work.

The major argument against this recommendation is that a great deal of market care is unsatisfactory. More specifically, many scholars believe that a substantial fraction of market care, especially that provided by unregulated relatives and informal family day-care operators—exactly the kind of care that must be used if work by poor mothers is to be profitable—is of low quality and is potentially harmful to children.

EFFECTS OF DAY-CARE QUALITY

It is precisely on the issue of day-care quality that researchers need to exercise the greatest caution. Very few policymakers or citizens are capable of understanding the technical studies that address this issue; they are, therefore, often at the mercy of whatever conclusions researchers draw and then, with the help of advocates, take to the public. Moreover, the public and most policymakers are ready to believe the worst about day-care quality. They are regularly exposed to media stories about neglect, maiming, and sexual abuse in day care — stories that zealots are only too anxious to dramatize. The U.S. Senate, for example, began its hearings on day care in 1990 by taking testimony from a panel of parents whose children had died in day care. If science is the antithesis of emotion, researchers have a special responsibility to be evenhanded in their analysis of day-care quality.

To provide a framework for evaluating studies of day-care quality, consider what most policy analysts want to see in studies that are to yield information for advising policymakers. Although no study conforms to the ideal in every particular, good studies feature:

- A large number of randomly selected subjects who represent a cross-section of a larger population.
- Random assignment of subjects to an experimental group and a control group.
- Manipulation of a treatment so that the experimental group receives one level while the control group receives another level.
- Measurement of the treatment's impact on subjects in both the experimental and control groups on several occasions over many years.

In the case of day-care quality, good research should be based on large and representative samples of children who were randomly assigned to a group that receives a higher level of quality and a second group that receives a lower level of quality. The children would then be tested or observed for differences in intellectual or social development over many years to determine whether the differences in day-care quality had either an immediate or a lasting impact.

In analyzing Clarke-Stewart's conclusion that high-quality care is potentially beneficial to preschool children's development, I examined the papers reviewed in her chapter as well as a body of studies reviewed by the National Research Council (1990) of the National Academy of Sciences in its recent study of day-care policy. There are now about 30 published, and a few unpublished, studies that report data on the impact of day-care quality on child behavior or development. If multiple reports on the same sample of children are discounted, the literature on day-care quality and child development consists of information on about 20 groups of children from the United States, Canada, Bermuda, Sweden, and Israel. How do these studies measure up against the standards just outlined?

First, none of the studies was performed on representative samples. One study was performed on nearly 600 children in day-care centers and family day-care homes in New York City (Golden et al., 1978), one was conducted on most of the preschool children in day care on the island of Bermuda (McCartney, 1984), and two of the studies were conducted with over 1,300 children in three American cities (Ruopp, Travers, Glantz, & Coelen, 1979; Travers & Goodson, 1980). The remaining studies, however, usually involved small numbers of children (range: 20 to 150; average: 66), selected from a small number of day-care facilities in one city. In summary, only a few of the studies can claim to be even moderately representative of American preschool children. The canons of science therefore dictate caution in interpreting results from such small and unrepresentative samples of convenience.

A second criterion of good social science is experimental manipulation. Of the published studies, only two contrasted experimental and control treatments. One study systematically varied teacher qualifications and staff–child ratios in 29 classrooms in eight centers in Atlanta (Travers & Goodson, 1980). Although neither teacher education nor staff–child ratios had significant impacts on child development, group size and teacher training in child development did. The second study (Field, 1980) varied staff–child ratios and classroom design and found no main effects of either variable on a host of social behaviors.

Given that the only two manipulative studies produced no evidence of impact for staff–child ratios, no evidence of impact for teacher education, and moderate evidence for impact of group size and teacher training in child development, it is difficult to see how an unbiased assessment could find more than moderate support for the notion that quality of care has an impact on child development. Neither study contained any information about the permanency of effects beyond the preschool years.

The final criterion of good studies is that they examine the impact of some measure of quality on children's development over a period of years. Researchers and day-care advocates often claim that studies show long-term effects: Good day care increases school achievement, leads to higher graduation rates, reduces teen crime and pregnancy, and increases adolescent and adult employment rates (see Schweinhart & Weikart, 1986). Advocates who make these arguments know that policymakers are especially attracted to programs that produce such long-term payoffs.

Only three of the published studies (Howes, 1988, 1990; Vandell, Henderson, & Wilson, 1988) reported data linking preschool day-care quality with behavior in the elementary school years. All three produced modest correlational evidence that day-care quality predicted social or academic competence. Two of the studies, however, had design or statistical problems, and the third found only one significant correlation between preschool quality and a teacher rating of classroom behavior. The oldest child observed across the studies was 8 years old. Thus, conclusions about the effects of day-care quality on children's development are not based on any evidence about development beyond age 8. Whether there are effects of day-care quality in the middle or late elementary school years, in high school, or beyond is completely unknown.

Thus, on the major criteria defining the types of studies that are suited to drawing policy conclusions—representative samples, random assignment, experimental manipulation, and long-term results—the body of research on child-care quality is limited.

Moreover, the review just presented provides little flavor of the actual findings on which many of the researchers based their conclusion that day-care quality has an impact on children's development. To be sure, a few of the studies are remarkable. The New York study (Golden et al., 1978) included extensive information on 577 children in 52 centers and day-care homes. In addition to spending several hours observing each child at his or her day-care facility, the authors of this study collected information on intellectual and language development, on social behavior with adults and peers, and on family background. Some of the measures of day-care quality, especially the indexes of the amount of social stimulation children received from caregivers, were related with child development at 24 or 36 months, but of the many such relationships examined, only a moderate number were statistically significant.

Two of the more impressive studies were conducted as part of the National Day Care study in the mid-1970s (Ruopp et al., 1979; Travers & Goodson, 1980). One of these featured thousands of hours of observation of children and their day-care teachers in 57 centers in three cities; another was an experiment in 29 classrooms in Atlanta in which both child–staff ratios and teacher education were systematically varied. As mentioned previously, none of these studies produced evidence that ratios or teacher education had an impact on child development; there was evidence, however, that group size and teacher training in child development had short-term impacts. Data from these excellent studies constitute the most impressive evidence that day-care quality influences development.

Just as the body of studies on quality included interesting and ambitious studies, so, too, did it include flawed studies. One of the latter (Vandell et al., 1988) was a follow-up study based on only 20 children from an original sample of 55 children. Another study (Carew, 1980) was based on 22 upper middle-class White children in centers that employed only teachers with college degrees. A third study (Howes, 1988) found no effects for quality in one analysis, but nonetheless concluded that quality had a strong impact on development because a second analysis produced some evidence, albeit unsupported by tests of statistical significance, of a correlation between day-care quality and behavior in kindergarten.

Nor does this review provide any indication of the inconsistency of findings across these studies. For almost every finding of a correlation between day-care quality and child development in one study, another study failed to find the same relationship. In fact, one published study (Kontos & Fiene, 1987) failed to find any effects of quality at all.

Clarke-Stewart drew the appropriate conclusion from this set of studies: Social science research has produced some evidence that quality of day care may, under some circumstances, have moderate impacts on children's development in the short run. She was even more terse, and in my view accurate, in an earlier review of several studies of day-care quality. On that occasion she characterized the link between day-care quality and children's development as "underwhelming" (1987, p. 114).

Perhaps my review of the evidence is too picky, and a roomful of impartial social scientists would decide that the scientific evidence does establish a strong link between day-care quality and child development. Would it follow that poor quality day care is an adequate basis for stronger regulation of the day-care market? Not necessarily. In addition to showing that poor quality care has an impact on children's development, the case for stronger regulation should rest on evidence that many children are in low-quality care and that such intervention can produce positive results.

Clarke-Stewart does not deal with the issue of whether the United States has lots of low-quality child care. The National Research Council (1990) took up this issue in its recent report recommending federal regulations, but other than a few references to expert opinion, the Council provided no evidence that vast numbers of children are in low-quality care. And for good reason. There are no nationally representative data on the average quality of care in day-care centers or homes in the United States. Nonetheless, there appears to be a widespread belief that lots of day care, particularly that provided by unregulated family day-care homes, is bad and perhaps deleterious to children's development. As it happens, there are fairly good data on just this type of care.

The National Day Care Home Study (Fosburg, 1981) made extraordinary efforts to locate a large sample of unregulated homes; their efforts included door-to-door canvassing to try to locate these informal, nonmarket facilities. More than 100 such facilities were located in San Antonio, Los Angeles, and Philadelphia. The researchers then spent thousands of hours interviewing and observing parents, teachers, and children in these 100 facilities, as well as parents, teachers, and children in another 200 regulated facilities.

Although there were some differences in the care provided by regulated and unregulated facilities, the authors concluded that unregulated care was of adequate quality. The investigators judged unregulated care not merely safe, but good enough that they informed the public that such care is "stable, warm, and stimulating," that it "caters successfully to the developmentally appropriate needs of children," that parents say it "meets their child care needs," and that the cost is "reasonable." Not surprisingly, the researchers recommended that policymakers use more public funds in these facilities (see p. 124).

CONCLUSION

Developmental psychologists and early childhood specialists who study day care are deeply committed to children's well-being. Clarke-Stewart (1990), noted that people who want to help children often use their professional skills to advance the children's cause. What researchers do is research. Thus, they conduct research to show that good day care helps children and bad day care hurts them.

This is not to say that researchers put their fingers on the scales of science as they conduct their studies. I trust that my review of the studies conveys my admiration for many of them. Even so, bias influences the interpretation: It causes the magnification of meager and conflicting results. Dispassionate evaluation of the body of research on day-care quality and children's development shows that there are no studies with representative samples, few experimental studies, and no information at all about the impact of quality beyond age 8. Combine this with the fact that the findings are often contradictory and that at least one study found no effects at all, and the conclusion that the effects are moderate and short-term seems appropriate. Moreover, there is no scientific information on the frequency of low-quality care in the United States, nor is there persuasive evidence that government regulations would actually increase quality.

In short, the case for using quality as a justification for interfering in the day-care market and insisting on conformity to strong standards is weak.

By contrast, there is abundant evidence that dependency on welfare is a major social problem and that welfare mothers can be helped by government programs to help them prepare for and take jobs in the private sector. If this approach to attacking dependency is to be successful, inexpensive day care is a must.

Reliable evidence from the Census Bureau indicates that most low-income and poor mothers already use inexpensive types of care. Moreover, the federal government is now spending well over $8 billion on day care, much of it directed to low-income families. In 1990, Congress enacted two new day-care programs that will provide about $1 billion per year to help low-income families pay for child care.

So, policymakers are faced with a tradeoff that will become even clearer as the Family Support Act and the new day-care programs are being implemented. On the one hand, advocates and many researchers are arguing that day-care quality is a problem and that children are at risk because most current state regulations are not strong enough and are not enforced with appropriate vigilance. They want the federal government to step in and require stronger regulations and more enforcement. Most people making this argument also hold that the federal government should supply additional funds to help the states put some teeth in their regulations and to do even more than it currently does to subsidize care for low-income families.

On the other hand, to the extent that low-income mothers are no longer allowed to place their children in informal, mostly unregulated arrangements, more and more mothers will have to pay higher and higher fees for child care.

As a result, the mothers will either fail to enter the labor force and thereby take an important step toward breaking their dependence on welfare or will choose the day care that best suits their needs and tastes and pay the bill themselves. Both are bad outcomes.

This tradeoff between the benefits and costs of stronger regulations is not merely academic. The state of Ohio, for example, has insisted that all providers, including relatives, meet state regulations before they can be reimbursed for caring for children of AFDC mothers. According to a recent report in *Public Welfare* (Offner, 1991), the result of this policy is that Ohio welfare mothers are having difficulty finding care. By contrast, welfare mothers in California are having little difficulty finding care because, like middle-class parents receiving a federal subsidy through the Dependent Care Tax Credit, they can choose whatever care best meets their needs. An evaluation by the Manpower Demonstration Research Corporation (Riccio, Goldman, Hamilton, Martinson, & Orenstein, 1989) found that only about 5% of welfare mothers not participating in the state's welfare-to-work program gave lack of day care as the reason. Moreover, 68% of the mothers with children under age 6 were using state-funded care.

The nation is now implementing policies designed to help as many poor families as possible to end their dependency on welfare by training for, finding, and securing employment. Congress has committed billions of dollars to helping these families find employment, pay for day care, and pay for medical insurance. Congress has also committed $53 billion for a 5-year period ending in 1995 to supplement the incomes of low-income families through the EITC. If this strategy succeeds, the payoff for the nation and for the families involved will be immense. Impeding the implementation of this policy because day care may harm some children under some circumstances is unwise. At the very least, social scientists who insist on putting every child in highly regulated day care must present stronger evidence showing how the benefits of such a policy exceed the costs.

REFERENCES

American Enterprise Institute. (1987). *A community of self-reliance: The new consensus on American welfare policy.* Washington, DC: Author.

Bane, M. J., & Ellwood, D. T. (1983). *The dynamics of dependence: The routes to self-sufficiency* (Department of Health and Human Services, Report No. HHS-100-82-0038). Cambridge, MA: Urban Systems Research and Engineering.

Brush, L. R. (1987). *Child care used by working women in the AFDC population: An analysis of the SIPP data base.* Unpublished manuscript, Analysis, Research and Training, McLean, VA.

Carew, J. (1980). Experience and the development of intelligence in young children at home and in day care. *Monographs of the Society for Research in Child Development, 45,*(6-7, Serial No. 187).

Clarke-Stewart, A. (1987). In search of consistencies in child care research. In D. A. Phillips (Ed.), *Quality in child care: What does research tell us?* (pp. 105-120). Washington, DC: National Association for the Education of Young Children.

Clarke-Stewart, A. (1990, August). *Discussion at APA Symposium on Child Care Policy and Research.* Paper presented at the annual meeting of the American Psychological Association, Boston, MA.

Clifford, R. M., & Russell, S. D. (1989). Financing programs for preschool-aged children. *Theory into Practice, 28,* 19-27.

Field, T. M. (1980). Preschool play: Effects of teacher/child ratios and organization of classroom space. *Child Study Journal, 10,* 191-205.

Fosburg, S. (1981). *Family day care in the United States: Summary of findings* (DHHS Publication No. OHDS 80-30282). Washington, DC: Department of Health and Human Services.

Golden, M., Rosenbluth, L., Grossi, M. T., Policare, H. J., Freeman, H., & Brownless, E. M. (1978). *The New York Infant Day Care Study.* New York: Medical and Health Research Association of New York City.

Greenstein, R. (1985, March 25). Losing faith in *Losing Ground. The New Republic, 192*(12), pp. 12-17.

Gueron, J. M., & Pauly, E. (1991). *From welfare to work.* New York: Sage Publications.

Haskins, R. (1988). What day care crisis? *Regulation, 12*(2), 13-21.

Haskins, R. (1991). Congress writes a law: Research and welfare reform. *Journal of Policy Analysis and Management, 10,* 616-632.

Himmelfarb, G. (1983). *The idea of poverty: England in the early industrial age.* New York: Vintage Books.

Howes, C. (1988). Relations between early child care and schooling. *Developmental Psychology, 24,* 53-57.

Howes, C. (1990). Can age of entry into child care and the quality of child care predict adjustment in kindergarten? *Developmental Psychology, 26,* 292-303.

Kontos, S., & Fiene, R. (1987). Child care quality, compliance with regulations, and children's development: The Pennsylvania study. In D. A. Phillips (Ed.), *Quality in child care: What does research tell us?* (pp. 57-79). Washington, DC: National Association for the Education of Young Children.

Kuttner, R. (1984, May 9). Declaring war on the war on poverty. *The New York Review of Books,* pp. 41-49.

McCartney, K. (1984). Effect of quality of day care environment on children's language development. *Developmental Psychology, 20,* 244-260.

Mead, L. (1991). The new politics of the new poverty. *Public Interest, 103,* 3-20.

Murray, C. (1984). *Losing ground: American social policy, 1950-1980.* New York: Basic Books.

National Research Council. (1990). *Who cares for America's children? Child care policy for the 1990s.* Washington, DC: National Academy Press.

Offner, P. (1991). Child care and the Family Support Act: Should states reimburse unlicensed providers? *Public Welfare, 49*(2), 6-9.

O'Neill, J., Wolf, D., Bassi, L., & Hannan, M. T. (1984). *An analysis of time on welfare.* Washington, DC: The Urban Institute.

Riccio, J., Goldman, B., Hamilton, G., Martinson, K., & Orenstein, A. (1989). *GAIN: Early implementation experiences and lessons.* New York: Manpower Demonstration Research Corporation.

Ruopp, R., Travers, J., Glantz, F., & Coelen, C. (1979). *Children at the center: Summary findings and their implications.* Cambridge, MA: Abt Associates.

Schweinhart, L. J., & Weikart, D. P. (1986). What do we know so far? A review of the Head Start Synthesis Project. *Young Children, 41*(2), 49–55.

Steiner, G. Y. (1971). *The state of welfare.* Washington, DC: Brookings.

Travers, J., & Goodson, B. D. (1980). *Research results of the National Day Care Study.* Cambridge, MA: Abt Associates.

U.S. Bureau of the Census. (1990). Who's minding the kids? Child care arrangements, 1986–87. *Current Population Reports,* Series P-70, No. 20. Washington, DC: U.S. Government Printing Office.

Vandell, D. L., Henderson, V. K., & Wilson, K. S. (1988). A longitudinal study of children with day-care experiences of varying quality. *Child Development, 59,* 1286–1292.

Consequences of Child Care—One More Time: A Rejoinder

ALISON CLARKE-STEWART
University of California-Irvine

In writing this rejoinder to the commentaries by Barbara Bowman, Jay Belsky, and Ron Haskins I am glad to have the opportunity to clarify, expand on my lead chapter and to acknowledge the contributions of my colleagues.

I think that Bowman is absolutely correct to suggest that we reconceptualize the results of much of our research on child care as demonstrating the effects of day care on children's learning rather than on children's development. I wish I had thought of this way of putting it myself. I was trying to make a similar point when I noted that the observed effects of day care on preschool children are not permanent. It would have strengthened the point to have suggested at the same time that because the effects are not permanent, they might be better thought of as effects on children's performance rather than on their competence, as effects on learning rather than on development. I make a similar point in suggesting that day care speeds up children's development rather than changing it in a basic way. All children learn their letters; it's just that children in day-care programs do it earlier. All children are eventually able to leave their mother's side to explore a new environment, but children in day care do it at younger ages. All children get over their inhibition with strangers; day-care children just do it faster. All children learn to cooperate with their peers; day-care children learn it sooner. Day-care children enter the world outside the home when they are very young, and their experiences in that outside world lead to their learning these skills. To reinforce Bowman's argument, more than simply learning new skills, they learn a different culture: a culture of interacting with groups of people, dealing with newcomers who have appeared and without friends who have disappeared, figuring out institutional rules, achieving academic success, and making decisions about what to do without Mother's advice. It is a culture into which children who stay home during the preschool years are not integrated until they get to school. It is a culture that is as different from the culture of being at home with mother as the American culture is different from the Mexican, the French from the English. I appreciate Bowman's bringing to our discussion these concepts of culture and learning; they offer a useful prism through which to view day-care effects.

I also appreciate Bowman's comment that "Today's fascination with day care and attachment may say more about the conservative longings in the country than about developmental consequences" (p. 97), although I have enough disagreements with another of my critics to make this statement myself. I, too, have suggested that ideology influences our research agendas and interpretations, and for this reason I have recommended that we examine in greater depth and with a broader array of measures the contemporaneous and long-term consequences of infant day care for children's psychological development, rather than focusing so fixedly on attachment to the mother.

This emphasis on attachment in the recent day-care debate could have been one reason to postpone the discussion of research on infant care to the last section of my chapter. In fact, it was not the reason I chose this organization. My reason was more straightforward and less political. I was simply going from what we know most about to what we know least about, and trying to offer some empirically based suggestions for improving day-care quality. I was not, as Jay Belsky claims, "orchestrating" the data to play up day-care pluses and play down day-care minuses.

I, too, am concerned about the possible risks of early extensive day care for infants (and their parents); that should have been clear in my cautious conclusions. Moreover, I, too, am in favor of parental leaves (they're good for parents whether or not they have measurable effects on infants' attachments), part-time employment (another boon for parents), and high-quality infant care (who wouldn't be?). I don't think we need an empirical basis to support these policy suggestions, and I don't think that we *have* one (in whatever order we discuss the data).

Belsky accuses me of "continuing to disregard" data in my presentation of the research, but although I may have omitted a study or two in my—extremely simple and brief—review, it was not for ideological reasons. I have no day-care axe to grind, and if Belsky could change his interpretation of the data from one year to the next (Belsky, 1984, 1986), with enough new and convincing data, so could, and would, I. All I have said all along is that we do not yet have enough evidence to reach conclusions about the effects of infant day care and that we should keep our minds open as we collect more data.

For one thing, I don't think that we have enough evidence to prove that available infant care is inadequate. Belsky infers from the "barely adequate" quality observed in the National Staffing Study (Whitebook, Howes, & Phillips, 1990) that infant care must be of concern, but that study was not a study of infant care and did not include the informal home-based care that the vast majority of infants in day care receive. I also don't think we have enough evidence to prove that infant day care has bad effects on children's development.

To justify my reservations about our knowledge base concerning the effects of infant day care, I will deconstruct Belsky's deconstruction of my chapter point by point. Belsky suggests that I separate research on aggression and noncompliance to sustain the argument that "(a) the linkage between attachment insecurity and early day care is an artifact of a separation-based methodology; (b) group differences in rates of insecurity are so small as to be meaningless; (c) aggression and noncompliance reflect assertive independence; and, thus, (d) most day care promotes social competence" (pp. 85–86).

First, let me respond to the question of whether (and why) I have argued that the link between attachment insecurity and early day care is an artifact of a "separation-based methodology." It is true that I have been critical of researchers' relying solely on the Strange Situation—a method that involves brief separations of infants from their mothers—for assessing the emotional development and well-being of infants in day care. If there is even the slightest possibility that day-care infants might react differently in this situation because they are more accustomed to being separated from their mothers, it makes sense to me to assess them in other situations as well. I have not disregarded the results of the Strange Situation, nor would I ever recommend doing so. I have merely argued that we need to collect other measures of children's fondness for their mothers and other evidence of emotional maladjustment.

I have not suggested that attachment classification depends only on physical closeness of infant and mother; I clearly stated in the chapter that the security of an infant's attachment is indicated by *going to or greeting* the mother. My concern is that day-care children might be less inclined to do either if they are more used to comings and goings by their mother, and so they might be misclassified as *avoidant* in the Strange Situation. I have never downplayed the usefulness of the Strange Situation as a tool for identifying problems in the mother–child relationship or for predicting later maladjustment in children whose main caregiver is the mother, but it is only logical not to use as the sole index of emotional health for day-care children a method of assessment that may not be equivalent for them.

Belsky's claim that he has collected evidence that is dramatically inconsistent with my suggestion that day-care children may not be comparably stressed by the Strange Situation is dramatically overstated, being based on a comparison of 11 infants in full-time care with 9 infants in part-time care. More subjects may not always be better (beyond 1,000 perhaps), but there are limits below which few is just too few. I continue to think it is an open question whether children's "avoidance" in the Strange Situation reflects the same kind of psychological pattern in day-care children as it does for home-reared children who are avoidant because their mother rejects them. I am not dismissing the issue; if I did I wouldn't be devoting all my research time to the National Institute of Child Health and Human Development (NICHD) Study of Early Child Care.

Next, let me respond to Belsky's suggestion that I think that the group differences in rates of insecurity between day-care and home-care children are so small as to be meaningless. I did not say that they were meaningless. What I said was that the likelihood of insecurity in day-care infants was within the normal range for assessments made around the world, and that how large the difference between groups is depends on who is in the sample. With more high-risk children in the sample, it is likely that the occurrence of insecurity will be *less* in day-care children than it is in home-care children, not greater (see Clarke-Stewart, 1989).

Belsky accuses me of indiscriminate data gathering for my tabulation of findings on this issue, and he's right. I did gather all the data I could find—indiscriminately—from all the studies I knew about that included information about maternal employment and children's behavior in the Strange Situation. I did not think it was necessary to be selective as long as the researchers knew the children's care status and coded their behavior in the Strange Situation blind to this knowledge. The unpublished data I was able to find to supplement Belsky's "carefully selected" studies may never be published as such; they were not gathered in studies of "day care" but rather in other longitudinal research on social development, by investigators unbiased by particular day-care or maternal-employment hypotheses. I am sorry that I did not ask about whether these children were in father-care while their mothers worked, as Belsky suggests I should have, but I do wonder why, if the argument is that children separated from their mothers are at risk for developing an insecure attachment to her, how being with Dad is better than being with a regular and loved nonrelated care provider.

Surely it is petty to fuss about the precise statistics on the rate of insecure attachment in day-care children; we all agree that the rate of insecurity (as assessed by the Strange Situation) is somewhat elevated. I prefer to leave open the question of how significant that elevation is.

The third point in Belsky's argument is that I have claimed that aggression and noncompliance are merely assertive independence. This is not true. I have claimed that aggression and noncompliance *go along with* assertive independence in children who have not been taught how to get what they want peacefully. He then credits me with a "well-established tradition of failing to evaluate the data in developmental context" (p. 89). This is also, I hope, untrue. The reason that I included the data on children's aggression and noncompliance in my discussion of the effects of preschool day care rather than in my discussion of the effects of infant care was that there is evidence that children who have attended day-care programs are likely to be more aggressive and noncompliant than children who have not, regardless of the age at which they begin day care. Belsky (correctly) points out that the "overwhelming majority of studies that have found linkages between day-care experience and heightened aggression and noncompliance are studies of children whose . . . care began in their first year of life" (p. 89). This does not mean, however, that studies of children whose day-care experience began *later* than the first year show that these children are *not* more aggressive and noncompliant. The "overwhelming majority" of these studies, too, show that day-care children are more aggressive and noncompliant. In one recent study of 600 children about to enter kindergarten, for example, Bates et al. (1991) found that day-care attendance at ages 1 to 3 was more predictive of aggression than day-care attendance in the first year of life. In another study, of 835 kindergarten children, Thornburg, Pearl, Crompton, and Ispa (1990) found no special effect of infant care on children's aggression and noncompliance; rather, care over the entire preschool period was associated with higher levels of aggression and noncompliance. In yet a third study, Park and Honig (1991) found that preschoolers who had been in full-time day care starting any time in the first three years were more aggressive and disobedient than preschoolers who had not had this day-care experience.

I do not condone aggression or claim that it is a sign of maturation and social competence; I abhor violence in my own or anyone else's child, but before we condemn infant day care — or day care at any age — we must also ask whether the aggression observed in day-care children reflects psychological maladjustment. There are four (empirically based) reasons that I suspect the aggression and noncompliance of day-care children is not as psychologically troublesome as Belsky claims. First, it has been observed that, although day-care children are more aggressive on the playground, they are not always considered by their teachers to be unlikable or difficult to manage (Haskins, 1985). Second, longitudinal studies show that, although day-care children are more aggressive from preschool through first or second grade, they are not more aggressive in the later school years (Egeland, 1991; Field, 1991; Haskins, 1985). Third, studies show that when family and child characteristics, such as socio-economic status and gender, are controlled (i.e., partialled out), infant day care contributes only minimally to children's aggression (Bates et al., 1991; Park & Honig, 1991). Fourth, the heightened aggression of day-care children can be eliminated by a day-care curriculum that focusses on teaching children social skills (Finkelstein, 1982).

Finally, Belsky argues that, because of the foregoing flaws in my organization and interpretation of the research, I fall into the trap of concluding that day care promotes children's social competence. My suggestion that day care promotes children's social competence, however, is not based on my interpretation of the research on attachment, aggression, or noncompliance. It is based on the research showing that children who are in day care are better able to cooperate and make friends with peers, to make overtures to unfamiliar adults, to do well in school, and to be liked by teachers (e.g., Field, 1991; Haskins, 1985; Park & Honig, 1991; Phillips, McCartney, & Scarr, 1987; Schwarz, Krolick, & Strickland, 1973), even if they also, at times, act aggressive and noncompliant.

In concluding his discussion, Belsky wonders why his sounding the alarm about infant care has not been used by psychologists or policy makers to make the argument that we need to improve the quality of infant care. There is, I think, a good reason for this oversight. Although it is politically correct to promote the cause of high-quality care, the evidence that Belsky has marshalled to raise the alarm about the possible negative effects of infant care does not demonstrate that any of these negative effects are less likely in high-quality care. The children who were observed to avoid their mothers and hit their peers were often in excellent day care—with in-home sitters (Barglow, Vaughn, & Molitor, 1987) or in model, university-based day-care centers (Field, 1991; Haskins, 1985; Schwarz, Strickland, & Krolick, 1974).

At least the idea that we should improve the quality of day care is one thing Belsky and I can agree on. Although we differ in our reading of the research literature, our politics (at least our politics regarding improving day-care quality) are compatible. In contrast, the third discussant of my chapter and I agree only in our appraisal of the research; our political views are substantially different.

Ron Haskins and I agree that most studies are limited because they are small scale, short-term, and non-experimental. Beyond this, however, we have a number of significant points of disagreement. First, I submit that, just because the experimental manipulations of day-care quality researchers have tried have not had strong effects on children's development, this does not mean that more extreme manipulations of quality would not have stronger effects. The extent of experimental manipulations researchers are permitted is limited by their need for approval by Human Subjects' Committees. Still, no one who saw the hidden camera exposé of day-care quality on "Prime Time" (ABC, June 20 and 27, 1991) could doubt that children in neglectful or abusive care would be likely to be strongly affected by their day-care experiences. There are undoubtedly extremes of low quality, such as the ones revealed in that program, that are damaging to children and would be documented as such, if they could be studied experimentally.

The second point of disagreement concerns Haskins' demand for research evidence that day care affects children's development *in the long term*. It is, of course, desirable to study children's development beyond the time they are in care, to probe for long-lasting consequences of their early experiences. Nevertheless, long-term effects should not be the only concern of a humane citizenry. Life should be minimally acceptable for children before they get to any long-term consequences. Even if, to use Haskins' analogy, children can't all live in a four-bedroom house in a nice neighborhood, they should all be able to live in a one-bedroom apartment in a decent neighborhood. Day-care "quality of life" as well as long-term consequences are issues for all children.

Most significantly, however, Haskins and I disagree about the role of the government in promoting high-quality day care. He downplays the role that government regulation can have in assuring quality care. Clearly regulation cannot create or guarantee high-quality care. Research showing that unregulated day care is of lower quality than regulated care (Fosburg et al., 1980; Goelman & Pence, 1987) or that quality is higher in states with more stringent regulations (Hofferth, Brayfield, Deich, & Holcomb, 1991; Kisker, Hofferth, & Phillips, 1990), however, does seem to suggest that regulation could help eliminate low-quality care.

Haskins also suggests that government regulation will not only not improve day-care quality but will decrease the likelihood that poor mothers will be able to work. "This is the heart of my argument: Strong federal day care regulations would raise the cost of care and make it more difficult for low-income families, especially single mothers, to achieve independence through work" (p. 107). Regulation of day care, he claims, presents a threat to reducing women's dependency on welfare because most poor mothers use relatives for day care and it would cost them more to send their children to a regulated day-care facility, but how, I ask, is federal regulation of day care going to change the likelihood that poor people will have grandmothers and aunts who can provide inexpensive care for their children? Federal regulation of day care does not mean that parents could not continue to make their own arrangements for care, or that if they were fortunate enough to have a willing relative they could not make an arrangement with that person for free care. Federal regulation of day care does not mean regulation of relatives. Federal regulation of day care does not mean that all children would be sent to centers.

Federal regulation also need not increase the cost of care provided by friends or neighbors. Providers who offer cheap care are not in the child-care business to make a lot of money. Therefore, if care were regulated so that the caregiver took in fewer children, or increased the safety of the setting by turning in the pot handles on the stove and barricading the stairs, or learned a bit more about how to care for and play with young children, or found out how to reduce children's aggression by teaching them social skills—all of which could be learned by watching community TV or getting some help from an organized day-care network or playground program—regulation would not increase the cost to the parents or the government. Regulations that require expensive physical changes to day-care homes or enrollment in community college courses could be eliminated to keep day-care costs down. If the purpose of regulation were to identify a reasonable *floor* of quality and to eliminate or modify care that fell below that floor, the enforcement of regulations might be more feasible and day-care costs would not increase. Federal regulation should at least serve to prevent the warehousing of large groups of children in unsafe and unstimulating facilities.

Haskins further suggests that the responsibility for regulating day care, if it is to be regulated, belongs to the states. This is fine if you live in California or Massachusetts, I suppose, but why should children in these states be assured of higher minimum standards of quality than those in Alabama or Texas? Across the states, adult–child ratios for infants range from 1:3 to 1:8; for preschoolers, from 1:5 to 1:20. These ratios reflect substantially different levels of quality, and at the low end, they undoubtedly reflect inadequate care. Setting a floor for quality that all states could agree with could only help ensure better and more equitable day care.

I do believe that regulation is invaluable for promoting quality day care. Still, I agree with Haskins that regulation is not the whole solution to the day-care issue. It alone will not guarantee high-quality care for all children. I also agree with Haskins that parents should have free choice of day-care arrangements. Unlike Haskins, however, I would emphasize parents' need to have something to choose from and information about how to choose well. Parents must be informed and vigilant about their children's experiences in day care. They, not the government, are their children's ultimate guardians. Finally, I agree with Haskins' recommendation that scientists present stronger evidence showing how the benefits of regulation exceed their cost. I would only add that the best way to do this is experimentally, by implementing regulation in some—randomly selected—communities and not in others. In the final analysis, then, regulation and research could work together to optimize the consequences of child care for all children.

REFERENCES

Barglow, P. B., Vaughn, B. E., & Molitor, N. (1987). Effects of maternal absence due to employment on the quality of infant–mother attachment in a low-risk sample. *Child Development, 58,* 945–954.

Bates, J. E., Marvinney, D., Bennett, D. S., Dodge, K. A., Kelly, T., & Pettit, G. S. (1991, April). *Children's day-care history and kindergarten adjustment.* Paper presented at the biennial meetings of the Society for Research in Child Development, Seattle, WA.

Belsky, J. (1984). Two waves of day care research: Developmental effects and conditions of quality. In R. Anslie (Ed.), *The child and the day care setting* (pp. 1–34). New York: Praeger.

Belsky, J. (1986). Infant day care: A cause for concern? *Zero to Three, 6,* 1–7.

Clarke-Stewart, K. A. (1989). Infant day care: Maligned or malignant? *American Psychologist, 44,* 266–273.

Egeland, B. (1991, August). *The relation between out-of-home care in infancy and outcomes in preschool and the school years.* Paper presented at the annual convention of the American Psychological Association, San Francisco, CA.

Field, T. (1991, August). *Quality infant day care and grade school behavior and performance.* Paper presented at the annual convention of the American Psychological Association, San Francisco, CA.

Finkelstein, N. W. (1982). Aggression: Is it stimulated by day care? *Young Children, 37,* 3–12.

Fosburg, S., Hawkins, P. D., Singer, J. D., Goodson, B. D., Smith, J. M., & Brush, L. R. (1980). *National Day Care Home Study.* Cambridge, MA: Abt Associates.

Goelman, H., & Pence, A. R. (1987). Effects of child care, family, and individual characteristics on children's language development: The Victoria Day Care Research Project. In D. A. Phillips (Ed.), *Quality in child care: What does research tell us?* (pp. 89–104). Washington, DC: National Association for the Education of Young Children.

Haskins, R. (1985). Public school aggression among children with varying day care experience. *Child Development, 56,* 689–703.

Hofferth, S. L., Brayfield, A., Deich, S., & Holcomb, P. (1991). *National Child Care Survey 1990.* Washington, DC: The Urban Institute.

Kisker, E. E., Hofferth, S. L., & Phillips, D. A. (1990). *A profile of child care settings: Early education and care in 1990* (Report submitted to U.S. Department of Education, Contract No. LC88090001). Princeton, NJ: Mathematica Policy Research.

Park, K. J., & Honig, A. S. (1991, August). *Infant child care patterns and later ratings of preschool behaviors.* Paper presented at the annual convention of the American Psychological Association, San Francisco, CA.

Phillips, D. A., McCartney, K., & Scarr, S. (1987). Child-care quality and children's social development. *Developmental Psychology, 23,* 537–543.

Schwarz, J. C., Krolick, G., & Strickland, R. G. (1973). Effects of early day care experience on adjustment to a new environment. *American Journal of Orthopsychiatry, 43,* 340–346.

Schwarz, J. C., Strickland, R. G., & Krolick, G. (1974). Infant day care: Behavioral effects at preschool age. *Developmental Psychology, 10,* 502–506.

Thornburg, K. R., Pearl, P., Crompton, D., & Ispa, J. A. (1990). Development of kindergarten children based on child care arrangements. *Early Childhood Research Quarterly, 5,* 27–42.

Whitebook, M., Howes, C., & Phillips, D. (1990). *Who cares? Child care teachers and the quality of care in America.* Berkeley, CA: Child Care Employee Project.

III

What Are the Consequences of Child-Care Practices and Arrangements for the Well-Being of Parents and Providers?

Consequences of Child Care for Parents' Well-Being

KAREN OPPENHEIM MASON
East-West Population Institute

LAURA DUBERSTEIN
University of Michigan

Every woman who has had a child during a time when she was committed to working outside the home knows that child care can be critical to parental well-being. Even those lucky enough to have supportive spouses and well-paid jobs may experience the doubts, distress, and anxiety caused by an inability to find child care, the breakdown of existing child-care arrangements, or suspicions that one's child care may be harming the child's health, happiness, and development. If this is how child-care problems can affect the lives of the relatively privileged, imagine how they affect the lives of individuals whose choices are far more constrained because of low income or lack of a helpful partner.

This chapter, thus, begins with a strong a priori conviction that child care is indeed critical to the well-being of parents, at least to parents in certain circumstances. Although we review the research literature on child care in relation to parental well-being, our aim is to refine our understanding of the paths through which child care affects well-being, rather than to question whether it does so at all. From personal experience, most of us know that our happiness as parents and human beings can depend critically on smooth-running, healthy child-care arrangements. As scholars, therefore, it is our task to understand why and for whom this is especially true, so that we can design more humane policies.

This chapter is organized as follows: We discuss, first, theoretical issues involved with assessing the impact of child care on parental well-being. This includes defining what we mean by *child care* and *well-being,* identifying those aspects of child care likely to affect well-being, and tracing the paths through which these aspects may influence well-being. The subsequent section reviews empirical studies. The final section discusses gaps in our knowledge and possible policy implications. The focus throughout the chapter is on the care of young children, especially those of preschool age, although many of the issues may be relevant for school aged children as well.

THEORETICAL BACKGROUND

In the most general usage, *child care* refers to a division of labor through which dependent children are reared, where this division of labor may involve only members of the child's family or household, or may include other individuals and institutions, as well. Of particular concern in the late 20th century are divisions of labor that involve nonfamily or non-household caregivers, especially when these arrangements are motivated by the mother's participation in paid work outside the home. Because the ideology of the 1950s prescribed that mothers be the sole caretakers of young children, the increased labor force participation of mothers of preschool-aged children has been perceived as problematic: Who will care for these children while their mothers are working for pay? Mothers are generally assumed to provide the best care their children can obtain, and it is in terms of this standard that the suitability of alternative caregivers is usually judged.[1] For this reason, the term *child care* is often used to refer to care provided by individuals other than the child's mother. In the current chapter, we use the term more generally, specifically referring to nonmaternal care when we wish to restrict our attention to arrangements in which the mother's care is supplemented by care from other sources.

The concept of *well-being* has several possible meanings, some more fully developed than others. In the current chapter, we use this term to refer to any aspect of the individual's psychological or material welfare. One problem in discussing the impact of child care on parental well-being is the possibility that the welfare of the husband and wife may not be similarly affected by particular child-care arrangements. Some arrangements may reduce the mother's welfare while leaving unchanged (or even enhancing) the father's, and others may have the reverse impact. In discussing the empirical literature, much of which focuses on mothers only, we try to identify likely

---

[1]This is at least true for white, middle-class mothers. The implicit assumption about the quality of care provided by lower-class or minority mothers often seems to be that their care is substandard, an attitude that has been actualized in policy through the creation of programs such as Head Start.

divergences between the welfare of mothers and fathers. As a working hypothesis, however, we posit that arrangements that are deleterious to the well-being of one parent are also likely to be deleterious to the well-being of the other parent because of the interdependency between parents, especially between parents of young children.

Two aspects of nonmaternal child care discussed in the literature are likely to affect parental well-being. These are the availability and affordability of child care of a particular quality, or as economists phrase it, the *cost per quality unit of care*. Availability and affordability involve both objective and subject elements. For example, whether a particular type of child care is available depends in part on its objective supply: Does the child have a grandmother alive and living nearby? Is there a day care center in the neighborhood? It also depends on parents' perceptions of availability and judgments about quality: Do they think the grandmother would be capable of providing acceptable child care? Do they regard day-care centers as appropriate for their child? Similarly, affordability reflects the market price of a particular kind of child care, but also depends on parents' judgments about the amount they can afford to spend, itself a function of their objective income, but also a function of their tastes for expenditures of different types. This dual nature of child-care availability and affordability makes their causal relationship to parental well-being complex. Characteristics of child care are not only exogenous to parents' household decisions, but are also endogenous to them.

In addition to being both exogenous and endogenous to household choice, child-care availability and affordability are intertwined with each other. In neoclassical economic theory, the availability of market-supplied child care reflects the price that consumers are willing to pay for it. If the consumer is willing to pay a high enough price, someone will supply the type of care desired. Similarly, subsidies that lower the price of particular types of care will, *ceteris paribus*, make that type of child care more available to the individual but less available in the aggregate; that is, there will be a shortage because demand will exceed supply (see Leibowitz & Waite, 1988). Quality and availability/affordability are also interdependent. Indeed, the choice that many parents may be making when they decide on a particular child-care arrangement is between types of care that are more readily available or less expensive but of lesser quality, and types that are less available or more expensive but are of higher quality.

Because availability and affordability per quality unit of care are intertwined, we treat them as a single dimension in the discussion that follows, referring to this dimension as the "costs" of child care. Figure 3.1 illustrates the primary paths through which child-care costs are thought to affect parental well-being. The right-hand side of the figure shows four proximate determinants of well-being: money, time, friends, and the satisfactions offered by particular roles, activities, or relationships (including the child-care

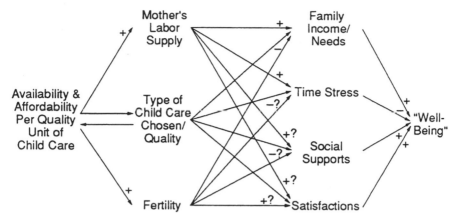

FIG. 3.1 Hypothesized effects of child care availability and affordability on parental well-being.

arrangement actually used by parents). These four proximate determinants form an admittedly crude approximation of the specific factors known to influence individual mental health and material well-being. Roughly speaking, however, having sufficient income relative to one's needs; having sufficient time in which to enact one's roles and enjoy some leisure; having friends, relatives, or other individuals who provide social supports; and engaging in activities that are personally satisfying are key ingredients influencing psychological and material well-being. Thus, if child care influences well-being, it is likely to do so through one of these four factors.

The left-hand side of Fig. 3.1 shows three factors that are thought to be influenced by the availability and affordability of child care and that, in turn, influence well-being via its proximate determinants. The first of these is the labor supply of the child's mother, that is, whether she participates in the paid labor force and if so, the amount of time she is employed. As we discuss further on, insofar as child care costs are exogenously determined, they appear to influence women's labor supply negatively: Higher costs discourage labor-force participation and reduce the hours of employment. Women's labor-force participation, in turn, exerts a positive effect on well-being via their earnings and possibly via the acquisition of friends who provide a source of social support. For some women, employment may also provide personal satisfactions.[2] Employment may exact a cost, however, in the form of

_____

[2]This and many of the generalizations we make here may be less true of women who are forced into the labor force and into the use of nonmaternal child care than of those who enter the marketplace voluntarily, even if out of economic need. This is important to keep in mind, given recent welfare reforms that emphasize the job training and employment of

increased time stress or overload (Staines & Pleck, 1983); that is, employed mothers may have less time in which to accomplish their domestic tasks and care for their children during nonwork hours than women who are not employed outside the home or who are employed for fewer hours.[3] Thus, whether child care ultimately enhances or detracts from well-being through its impact on mothers' labor supply depends on the balance between earnings, social supports, and the direct gratification of working, on the one hand, and time stress, on the other. Given extremely high and growing rates of labor-force participation among mothers of preschool-aged children in the United States, the balance seems likely to favor earnings, social supports, and direct gratification, rather than time stress, although the existence of the last is undeniable.

A second path through which child care may affect parental well-being is via the type and quality of child care that parents actually end up choosing. Several types of care are of interest here. One is exclusive care by the child's mother, a choice that implies lower family income, but that may also involve less time stress for the mother and, for many women, greater personal satisfaction or peace of mind (i.e., higher quality care) than alternative child-care arrangements.[4] Thus, whether the net balance of maternal care for parental well-being is positive or negative is unclear. The same is true for another type of care of interest here: father care. As we review later in the chapter, when dual-earner couples work different shifts so that fathers can care for their children while mother's work for pay, family income may be enhanced and out-of-pocket child-care expenditures reduced, but time and other stresses for the married couple may increase. Furthermore, whether the father's satisfaction is enhanced by increased involvement with childrearing may depend on whether the choice of this child-care arrangement is driven primarily by financial considerations or by personal tastes. Thus, neither form of parental child care has a clearly defined relationship to parental well-being.

Another type of child care of interest here is the mother's self-employment

---

AFDC recipients, including those with young children (see Maynard & McGinnis, this volume).

[3]The concept of *time stress* is similar to the idea of *role strain* used in the sociological literature on the family.

[4]The implications of full-time mother care for social supports is unclear, because it is likely to depend critically on whether such care isolates the mother from family and friends or, instead, permits her to spend more time with them. The evidence from some sources (e.g., Mason & Kuhlthau, 1989) that a majority of mothers of preschool-aged children believe that parental care is the best type of care for all children prior to their entering first grade is consistent with the hypothesis that many women gain personal satisfaction from caring for their children full time.

as a child-care provider. Connelly (1990) has developed a microeconomic model of women's choice between home work, market work, and work that allows them to care for their children themselves while working, including work as a self-employed child-care provider. Although the total proportion of the female labor force self-employed in child care is small, these women provide a substantial portion of the child care purchased by other employed mothers. Understanding why some mothers respond to problems of child-care availability and affordability — and to the need to earn income — by caring for other women's children is, therefore, of theoretical interest. Like any form of employment, self-employment should positively affect parental well-being by increasing family income relative to needs, but its effects on time stress and social supports may differ from the effects of employment outside the home. Because women who work at home often care for their own preschool-aged children while earning money, they may face less time stress than women employed outside the home. Like nonemployed mothers, they may also feel they have acquired higher quality child care by providing it themselves. Their comparative social isolation, however, may lower their access to social supports gained through having a job. Whether the net balance favors the positive effects of earnings and decreased time stress or the negative effects of lack of social supports is unclear, although high turnover in the family day-care industry suggests that the balance may be negative.

In addition to being influenced by mother care and father care, parental well-being may also be influenced by different types of nonparental child care, including care by relatives and various forms of market child care. Although approximately half of those using relative care pay something for that care (Hofferth & Wissoker, 1990), relative care is generally less expensive than market care, which may thereby improve the economic well-being of parents. In terms of different types of market care, parents of older preschoolers often express a preference for care that enhances their child's educational opportunities (primarily, organized group care provided by preschools, nursery schools, or day care centers). This type of care is more expensive than many other types of market-provided child care (O'Connell & Bloom, 1987), and may therefore influence parents' economic well-being negatively. That it is preferred by parents over less formal types of market care, however, may mean that it offers greater psychic benefits to parents than do other forms of care. Quality of care, whatever its type, should also affect parents' satisfaction and hence well-being positively, because parents presumably want the best possible care for their children. We review further on studies of parental satisfaction with child care in an attempt to test these speculations.

The third factor thought to be influenced by child-care availability and affordability is women's fertility, that is, whether they bear additional children. In principle, inexpensive child care should encourage childbearing, because it lowers both the direct and opportunity costs associated with rearing additional children: It becomes relatively easy for the mother to earn money, and her out-of-pocket expenses for child care will be relatively low. What is theoretically less clear, however, is whether additional children have the net effect of lowering or raising parental well-being. One might argue that if the choice to bear the additional child was made deliberately, rather than resulting from an accidental or unintended pregnancy, then the net benefits of the additional child are, by definition, perceived by the parents to be positive. Whether this necessarily turns out to be the case, however, is unclear, especially for families already at the margin in terms of income relative to needs or time stress. Thus, whether the net effect of child care on well-being via fertility is positive or negative is an open question.

The factors shown on the left-hand side of Fig. 3.1 are not the only variables pertinent to well-being that might be influenced by child-care availability and affordability. For example, in Japan, there is some evidence suggesting that household composition — specifically, doubling up with the wife's or husband's parents — may reflect the availability and affordability of nonfamilial child care (Morgan & Hiroshima, 1983). In the United States, however, the factors shown in Fig. 3.1 are most frequently studied and are the three for which there is evidence of the influence of child-care costs. (Doubling up with relatives in order to obtain inexpensive child care appears to occur infrequently in the United States and only for a very limited portion of the family cycle; see Parish, Hao, & Hogan, 1991.) For this reason, the review that follows focuses on these factors.

WHAT PAST STUDIES HAVE SHOWN

There are very few studies that have addressed directly the question of how child-care problems influence parents' well-being. Instead, most have focused on the links between child-care costs and the three intermediate variables shown in Fig. 3.1, namely, mother's labor supply, type or quality of child care chosen, and fertility. In this section, we first review studies (most of them quantitative) concerned with the relationship between child-care costs and women's labor supply or fertility. We then turn to the more complex subject of how child-care costs are related to type and quality of care, a rubric under which, among other things, we consider shift-work among dual-earner couples as a child-care arrangement. We end with a review of studies that have attempted to relate child care directly to measures of parental well-being, including studies of satisfaction with child care as well as the one or two studies that have used direct measures of parents' psychological well-being.

Child Care Costs in Relation to Mother's Labor Supply
and Fertility

Studies investigating whether the availability and affordability of child care
constrain women's labor supply or fertility have used two main approaches: in
one, quantitative measures of child-care costs are developed and related to
women's labor supply or fertility; in the second, women are asked directly
whether or to what extent problems with child care have constrained their
employment or childbearing. In the first type of study, three alternative types
of cost measures have been used, each one implicitly representing a particular
conceptualization of costs. Several studies (Blau & Robins, 1988, 1989;
Gustafsson & Stafford, 1988; Klerman & Leibowitz, 1990) have used *areal*
measures of costs, an approach that estimates the market price of child care
in a local area. For example, Blau and Robins (1988; see also Klerman &
Leibowitz, 1990) used the wage level of child-care workers in the respondent's
local area as reported in the most recent U. S. Census, whereas Gustafsson
and Stafford (1988) used the fees charged by government child-care centers in
Sweden. Because areal measures like these are independent of women's
personal and household characteristics, they are clearly intended to measure
the price of market-supplied child care, rather than aspects of availability or
affordability that depend on women's incomes, preferences, or family
structure. They are, thus, exogenous to parents' choices about child care.

A second type of measure, although based in part on women's personal and
family characteristics, also taps costs that are independent of parental
preferences and choices. This type of measure is the maximum child-care tax
credit that a mother would be eligible to receive from the federal or state
government were she to work full time (used by Blau & Robins, 1989, and
Klerman & Leibowitz, 1990). Such measures are based on the state in which
the woman lives and on individual and household traits that determine tax
credit eligibility, such as the level of household income, the woman's wage
rate, and family composition. Such measures tap the subsidy for paid child
care available to the respondent from governmental sources, that is, the
amount by which the local market price of child care would effectively be
lowered were she to use such care while working for pay full time.

The third type of measure of child-care costs involves individual-level
estimates of how much the respondent could be expected to pay for child care
were she to work and pay what employed women with similar personal and
household characteristics currently pay for child care (see Connelly, 1989;
Duberstein & Mason, 1991; Hofferth & Wissoker, 1990; Maume, 1989).
Unlike the areal and tax credit approaches, this approach measures likely
child-care expenditures, and is thus endogenous to parents' choices about
child care. In other words, it rests on the assumption that there are consistent
socio-demographic predictors of the type and amount of child care women

purchase, and hence the approximate amount they spend, when they enter the labor force during their children's preschool years. There are several specific approaches that can be used in computing this type of measure, but all share the implicit assumption that a particular kind of couple is likely to purchase a particular "bundle" of child care services when the mother goes to work.[5]

Table 3.1 summarizes the major quantitative studies published since 1980 that have related child-care availability or affordability to women's employment and fertility. The first part of the table shows studies using one or more of the measures of child-care costs just described; the second part shows studies that have used attitudinal questions asking women directly about the constraints on employment or fertility posed by child-care problems, or inquiring about the reasons for their nonparticipation in the labor force.

Regardless of the type of cost measure used, almost all studies relating child-care costs to women's labor supply find a negative relationship, even after other known determinants of labor supply have been held constant. In other words, the higher the price of or likely expenditure on child care, the lower is the probability of labor-force participation, exactly the relationship that economic theory predicts. The strength of the relationship estimated in different studies varies greatly, however, even if the direction of the relationship does not. Especially strong relationships are found in studies that employ areal measures of child care costs (Blau & Robins, 1988, 1989; Gustafsson & Stafford, 1988). For example, one model estimated by Blau and Robins (1988) suggests that if child care were to cost married mothers nothing, then 87% of them would participate in the labor force, whereas if it cost them $40 per week, only 17% of them would do so. Effects of this magnitude are suspiciously large, and suggest that areal child-care measures may pick up other types of areal effects on women's employment, such as the local supply of jobs.[6] Although it is reasonable to expect the price of

---

[5]The most common approach used in computing this type of measure is statistically similar to the approach used by economists to estimate nonworking women's wage levels. The labor force nonparticipation of many mothers of preschool-aged children may be caused by the high cost of child care they face. Because of this, one cannot simply impute to these women the expenditures for child care made by currently employed women having the same socio-demographic traits. Instead, it is necessary to adjust for the selectivity of employment with respect to child-care costs. Heckman (1976, 1979) has suggested a two-stage method for making this adjustment, in which the determinants of labor-force participation are first modeled using Tobit or probit analysis (Maddala, 1983), and the error structure from that model is then used as a selectivity adjustment to an Ordinary Least Squares (OLS) model predicting child-care expenditures on the basis of employed women's characteristics. The coefficients from this model are then used to impute a predicted child-care cost value for all women, regardless of their labor-force status.

[6]None of the studies here that used areal measures of child care costs controlled for characteristics of the labor market that might independently influence women's labor supply, such as the local industry mix or the unemployment rate.

TABLE 3.1

Studies Relating Child-Care Costs to Female Employment or Fertility

Study	Date and Sample	Universe	Cost Measure Used	Effects on Employment	Effects on Fertility	Comments
Blau & Robins 1988	1980 EOPP; N = 6170 PSUs = 20	Married, spouse present, women <45 with child <14.	1) Average $ paid for care per PSU; 2) wage of child-care workers in PSU.	Negatively related, especially when child care is purchased.	Not studied.	Employment & fertility and use of purchased child care modeled jointly; effects too strong.
Connelly, 1989	1984 SIPP; N = 2781.	Married women 21-55 with child <13.	Predicted costs based on 2-stage Tobit of actual costs.	Negatively related.	Not studied.	Predicted child-care costs adjusted for selectivity bias.
Duberstein & Mason, 1991	1986 DCCS; N = 937.	Non-black women 15-39 with preschool child.	Predicted costs based on actual costs.	Negatively related to work plans (strength varies).	Not studied.	Predicted child care costs adjusted for selectivity bias.
Gustafsson & Stafford, 1988	1984 nat'l sample of Swedish households; N = 166.	Women in 2-parent house-holds with one preschool child.	1) Public child-care fees in area; 2) spaces per child in area.	Where spaces adequate, fees negatively related to employment.	Not studied.	15+ hrs/wk; no controls for other areal traits.
Klerman & Leibowitz, 1990	1987 NLS-Y; N = 1523.	Women 14-29 with 1st birth & worked 20+ hrs/wk at some time in the past.	1) Relatives in household; 2) child-care worker wages in area; 3) federal tax credits; 4) state tax credits.	Some measures related to quick return to work after 1st birth; other not.	Not studied.	Return to work by 3 or 24 months post-birth and use of relative vs. nonrelative child care modeled together.

Study	Data	Sample	Measures	Results		Notes
Leibowitz et al., 1988	1977 NLS young women; N = 1763.	Employed women 23–34 with child <6.	1) Avail of relatives; 2) how much care needed (child's age, #s); 3) availability of formal care; 4) preferences.	Some measures related to labor supply as expected; other not.	Not studied.	Analysis done separately by youngest child's age (0–2 vs 3–5); results vary by age.
Maume, 1989	1986 SIPP; N = 658.	Women 15–45 with child <13, employed in 1985 and not unemployed in 1986.	Predicted costs based on 1985 expenditures.	Negative (but weak) relation to voluntarily exiting from the labor force.	Not studied.	Modeled exiting from the labor force between 1985 and 1986.
Parish et al., 1991	1984 NLS-Y; N = 1787.	Black & non-Hispanic white women 19–26 with child <6.	1) Employed relatives in household; 2) nonworking relatives in household; 3) relatives in neighborhood.	Measure #1 positively related to labor force entry; #2 negatively related to labor force entry; #3 no relation with LF entry.	Not studied.	Results interpreted in terms of family's "culture of employment."
Blau & Robins, 1989	1980 EOPP; N = emp = 6170; N not emp = 8940 PSUs = 20	"Married women."	1) Average $ paid for care per PSU; 2) fed tax credits possible.	Measure #1 positively related to leaving labor force; negatively related to entering; #2 ns.	Measure #1 negatively related to add'l birth among nonemployed only; #2 ns.	Event-history models over 22-month period, effects too strong, may reflect lack of areal controls.

(continued)

TABLE 3.1 (*Continued*)

Study	Date and Sample	Universe	Cost Measure Used	Effects on Employment	Effects on Fertility	Comments
Lehrer & Kawasaki, 1985	1976 NSFG; $N = 599$.	Fecund employed mothers in 2-parent households with child <6, using only 1 type of child care.	Type of care used (relative, sitter, organized facility).	Not studied.	Using relatives associated with intending add'l birth (but coefficients are ns).	Whether intends another birth is dependent variable, modeled jointly with child-care type.
Bloom & Steen, 1990	June 1982 CPS.	Women 18–44 with child <5.	If satisfactory child care available at a reasonable cost, would you work?	Potential rate of 62% vs. actual rate of 48%.	Not studied.	Potential rate estimated by adding positives responses to Q to actual rate. See Bloom and Steen, 1990.
Kisker et al., 1989	1988 probability sample of Camden and Newark, NJ, South Chicago, IL: N unknown.	Mothers of preschool children.	If satisfactory child care available at a reasonable cost, would you work?	Potential rate of 71% vs. actual rate of 52%.	Not studied.	
Mason & Kuhlthau, 1991	1986 DCCS; $N = 1022$.	Women 15–39 with preschool child, not unemployed.	Whether past or current labor supply and fertility constrained by child-care problems.	One third say labor supply was or is constrained by child-care problems.	10% say fertility was or is constrained by child-care problems.	Q similar to the June CPS Qs used, but other Qs also used.

Presser & Baldwin, 1980	June 1977 CPS.	Women 18–44 with child <5.	If satisfactory child care available at a reasonable cost, would you work?	Potential rate of 46% vs. actual rate of 35%.	Women who report a child-care constraint less likely to expect add'l birth.	First study to ask child-care constraint Q
Kisker et al., 1990	1987–1990 Teenage Parent Demonstration Project (TPDP) in NJ and IL; N = 600.	Teenage women with preschool child, enrolled in or applied for the TPDP.	Reasons for not working, being in school or in job training.	Child-care problems (availability, cost) main reason given.	Not studied.	No difference between enrollees and control group.

Note. From EOPP—Employment Opportunity Pilot Projects baseline household survey, a non-probability sample in 20 PSUs across 11 states with low-income households oversamples; SIPP—Survey of Income and Program Participation, national probability panel study with low-income and minority households oversampled; DCCS—Detroit Child Care Survey, probability sample of women 15–39 with at least one child born January, 1980, or later living in the Detroit metropolitan area; NLS-Y—National Longitudinal Survey of Labor Market Experience, Youth Cohort, national probability panel study of individuals 14–21 in 1979, with minorities oversampled; NLS Young Women—National Longitudinal Survey of Labor Market Experience, Young Women, national probability panel study of women 14–25 in 1968; NSFG—National Survey of Family Growth, national probability sample of women under age 50 ever-married or with at least one birth; CPS—Current Population Survey, national probability sample of households.

market-supplied child care to influence women's decisions about labor force participation, the heavy reliance on nonmarket child care in the United States (Bloom & Steen, 1990), and the importance of personal and household traits for determining the type of care that is used, both suggest that market prices are unlikely to have more than a moderate effect on the type of child care that is used, and hence on women's labor supply decisions.

That child-care availability and affordability play a role in determining women's employment, at least when they have dependent children at home, is further confirmed by studies asking women direct questions about the constraints posed for employment by child care. In 1977, the National Institute for Child Health and Human Development and the U.S. Census Bureau cosponsored a question in the June Current Population Survey (CPS) that asked women who were out of the labor force: "If satisfactory child care were available at reasonable cost, would you be looking for work at this time?" Identical or similar questions were included in subsequent CPSs and in several other national and regional surveys.

As entries 11 through 14 in Table 3.1 indicate, a substantial proportion of the women answering such questions have responded positively. Many women believe their labor-force participation to be constrained by the unavailability or expense of child care, enough so that the female labor-force participation rate would rise between 9 and 19 percentage points if every woman responding "yes" to the question were actually to enter the labor force. In the 1986 Detroit Child Care Survey (Mason & Kuhlthau, 1991), this question was followed by a question asking what types of child care would be acceptable. Of the women who said that they would be working if they could find acceptable child care, 23% indicated that relatives constituted the only type of acceptable caregivers for their children. The remaining 77% named at least one type of unrelated caregiver as acceptable. Thus, whereas government policies to increase the supply of market child care are unlikely to draw *all* women currently constrained from working by the unavailability of child care into the labor force, they could have this effect for a substantial proportion of nonworking women.[7]

---

[7]Although it is often assumed that government policies could increase the supply of nonrelative caregivers (e.g., by increasing parents' purchasing power in the child care market), it is often implicitly assumed that the supply of relatives would not be similarly affected. Whether this latter assumption is correct, however, depends on the reasons that relatives are unavailable for child care. If it is that they do not live in the same geographic area, themselves work, are too feeble or unhealthy to care for a young child, are uninterested or unwilling to care for a grandchild or other related child at any price, or are viewed by the child's parents as incompetent caregivers, then government policies or programs would probably do little to increase the supply of related caregivers. On the other hand, if the lack of relative care reflects a lack of economic incentives to them for providing care, then government policies might, indeed, be able to increase their supply. Data from

Several qualitative studies of employment among mothers of young children also confirm the importance of the availability and affordability of child care in determining whether women enter employment during this period of their lives. For example, Glezer (1988, pp. 77–79), using Australian survey data for women who gave birth during May of 1984, reports that many women blamed their failure to return to the labor force after childbirth on the lack of adequate and affordable child care. An intensive study of 40 Puerto Rican mothers living in New York City reported similar statements, although the women who either had an extremely strong financial need to work or a strong professional career orientation said that they would work regardless of child-care availability or costs (Hurst & Zambrana, 1982). The study by Kisker, Silverberg, and Maynard (1990) shown at the bottom of Table 3.1 also found that child-care problems were the main reason given for nonparticipation in employment, schooling, or job training by a sample of teenaged mothers with preschool children.

The number of studies relating child-care costs to fertility is far smaller than the number relating these costs to women's labor supply. The methods used in these studies are also quite varied (Blau & Robins, 1989; Lehrer & Kawasaki, 1985; Mason & Kuhlthau, 1991; Presser & Baldwin, 1980). Generalizing from them is, consequently, difficult. None of these studies, however, shows a strong effect of child-care costs on fertility, although most of them found some effect. For example, in Blau and Robins' (1989) analysis relating the average amount paid for child care in the local area to the birth of an additional child, the expected negative effect was found, but this effect occurred only for women not in the labor force at the start of the study; a second areal measure of the price of child care had no effect for any group. Similarly, in an analysis by Lehrer and Kawasaki (1985) that used the type of child care to proxy child care costs, women using relatives to care for their children were more likely to expect another child than women using babysitters or organized forms of child care, but the coefficients involved did

---

the Detroit Child Care Survey suggest that little of the unavailability of relatives for child care reflects a lack of economic incentives to them to act as caregivers. Only 6% of the Detroit sample said they had a relative who was theoretically available as a caregiver whom they would not feel free to ask to take on this task (these women constituted 22% of those with a relative locally available and theoretically able to provide child care). In contrast, 23% of the sample had no relative living nearby and another 35% had relatives living nearby who were not available to provide child care. Based on patterns in Detroit, at least, this suggests that government policies to increase the supply of related potential caregivers are likely to generate relatively few caregivers unless the total compensation offered for providing child care were to exceed what these relatives are able to earn in the labor market. On the other hand, that many relatives are paid for their child-care services (Hofferth & Wissoker, 1990; Presser, 1989) suggests that subsidies might indeed draw others into providing care.

not reach statistical significance. In the study by Mason and Kuhlthau (1991), which analyzed questions asking women whether birth spacing or numbers of children had ever been constrained by child-care problems, only 10% of women reported that they had, as compared to 34% of the sample reporting child-care constraints on their employment. Thus, if child-care costs directly depress fertility, they appear to do so only weakly or in relatively few cases.[8]

In sum, there is clear evidence that the availability and affordability of child care often influence the labor supply of women with preschool-aged children. It would also appear that child-care costs can influence women's fertility decisions, although less often than they influence their employment decisions. Less well understood is how employment and fertility themselves are related to parental well-being, topics that are beyond the scope of the current review.

Child Care Costs in Relation to Type
or Quality of Child Care

We now turn to the issue of how child-care availability and affordability influence the type and quality of child care actually chosen. As was noted earlier, there are several types of child care that are of interest here:

1. exclusive care by the mother (including the choice to become a self-employed child care provider);
2. care by the father as well as by the mother;
3. care by other relatives; and
4. care by nonrelatives, especially the nursery schools, preschools, and day-care centers preferred by parents of older preschool-aged children.

Quality of child care can also be studied independently of type of care.

Maternal Care.   There are few studies that focus on the choice between exclusive care of children by the mother versus any other form of care. This

---

[8]As Lehrer and Kawasaki (1985) pointed out, however, the cost of child care may have an indirect effect on fertility via its effect on women's employment, in which case the effect would most likely be *positive*. If the high costs of child care discourage labor-force participation, and if this in turn encourages childbearing (as past studies suggest it does), then costly child care might actually increase fertility rather than depressing it. Consistent with this speculation is the finding in Mason and Kuhlthau (1991) that the only factor predicting whether women reported a child-care constraint on their fertility was their labor-force attachment. Women strongly committed to working for personal or financial reasons were more likely than other women to have postponed or avoided a birth because of their inability to find affordable child care of acceptable quality.

no doubt reflects the (erroneous) assumption that there is a one-to-one correspondence between employment and child-care decisions, an assumption that leads to the study of women's employment decisions rather than their choice to provide all child care themselves.[9] Although it is true that the great majority of employed women use nonmaternal child care, a minority does not. For example, in 1986, 8% of the employed mothers of preschool-aged children in the Detroit metropolitan area provided all regularly scheduled child care while working (Kuhlthau & Mason, 1991); the comparable figure in the 1988 National Health Interview Survey on Child Health was 5% (Dawson, 1990). In addition, there are many nonemployed women who use nonmaternal child care on a regularly scheduled basis (44% in the Detroit survey, 20% in the 1988 National Health Interview Survey). Thus, although the impact of child-care availability and affordability on the mother's employment provides partial information about the decision to rely exclusively on maternal child care, it does not tell the whole story.

Probably the question of greatest interest in studying the choice for exclusive maternal care is whether this choice is economically driven, that is, whether it is an economic necessity for parents who cannot afford market child care and who do not have relatives available to provide nonmarket care, or is instead driven by preferences for maternal care and is a luxury that only relatively affluent families can afford. The literature on the labor supply of married women suggests that full-time child care by mothers is, if anything, a relative luxury that only higher income families can afford. Once a woman has left the labor force after a child is born, however, her decision to provide all child care herself may reflect, in part, an inability to pay for group care, as an analysis by Kuhlthau and Mason (1991) suggests. In that analysis, only two variables predicted whether nonemployed women supplemented their own care with a preschool, nursery school, or kindergarten: the child's age and the household's income (both were inversely related to the exclusive use of maternal care). Thus, among nonemployed mothers, the cost of the relatively expensive forms of care that these mothers favor as an alternative to their own influences whether they provide all child care themselves.

One way in which women can simultaneously earn money and care for children themselves is to become self-employed, particularly as a child care provider. In an analysis of this choice in a national sample of employed women (SIPP data), Connelly (1990) found that white, married women from higher income families with relatively large numbers of children (both preschool and school age) were most likely to become self-employed, both in

---

[9]This assumption is built into a number of recent surveys, such as the Survey of Income and Program Participation (SIPP), which ask about child-care arrangements only if the mother was employed.

general and specifically as child-care providers. Thus, the decision to enter self-employment does not appear to be driven by an inability to purchase market child care. If anything, this decision is facilitated by the income security that having a relatively high-earning husband provides. Thus, although we do not know whether the choice for self-employment enhances the well-being of either the mothers who are self-employed or their husbands, that the choice to become self-employed appears to be driven more often by a desire to rely on maternal care rather than by sheer economic necessity suggests that it may provide satisfaction to parents and consequently enhance their well-being.

Father Care. As the pioneering work of Harriet Presser (1986, 1988; Presser & Cain, 1983) has made clear, a substantial proportion of dual-earner couples with preschool-aged children in the United States provide most or all child care themselves, a feat achieved by the mother working part time and/or working different shifts than the father.[10] The national data analyzed by Presser do not permit one to determine whether it is the desire to rely on parental care that causes the parents to work different shifts, or the predetermined fact of shift work that leads them to decide to involve the father in child care. Unpublished data from the Detroit Child Care Survey, however, suggest that child-care preferences frequently determine work shifts. In response to questions asking whether the father or mother had deliberately arranged their work schedules so the father could help take care of their preschool-aged children, 55% of the 605 wives in dual-earner couples said they had. Thus, father's care of preschool-aged children is not only common, but is often deliberately chosen. The question is why couples choose this arrangement, and what consequences it has for their well-being.

In statistical studies of whether fathers help care for their preschoolers, one of the most consistent findings is that fathers are more likely to participate in child care when they or their wives work fewer hours (Christian, 1990; Presser, 1986, 1988; Yeager, 1979). Fathers are also more likely to participate when the wife works evenings, nights, or on weekends (Christian, 1990; Presser, 1988; Yeager, 1979).[11] These results are equally consistent with the idea that the father's availability for child care during the hours when his wife is at work influences his likelihood of actually providing such care, and the

---

[10]In the 1988 National Health Interview Survey on Child Health, the main source of care for children under 5 was the child's father in 13% of the cases (Dawson, 1990).

[11]The father's own work shift does not have a consistent relationship to his propensity to participate in child care. In some studies (Christian, 1990; Hofferth & Brayfield, 1991), the father's working a non-day shift increases his likelihood of providing child care, but in others (Presser, 1988), it decreases this likelihood.

notion that parents deliberately arrange their work schedules in order to facilitate parental care of children. One study (Hofferth & Brayfield, 1991) has shown that the presence of adults other than the parents in the household lowers the probability of the parents providing all child care themselves, a pattern seemingly consistent with the idea that dual-earner parents would prefer to rely on other kin for child care than provide all care themselves. There is other evidence, however, that a majority of parents think parental care is better for preschoolers than the care provided by other caregivers (Mason & Kuhlthau, 1989), a belief that appears to influence whether fathers participate in child care (Christian, 1990).

Another consistent finding in studies of fathers' participation in child care is that having more preschool-aged children is associated with a higher likelihood of father care (Baruch & Barnett, 1983; Hofferth & Brayfield, 1991; Presser, 1986, 1988). This could reflect a tendency for child-oriented couples both to have more of them and to participate more in their care than other couples do, but it is also consistent with the idea that, as child care costs rise, parents are more likely to provide all care themselves. In support of the latter is a tendency for parents with more preschool-aged children to use other forms of free or inexpensive care than parental care alone, such as care provided by relatives or in family day-care homes rather than in day-care centers (Blau & Robins, 1988, 1990; Floge, 1985; Lehrer, 1983, 1989; Lehrer & Kawasaki, 1985). This suggests that the use of father care may be driven by economic considerations, rather than by preferences.[12]

To some extent, however, this conclusion is contradicted by the results for measures of the couple's socioeconomic status, which fail to show a consistent relationship to the use of father care. Across studies, the father's occupation (Christian, 1990; Presser, 1988) and income (Presser, 1986; Yeager, 1979) either have no relationship to his participation in child care, or have inconsistent relationships. Although there is a consistent tendency for husbands of better educated or higher earning wives to be less involved in child care (Christian, 1990; Hofferth & Brayfield, 1991; Hofferth & Wissoker, 1990; Yeager, 1979), it is not clear whether this reflects the ability of higher earning women to pay for nonfamilial care, the preferences of better educated mothers for more educational forms of child care (Leibowitz, Waite, & Witsberger, 1988), or a tendency for higher earning women to work more

---

[12]Consistent with this is Presser's (1986) finding that mothers who relied on the father as the primary caregiver while they were employed were more likely than other women to say that their employment was constrained by lack of adequate child care. In a later analysis (Presser, 1988), however, this was not found to be the case. Instead, it was women who relied on other relatives who were significantly more likely to report a constraint on their working caused by inadequate child care, not the women who relied on the child's father.

hours. Thus, what it is that leads employed parents to involve the father in child care — economic need or a matter of preference — is unknown. Quite possibly there are some parents who rely on father care out of economic necessity and others who rely on it out of preference.

Care by Relatives.   There is consistent evidence that the availability of relatives has a strong impact on whether they are chosen as caregivers (Blau & Robins, 1990; Kuhlthau & Mason, 1991; Leibowitz et al., 1988; Parish et al., 1991). Whether the measure used pertains to adults living in the child's home or living nearby, children that have kin available are more likely to be cared for by them than are children without nearby kin. This relationship is partly mechanical — if one has no kin, then one cannot possibly have them care for one's children — but it also reflects a choice by those with kin to have them care for their children. In other words, not every family with a working mother and relatives nearby actually chooses relatives for child care. That a high proportion do indicates that they value either the intimate relationship these caregivers offer, their low price, or both.[13]

Another variable consistently related to care by relatives is child-care cost, as indicated by numbers of children. In most studies, the greater the number of preschool-aged children in the family, the greater is the likelihood that the family relies on relatives for child care (Blau & Robins, 1990; Lehrer, 1983; Lehrer & Kawasaki, 1985). Because there are few quantity discounts in the world of market child care, especially for children of different ages needing different types of care, it is easiest to interpret this relationship in terms of the economics of child care.

The family's income, and hence whether paying non-relatives for child care is affordable, also has a relatively consistent relationship to the use of relatives for child care. Several studies have found a negative relationship between relative care and the household's income minus what the mother contributes (Blau & Robins, 1990; Lehrer, 1983; Lehrer & Kawasaki, 1985), although the relationship is sometimes weak or nonexistent (Hofferth & Wissoker, 1990; Kuhlthau & Mason, 1991; Leibowitz et al., 1988). A number of studies have also reported a negative relationship between the mother's wage or earnings and the use of relative care (Blau & Robins, 1990; Hofferth & Wissoker, 1990; Lehrer, 1983; Lehrer & Kawasaki, 1985; Leibowitz et al., 1988), and in some studies (Lehrer, 1983; Lehrer & Kawasaki, 1985; Leibowitz et al., 1988), the

---

[13]A number of studies also find that African-American mothers are more likely to rely on relatives for child care than are economically similar white mothers (Blau & Robins, 1990; Hogan, Hao, & Parish, 1990; Lehrer, 1989; Lehrer & Kawasaki, 1985; Parish et al., 1991). As the study by Hogan et al. (1990) indicates, this at least partly reflects the greater availability of relatives among African-Americans than among non-Hispanic/non-Asian Whites.

mother's hours of work had an inverse relationship to the use of relative care, a finding that, in the absence of a control for earnings, also implies an inverse relationship between income and the use of relatives for child care. All of these relationships suggest that when families have more money, they are less inclined to rely on relatives for child care. Thus, it would appear that some parents choose relative care primarily because of its low cost, rather than because of their preferences.

Other Types of Child Care. Studies of whether parents choose group care versus other forms of market child care generally find patterns similar to those for the use of care by relatives, perhaps because organized group care typically is more expensive than most other forms of non-relative care.[14] Having a larger number of children tends to be associated with less use of organized group care (Floge, 1985), as is a low maternal wage level (Hofferth & Wissoker, 1990; Lehrer, 1989; Robins & Spiegelman, 1978), a low level of education (Floge, 1985), or a small number of hours worked (Lehrer, 1989). Thus, the more that parents can afford to spend on child care, either because they have only one child to care for or because they have a relatively high income, the more likely they are to choose organized group care over other forms of nonrelative care. This may be especially true when their children are over 2 years of age (Leibowitz et al., 1988), because of the greater suitability of organized group care for older preschool-aged children; it also is likely to reflect a widespread preference among parents for this type of care (Sonenstein, 1990).

Quality of Care. Child-care quality is a complex, multidimensional phenomenon that is difficult to measure in its entirety. Child development specialists agree that group size, formal training of caregivers, the ratio of caregivers to children, and the educational richness of the physical environment all are important — and readily measured — aspects of child-care quality (Clarke-Stewart, this volume), but equally important for children's well-being are such difficult-to-measure qualities as the caregiver's warmth toward children. In addition, from parents' point of view, it is not only the caregiver's qualities and the environment in which care is given that count: Such practical factors as the location of the care, the hours it is offered, and the convenience of transportation to and from the child care site are also important. This complexity in determining child-care "quality" makes it difficult to study the

---

[14]Full-time, in-home caregivers — nannies — are sometimes reported to be the single most expensive form of care (O'Connell & Bloom, 1987), but because they are rare compared to family day-care homes, which are relatively inexpensive, the average amount paid in the non-relative, non-group category tends to be lower than the average amount paid for organized group care.

relationship between child-care costs and quality, or between quality and parental well-being. For this reason, most studies can, at best, be considered partial views of the relationships among child-care costs, its quality, and parental well-being.

One of the most important findings in the literature on child-care quality is that type of care and quality do not have a simple, one-to-one relationship with each other, regardless of whether quality is measured objectively, in the terms emphasized by child development specialists, or is judged subjectively, by parents themselves. For example, Waite, Leibowitz, and Witsberger (1988), using mothers' reports of three objective features of child-care (group size, ratio of adults to children, and caregiver training), found that organized group facilities often fail to meet the federally recommended standards for group size and ratio of adults to children. Parents, relatives, and family day-care homes all rate higher on these dimensions, although these caregivers are less likely to have formal child-care training. In a study of mothers receiving Aid to Families with Dependent Children (AFDC), Sonenstein and Wolf (1991) reported a similar result using mothers' own evaluations of the quality and convenience of care. Each type of child care considered was judged positively by mothers on some criteria, but negatively on others. Thus, although parents often state a preference for organized group care, there is little evidence that this care is rated highest by parents on all dimensions of quality and convenience.

Because both expensive and inexpensive forms of child care rate highly on some quality dimensions, the relationship between child-care quality and child-care costs is weak (Waite et al., 1988). Indeed, for some dimensions of quality, there is an inverse relationship, indicating that it is often relatives or the child's father who score highest on quality measures but cost the least in monetary terms. Thus, although there is evidence that the availability and affordability of child care may influence the *type* of care that is chosen, it is difficult to conclude that it influences the *quality* of care chosen. Independent evidence suggests, however, that holding availability and affordability constant, parents usually choose higher quality care (Hofferth & Wissoker, 1990).

Impact of Child-Care on Parental Well-Being

Thus far, this discussion has focused on whether child-care costs influence employment, fertility, or the type or quality of child care that parents actually use. Although these relationships are relevant to our ultimate understanding of how child care affects parental well-being, the evidence examined thus far for the evaluation of well-being has been indirect. In this section, we turn to the rather sparse evidence directly concerned with the link between child care and parental well-being. We first discuss satisfaction with child care as an indicator of parental well-being, then turn to studies that measure parents' economic and psychological well-being more directly.

Satisfaction With Child Care. When representative samples of parents are asked to report on their overall satisfaction with their current child-care arrangements, the overwhelming response is usually extremely positive (Sonenstein, 1990). For example, in the Detroit Child Care Survey of mothers of preschool-aged children, 51% said they were "extremely satisfied" with their primary nonmaternal child-care arrangement for their youngest child, and another 35% said they were "very satisfied" (12% were "fairly satisfied" and a mere 2% "not too satisfied"). Even when studies have asked parents whether they would like to switch arrangements — a question that may be less loaded emotionally than a direct question about satisfaction — the percentages reporting they would like to change are generally small (Sonenstein, 1990). Thus, although we know that a substantial minority of mothers find their current child care inadequate, in terms of permitting them to work or to work as much as they would like (see in Table 3.1), most apparently think that the care they are currently using is, overall, highly satisfactory.

One exception to this generalization, however, is found in low-income samples. For example, in a study of mothers living in three low-income cities (Kisker, Maynard, Gordon, & Strain, 1989), one third of the women using nonmaternal child care reported they would change arrangements if the type of care they preferred was available free of charge. (This figure is higher than is reported in studies with more general populations: For example, in the Detroit Child Care Survey, only 17% of women said they would prefer an alternative arrangement for their youngest child if they could afford to spend any amount on child care.) Similarly, Sonenstein and Wolf (1991) reported that only half of the women in their AFDC sample were fully satisfied with their current child-care arrangement, in contrast to the 80% to 90% usually found to be satisfied in more general samples. Analyses of whether child care is reported to constrain women's employment also typically find such reports to be more frequent among poor mothers than among more affluent mothers (Mason & Kuhlthau, 1991; Presser & Baldwin, 1980). Thus, it would appear that the inability to afford more expensive forms of child care not only may impede women's employment and consequently lower their incomes, but may also reduce their overall satisfaction with their child-care arrangements.

An issue of interest from a policy point of view is whether satisfaction with child care varies according to the type of care currently being used. In the Detroit sample, the primary type of nonmaternal care being used for the youngest child was significantly related to reported satisfaction, but the differences among types were fairly small (see Table 3.2). For example, on a

TABLE 3.2

Coefficients Relating Type of Primary Child Care and Personal and Family Characteristics to Whether Child Care has Broken Down in Past Year and to Level of Satisfaction With Child Care: Detroit Child Care Survey, 1986.[a]

Predictor Variables	Whether Child Care Broke Down[b]	Satisfaction With Child Care[c]
Type of primary child care		
Father	—	—
Other Relative	.03	.20***
Sitter, Nanny, Family Day Care	.09	− .03
Organized Group Care	− .45	− .02
Kindergarten	− 1.09***	− .26***
Whether Child Care Broke Down	—	− .08
Hourly Cost of Child Care	− .01	.05
Whether Child Care is Free	− .52**	.18**
Number of Hours of Child Care	.01*	—
Lower Third on Hours of Care	—	—
Middle Third on Hours of Care	—	.07
Upper Third on Hours of Care	—	.06
Mother's Employment Status		
Not Working	—	—
Working Part Time	.70***	− .16*
Working Full Time	.53*	− .14
Mother's Education		
Some College or more	—	—
High School Graduate	− .14	.01
Less than High School Graduate	− .09	− .20**
Household Income ($100s)	− .01	.00
Whether Living With a Husband	− .19	.11
Whether African-American	− 1.12***	.00
Whether Child is 3 or Older	− .27	.06
Sampling Weights		
Weight 1	− .14	.01
Weight 2	.11	− .14
Weight 3	—	—
Likelihood Ratio Test/17 *df*	119	—
Adjusted R^2	—	.04
Number of Cases	773	773

*Coefficient is significantly different from zero, $p < .10$.

**Coefficient is significantly different from zero, $p < .05$.

***Coefficient is significantly different from zero, $p < .01$.

[a]Based on a probability sample of women ages 15–39 with at least one child born January, 1980, or later, residing in the greater Detroit metropolitan area in spring of 1986. Only women currently using some form of regularly scheduled, nonmaternal child care are included. Type of primary child care is that used for the youngest child receiving care.

[b]Coefficients in this column are estimated from a logistic response model using maximum likelihood. Each coefficient shows the log odds of having experienced a child-care breakdown associated with a one unit increment in the predictor variable.

[c]Coefficients in this column are estimated from an ordinary least square regression model. Satisfaction with child care is scored 1 if the mother is not too satisfied or fairly satisfied; 2 if she is very satisfied; and 3 if she is extremely satisfied.

scale that has a range of three points, mothers whose youngest child was in kindergarten (the least satisfied group) were only half a point less satisfied on average than were mothers whose youngest child was cared for by a relative (the most satisfied group). It is interesting to note that father care (the excluded category) is associated with somewhat lower levels of satisfaction than is care by another relative, perhaps because father care is chosen out of economic necessity rather than as a matter of preference. Also of interest is that care in an organized group facility breeds no greater satisfaction than care by the father or in a family day care home, a finding surprising in light of the stated preference of many parents for this type of care. Noteworthy, too, is that experience with child-care breakdowns has no relationship with child-care satisfaction, evident from the fact that kindergarten is the arrangement least prone to breakdowns but with which mothers are least satisfied. The only other characteristic of child care associated with satisfaction is whether it is free. Mothers who are getting their primary child-care arrangement free of charge are somewhat more satisfied than are mothers who are paying, but whether those paying are spending a little or a lot makes no difference vis-à-vis their satisfaction.

In the study of AFDC mothers by Sonenstein and Wolf (1991), type of child care had no relationship to satisfaction with care. In that study, however, there were several dimensions of quality and convenience that were related to satisfaction. In particular, for younger preschool-age children, the adult-to-child ratio and the convenience of the care location were both important for mothers' satisfaction; for older preschoolers, learning opportunities, the child's happiness with the arrangement, and convenience of location were important. On the basis of this study and the results from the Detroit study, it would appear that type of child care is less important for parents' satisfaction than is the nature of the particular arrangement and the parents' ability to purchase the care they desire.

Economic and Psychological Well Being. We have already reviewed the evidence that child-care problems may contribute to a reduction of family income via restrictions on the mother's labor supply. In this section, we also note the possibility that problems with child care can impair women's long-term earning prospects. This assertion grows out of a paper by Dalto (1989) concerned with the effects of maternity leave on women's human capital formation and returns to human capital, a paper whose key points can be generalized to the case of child care. Dalto argued that the provision of guaranteed maternity leave by women's employers reduces the impact on earnings of absences from the labor force caused by childbearing and child-rearing by providing job continuity in the face of labor-force discontinuity. Guaranteed maternity leaves should, thus, have the effect of improving the monetary payoffs to women's total years of employment and formal training.[15] Insofar as affordable and readily available child care also helps to reduce the intermittent nature women's labor-force involvement, it, too, should improve the monetary returns to employment experience. An especially important implication of this hypothesis is that public provision of child care might help to improve the long-term earning prospects of the very women who are most in need of such improvements, namely, women from poverty backgrounds.

At the start of this chapter, we suggested that child care was important for parental well-being because it could influence time availability or stress. Unfortunately, this topic does not appear to have been studied empirically other than in one small-scale study conducted in a middle-class suburb of Boston in the early 1980s (Barnett & Baruch, 1984; Baruch & Barnett, 1983). In this study, a measure of husband's and wife's "role strain" (approximately equivalent to the concept of time stress used here, i.e., not having sufficient time to enact all required roles) was related to the relative participation in child care of the husband and wife. Although the wife's relative participation had no impact on her own role strain, it did affect her husband's. The more child care was performed by the wife, the less the husband reported suffering from role strain. This study illustrates the problem discussed earlier: that some forms of child care may enhance the well-being of only one parent, perhaps at the expense of the other parent. In this particular study, whether the enhancement of the father's well-being was achieved at the mother's expense was not made clear. Further studies of time stress, especially on a larger and more representative sample of the population, would be highly worthwhile.

Seemingly consistent with the Barnett and Baruch results for time stress are the results of a study by White and Keith (1990) of the impact of shift work on the quality of the marital relationship. Although White and Keith were not concerned with the father's participation in child care per se — it was shift work, not child care, that they focused on — the association between shift work and the father's participation in child care among dual-earner parents of young children suggests their results are applicable to father's participation in child care. For a national sample of couples, White and Keith found that, when at least one partner worked nonday shifts, the marriage was more likely to experience difficulties and a subsequent divorce than when both partners worked day shifts. This suggests that reliance on fathers for the care of preschool-aged children may be problematic from the parents' point of view. In some cases, although by no means in all of them, it may produce time stress for the father and may lead to a deterioration of the marital relationship; it may also produce dissatisfaction for the mother (see Table 3.2). Whether the

---

[15]The results of an analysis by Dalto of data from the 1977 Quality of Employment Survey were consistent with this expectation (Dalto, 1989).

circumstances that lead to shift work, and hence the father's involvement in child care, affect these outcomes is unknown and would be worth studying.

The final study we review here speaks directly to the issue of how child care problems affect parents' (or at least, mothers') psychological well-being. This is an analysis by Ross and Mirowsky (1988; also reported in Mirowsky & Ross, 1989) of factors contributing to depression, as measured through a survey instrument. Using a multi-item depression scale administered in telephone interviews to a national probability sample of American women, Ross and Mirowsky found one group with significantly elevated depression scores: employed mothers who reported that their husbands did not share child care and who said that finding adequate child care was difficult. This suggests that child-care availability can have a strong impact on women's mental health, although the impact can be mitigated by the presence of a helpful spouse or, presumably, an income high enough to make child care more available. It would be overstating the case to say that every mother who experiences child-care problems suffers clinical depression, but Ross and Mirowsky's findings suggest that child-care problems can indeed have serious consequences for women's psychological well-being.[16]

In sum, then, although studies that directly link child-care problems, child-care type, or child-care quality to parental well-being are relatively rare, they suggest that there may indeed be important links here. Whether child-care problems affect social supports has yet to be studied.

CONCLUSIONS

This review of existing studies shows there to be considerable evidence for the idea that child-care availability and affordability affect the well-being of mothers and fathers. Some of the possible links between child-care problems and parental well-being are under-studied, however, and would benefit from further investigation. It would be useful to know more about parents' preferences for child care (Sonenstein, 1990): specifically, how parents weigh costs, time constraints, income needs and their perceptions of what will be best for their children in deciding how to care for their children. We also need to learn more about parents' satisfaction with child care, using more detailed questions than have been used in past studies. We do not really understand why studies of the general population yield such high rates of satisfaction, nor

---

[16]A possibility that Ross and Mirowsky do not discuss but that should be recognized is that it may be that depression contributes to difficulties in finding child care rather than that child-care difficulties contribute to depression. That depression was associated with child-care difficulties only when the husband provided no child-care help, however, suggests that it is child-care problems that contribute more to depression than the reverse.

do we know how parents weigh their child's needs against their own needs in judging the adequacy of particular child-care arrangements.

Another under-studied area is child care provided by fathers: not only its extent, but what leads parents to choose this form of care and what consequences it has for children and parents themselves. Thanks to Presser's papers (1986, 1988) on shift work and father care, we have become more aware of the important role that fathers often play in caring for children while mothers are at work, but we do not understand very well what leads parents to choose this arrangement, nor what consequences it has for family life. Indeed, the issue of time stress in family life is generally poorly understood. Parents in dual-earner marriages commonly complain about the time stresses they suffer, but we have little systematic evidence about the causes and consequences of this stress and whether nonfamilial child care plays a role in contributing to it or relieving it.

Finally, further information on the impact of child-care availability and costs on women's long-term patterns of employment and returns to human capital would be very worthwhile. Are women who are confident that a trustworthy and affordable caregiver is available more likely to work continuously and enjoy greater financial and social rewards from employment than women who find the supply, price, or quality of child care problematic? We do not yet fully understand the rewards of employment to women, including nonmonetary rewards, such as the development of friendships that provide social supports. Understanding how the supply, quality, and price of child care affects women's work lives is important. As a number of studies have noted, child care is most likely to prove problematic for the very parents who most require it because they lack partners to help with the care of their children or lack the financial resources to purchase care. Poor women and women raising children without partners are especially likely to find child care unavailable or unaffordable, to report that they are constrained from working by this lack of availability, and to suffer psychologically and economically as a result. Understanding how better quality, more affordable, convenient, and reliable child care would affect these women's work lives is very important.

As we stated at the start of this chapter, even relatively affluent parents with supportive partners often face child-care problems, and when they do, they are likely to suffer psychologically, at least in the short run. The research evidence suggests these problems are far more serious for the more deprived members of our society. Although it is beyond the scope of the present paper to consider policy alternatives that might be enacted to alleviate this problem, it seems clear that some form of public sector intervention is warranted. When parents suffer, children suffer, and when inadequate child care prevents poor women from entering the labor force, other taxpayers are burdened (Bloom & Steen, 1990). The United States has lagged behind many European nations in its support for children and families, in general, and for alternatives to maternal child care, in particular (Ergas, 1990). We hope that this volume helps to bring about reforms that make high-quality child care more available and affordable for parents and children from all walks of life.

ACKNOWLEDGMENTS

We thank Alan Booth, Alison Clarke-Stewart, Sandra Hofferth, and Rebecca Maynard for their suggestions. Parts of the research reported here were supported by grant RO1-HD20260 from the National Institute of Child Health and Human Development.

REFERENCES

Barnett, R. C., & Baruch, G. K. (1984). *Mother's participation in child care: Patterns and consequences* (Working Paper No. 137). Wellesley, MA: Wellesley College Center for Research on Women.

Baruch, G. K., & Barnett, R. C. (1983). *Correlates of father's participation in family work: A technical report* (Working Paper No. 106). Wellesley, MA: Wellesley College Center for Research on Women.

Blau, D. M., & Robins, P. K. (1988). Child-care costs and family labor supply. *Review of Economics and Statistics, 70,* 374–381.

Blau, D. M., & Robins, P. K. (1989). Fertility, employment, and child-care costs. *Demography, 26,* 287–299.

Blau, D. M., & Robins, P. K. (1990, May). *Child care demand and labor supply of young mothers over time.* Paper presented at the annual meeting of the Population Association of America, Toronto, Ontario.

Bloom, D. E., & Steen, T. P. (1990). The labor force implications of expanding the child care industry. *Population Research and Policy Review, 9,* 25–44.

Christian, P. B. (1990, May). *Determinants of child care arrangements: Shift work as a type of child care.* Paper presented at the annual meeting of the Population Association of America, Toronto, Ontario.

Connelly, R. (1989). *The effect of child care costs on married women's labor force participation.* Unpublished manuscript, Bowdoin College, Brunswick, ME.

Connelly, R. (1990, May). *Self employment and providing child care: Employment strategies for mothers of young children.* Paper presented at the annual meeting of the Population Association of America, Toronto, Ontario.

Dalto, G. C. (1989). A structural approach to women's home-time and experience-earnings profiles: Maternity leave and public policy. *Population Research and Policy Review, 8,* 247–266.

Dawson, D. A. (1990, October 1). Child care arrangements: Health of our nation's children, United States, 1988 (Number 187). *National Center for Health Statistics Advance Data.*

Duberstein, L., & Mason, K. O. (1991, March). *The impact of child care costs on women's work plans*. Paper presented at the annual meeting of the Population Association of America, Washington, DC.

Ergas, Y. (1990). Child-care policies in comparative perspective: An introductory discussion. In Organisation for Economic Co-operation and Development [OECD] (Eds.), *Social policy studies: Vol. 8. Lone parent families: The economic challenge* (pp. 173–199). Paris: OECD.

Floge, L. (1985). The dynamics of child-care use and some implications for women's employment. *Journal of Marriage and the Family, 47,* 143–154.

Glezer, H. (1988). *Maternity leave in Australia: Employee and employer experiences. Report of a survey* (Monograph No. 7). Melbourne: Australian Institute of Family Studies.

Gustafsson, S., & Stafford, F. (1988). *Daycare subsidies and labor supply in Sweden.* Unpublished manuscript, Arbetslivcentrum, Stockholm, and Institute for Social Research, Ann Arbor, MI.

Heckman, J. J. (1976). The common structure of statistical models of truncation, sample selection and limited dependent variables and a simple estimator for such models. *Annals of Economic and Social Measurement, 5,* 475–492.

Heckman, J. J. (1979). Sample selection bias as specification error. *Econometrica, 47,* 153–161.

Hofferth, S. L., & Brayfield, A. A. (1991, March). *Making time for children: Family decisions about employment and child care.* Paper presented at the annual meeting of the Population Association of America, Washington, DC.

Hofferth, S. L., & Wissoker, D. A. (1990, May). *Quality, price, and income in child care choice.* Paper presented at the annual meeting of the Population Association of America, Toronto, Ontario.

Hogan, D. P., Hao, L., & Parish, W. L. (1990). Race, kin networks, and assistance to mother-headed families. *Social Forces, 68,* 797–812.

Hurst, M., & Zambrana, R. E. (1982). Child care and working mothers in Puerto Rican families. *Annals of the American Academy of Political and Social Science, 461,* 113–124.

Kisker, E. E., Maynard, R., Gordon, A., & Strain, M. (1989). *The child care challenge: What parents need and what is available in three metropolitan areas.* Executive summary. Princeton, NJ: Mathematica Policy Research.

Kisker, E. E., Silverberg, M., & Maynard, R. (1990). *Early impacts of the teenage parent demonstration on child care needs and utilization.* Princeton, NJ: Mathematica Policy Research.

Klerman, J. A., & Leibowitz, A. (1990). Child care and women's return to work after childbirth. *American Economic Review, 28,* 284–288.

Kuhlthau, K., & Mason, K. O. (1991). *Type of child care: Determinants of use among working and non-working mothers.* Unpublished manuscript, East-West Population Institute, East-West Center, Honolulu.

Lehrer, E. L. (1983). Determinants of child care mode choice: An economic perspective. *Social Science Research, 12,* 69–80.

Lehrer, E. L. (1989). Preschoolers with working mothers: An analysis of the determinants of child care arrangements. *Journal of Population Economics, 1,* 251–268.

Lehrer, E. L., & Kawasaki, S. (1985). Child care arrangements and fertility: An analysis of two-earner households. *Demography, 22,* 499–513.

Leibowitz, A., & Waite, L. J. (1988). *The consequences for women of the availability and affordability of child care* (Report for the Panel on Child Care, National Research Council, National Academy of Sciences). Santa Monica, CA: The Rand Corporation.

Leibowitz, A., Waite, L. J., & Witsberger, C. (1988). Child care for preschoolers: Differences by child's age. *Demography, 25,* 205–220.

Maddala, G. S. (1983). *Limited-dependent and qualitative variables in econometrics.* Cambridge: Cambridge University Press.

Mason, K. O., & Kuhlthau, K. (1989). Determinants of child care ideals among mothers of preschool-aged children. *Journal of Marriage and the Family, 51,* 593–603.

Mason, K. O., & Kuhlthau, K. O. (1991). *The perceived impact of child care costs on women's labor supply and fertility.* Unpublished manuscript, East-West Center Population Institute, Honolulu.

Maume, D. J., Jr. (1989). *Child care costs and women's employment turnover.* Unpublished manuscript, University of Cincinnati, Department of Sociology, Cincinnati.

Mirowsky, J., & Ross, C. E. (1989). *Social causes of psychological distress.* New York: Aldine de Gruyter.

Morgan, S. P., & Hiroshima, K. (1983). The persistence of extended family residence in Japan. *American Sociological Review, 48,* 269–281.

O'Connell, M., & Bloom, D. (1987). Juggling jobs and babies: America's child care challenge. *Population Trends and Public Policy, 12,* 1–16.

Parish, W. L., Hao, L., & Hogan, D. P. (1991). Family support networks, welfare, and work among young mothers. *Journal of Marriage and the Family, 53,* 203–215.

Presser, H. B. (1986). Shift work among American women and child care. *Journal of Marriage and the Family, 48,* 551–563.

Presser, H. B. (1988). Shift work and child care among young dual-earner American parents. *Journal of Marriage and the Family, 50,* 133–148.

Presser, H. B. (1989). Some economic complexities of child care provided by grandmothers. *Journal of Marriage and the Family, 51,* 581–591.

Presser, H. B., & Baldwin, W. (1980). Child care as a constraint on employment: Prevalence, correlates, and bearing on the work and fertility nexus. *American Journal of Sociology, 85,* 1202–1213.

Presser, H. B., & Cain, V. (1983). Shift work among dual-earner couples with children. *Science, 219,* 876–879.

Robins, P. K., & Spiegelman, R. G. (1978). An econometric model of the demand for child care. *Economic Inquiry, 16,* 83–94.

Ross, C. E., & Mirowsky, J. (1988). Child care and emotional adjustment to wives' employment. *Journal of Health and Social Behavior, 29,* 127–138.

Sonenstein, F. L. (1990). The child care preferences of parents with young children: How little is known. In J. S. Hyde & M. J. Essex (Eds.), *Parental leave and child care: Setting a research and policy agenda* (pp. 337–353). Philadelphia: Temple University Press.

Sonenstein, F. L., & Wolf, D. A. (1991). Satisfaction with child care: Perspectives of welfare mothers. *Journal of Social Issues, 47,* 15–31.

Staines, G. L., & Pleck, J. H. (1983). *The impact of work schedules on the family.* Ann Arbor, MI: University of Michigan, Institute for Social Research, Survey Research Center.

Waite, L. J., Leibowitz, A., & Witsberger, C. (1988, March/April). *What parents pay for: Quality of child care and child care costs.* Paper presented at the annual meeting of the Population Association of America, Baltimore, MD.

White, L., & Keith, B. (1990). The effect of shift work on the quality and stability of marital relations. *Journal of Marriage and the Family, 52,* 453–462.

Yeager, K. E. (1979). Cost, convenience and quality in child care demand. *Children and Youth Services Review, 1,* 293–313.

The Impact of Child Care on Parents

ELLEN GALINSKY
Families and Work Institute

T he National Symposium on Child Care in the 1990s: Trends and Consequences includes the topic of child care and parental well-being, and Karen Oppenheim Mason and Laura Duberstein have posed a conceptual model for these relationships. This represents an important step forward in our field. The rapid increase in the number of mothers in the workforce has given rise to a substantial literature on the impact of family structure and job characteristics on workers' well-being (Galinsky, 1986; Hughes, Galinsky, & Morris, in press; Jackson, Zedeck, & Summers, 1985; Piotrkowski, 1979; Piotrkowski & Katz, 1983; Quinn & Staines, 1979; Repetti, 1987; Shinn, Ortiz-Torres, Wong, & Simko, 1989; Voydanoff, 1988). Likewise, there has been a great deal of attention given to the ways in which child care affects children's well-being and development (Gamble & Zigler, 1986; Hayes, Palmer & Zaslow, 1990; Howes & Stewart, 1987; Kontos, in press; Phillips, 1987; Whitebook, Howes, & Phillips, 1990). There has, however, been an unfortunate and noticeable lack of attention given to the ways in which child care can affect parents. Do similar or different aspects of child care have an impact on children and parents? Which characteristics of child care are most salient? In what ways do these affect parental well-being? How should well-being be defined? Is parental performance on the job affected?

On the basis of the research that my colleagues and I at the Families and Work Institute investigating these questions, both in terms of qualitative and quantitative research, I would argue for a different conceptual model than the

159

one posed by Mason and Duberstein. I can understand the utility of their model in an economic context, but when one considers the well-being of parents, other complexities come into play. Thus, I contend that such models should separate finding child care and maintaining child care. I define well-being as including measures of health, stress, work–family conflict, marital and parenting satisfaction, psychological well-being, and workplace effectiveness.

OBTAINING CHILD CARE AND PARENTAL WELL-BEING

The definition of child-care availability differs, depending on whether one takes an economic or a psychological perspective, although these two are often confused. From a psychological vantage point, one has to consider the process of finding child care as quite distinct from the processes of maintaining the arrangements that one selects. Notice that the word *arrangements* is plural. Unfortunately, most of the research on child care is conducted as if parents have only one arrangement or as if it is only the primary arrangement that counts. We now know from the *National Child Care Survey 1990* (Hofferth, Brayfield, Deich, & Holcomb, 1990) that 83% of parents of preschoolers have more than one arrangement. Two out of every three of these second arrangements are parent care (67%), then relative care (15%), and centers (6%).

There are three stages in the process of finding child care that must be considered: Deciding whether to return to work, finding out about the available child care, and judging the child care and making a decision. Although these can be conceptualized as different, in fact, there can be considerable overlap. For example, although a mother may think she wants to return to work, when she sees the available child care, she may change her mind.

Deciding Whether to Return to Work

Demographic factors are important in the decisions that women make about returning to work. In a study that investigated the leave-taking patterns of new mothers in four states, the Families and Work Institute found that mothers most likely to return to their jobs had higher salaries or earned a large share of their household's income. In other words, both higher and lower income women were more likely to return than middle-income women, (Bond, Galinsky, Lord, Staines, & Brown, 1991). In addition, as Mason and Duberstein state, the number of children and the education of the employee are also important factors.

Attitudes clearly affect the decision-making process. In the four-state study

(Bond et al., 1991) women who felt that working was important to their image of themselves were more likely to return their jobs. Although it was not assessed in this study, the husband's feelings about whether mothers should work and what this connotes about his role as a breadwinner play a crucial role in the decision-making process. I suspect that mothers who feel forced to return to work by economic necessity react completely differently from mothers who want to return, or who at least feel they have a choice.

There is concern in the business sector that women who take leaves planning to return to work will change their minds once the baby is born and then quit their jobs. Although this does happen sometimes, it is far less frequent than is generally assumed. In a study of a large corporation, only 6% of women took a leave and subsequently decided not to return. Four factors are predictive of this change of plans: the occurrence of complications in the pregnancy, in the birth or in the child's health, and poor employee performance ratings (Staines & Galinsky, in press).

Company policies and culture also play a role in decision-making. Interestingly, the company just referred to had a very generous parental leave policy, providing one year off with a job guarantee and continuation of health benefits. This company had a retention rate of 94%, much higher than the standard 85% rate (Staines & Galinsky, in press). Research has revealed that companies with more accommodating policies reap a return on this investment: Pregnant women work longer into their pregnancies, miss less time, are sick less often, take work home more frequently, and are more likely to return to work (Bond, in press). Among the company policies that affect retention rates are the length of the job-guaranteed leave, the possibility of a part-time transition back to work, and flexibility in daily arrival and departure times. Research reveals that family-supportive company policies, in and of themselves, are not sufficient. The company culture makes a difference, too. In the four-state study, the supportiveness of co-workers and the supervisor, and the degree to which the company was perceived as "family-friendly" during the employee's pregnancy were predictive of whether or not she returned to work (Bond et al., 1991). Mason and Duberstein mention co-workers in their conceptual model. On the basis of the research just described, I would argue that the support of supervisors and a family-friendly atmosphere are also salient.

Availability of child care also figures heavily into the decision of whether to return to work. New mothers in the four-state study were more likely to return to work if they had friends or relatives nearby who could provide child care (Bond et al., 1991).

Finding out About Available Child Care

Parents report that finding out about available sources of care is like entering a secret society: Parents are often unsure about where to turn for information and how to judge the information they receive. In a survey of 1,470 parents employed in a communication company, 39% reported that it was "difficult" or "very difficult" to find out about the available child care. This process can be even more problematic if one is looking for more specialized forms of care, such as infant care or before- and after-school care (Galinsky, 1988a). The *National Child Care Survey 1990* (Hofferth et al., 1991) revealed that most parents turn to friends and relatives to locate child care rather than using more formal means such as child-care resource and referral services.

Judging the Available Care and Making a Decision

Studies reveal that most parents look at more than one arrangement before making a selection. In a study of a representative group of mothers using child-care centers in Atlanta, only 6% of the mothers had enrolled their child in the first and only center they considered. Although the vast majority had made an effort to find alternatives, few parents were satisfied with the available choices. Of those who would have preferred home-based care, 74% found no other acceptable choices that they could afford. Of those who preferred centers, 78% felt they had no other acceptable alternatives. Although this sample of mothers — like others reported by Mason and Duberstein — reported high satisfaction with their current arrangements (80% would choose their current arrangement again without hesitation), when they thought back to the moment of decision-making, the majority (53%) would have selected some other program if they had had more choice (Galinsky, 1989). Therefore, it is clear that a sizeable number of parents find their choices limited.

What factors do parents consider in making a choice? As Mason and Duberstein point out, little is known about this process, and more research is called for. I am pleased to say that the Families and Work Institute was funded to conduct such a study in three communities in a project begun in the fall of 1991. In the meantime, other studies do indicate some of the factors of importance: The type of care preferred is salient. Resource and referral agencies indicate that parents seem to prefer one form of care other another, although this varies by income level, community resources, and age of child (Zinsser, 1990). From the actual choices they make, parents of infants and toddlers seem to want family care: If not care in their own homes, then care by relatives, not strangers. Parents of children 3 and older seem to want institutionally based care. At that age, perhaps, children are seen as ready to learn and, therefore, should be in school-like settings (Hofferth et al., 1991).

Another factor of importance in selecting child care is the perceived effect of the care on the child. Regardless of the age of the child or the type of care preferred, the *National Child Care Survey 1990* found that the teacher-caregivers' relationship with the child is of critical importance to parents in making a selection (Hofferth et al., 1991). Our own research at the Families and Work Institute corroborates this finding (Galinsky, 1988a). Parents seem to be looking for a warm teacher-caregiver who will nurture their child. Little is known about whether parents are looking for shared culture and values. Parents also care about the child-care facilities; they assess whether they are clean and safe, and whether the activities are geared to the children (Galinsky, 1988a, Klein, personal communication, June, 1991). Some parents are attuned to group size and staff-to-child ratios, whereas the training of teachers or caregivers seems to be of no importance (Shinn, Galinsky, & Gulcur, 1990; Klein, personal communication, June, 1991). In fact, recent focus groups indicate that parents oppose the notion of trained providers: They see taking care of children in child care much like parenting. As one parent put it, "If child care providers need training, does this mean I need training?" (Klein, personal communication, June, 1991). It is not known if parents care about whether centers are licensed or accredited; or whether family child-care providers are registered, licensed, or accredited; or even the extent to which parents are aware that these state and professional association protections exist.

In addition to factors that affect children, the perceived effect of the care on the parent is also important in the selection process. This includes location, hours, flexibility, and cost. Company needs assessments reveal that although most parents prefer to have their children cared for close to home, some — especially those with very young children — would like their child care to be at or near the workplace. The hours the program is open must fit into the parents' job schedules and the arrangement must offer flexibility when and if the employee must work overtime. Clearly, cost is one of the most important factors that parents must take into account. Mason and Duberstein have conducted a thorough review of the research on cost. There is, however, a psychological component to cost considerations. Families tend to use the mother's salary as the yardstick for determining what is affordable: The cost must not exceed what the mother can earn thus prices have remained low. However, families who are poor pay a much greater share of their income on child care (23%) than do families with high incomes (6%); Hofferth et al., 1991).

Little is known about how parents determine these cost–quality tradeoffs. Do they preselect care of a certain cost and then look for quality within those constraints? Do they look for quality first, then make cost decisions? Do various types of families approach these issues differently? What considerations cause parents to shift their priorities? Research is needed into these dimensions of the choice process.

The recent passage of comprehensive child-care legislation and its philosophical emphasis on the importance of parental choice make it clear that the policy thrust in this country will be on demand-side interventions into the child-care marketplace. However, the growing knowledge that many children are in poor quality arrangements that are likely to both compromise the children's future development and be expensive to remediate has stimulated a response, especially by business leaders. There is a growing corporate interest in affecting consumer behavior. The recent $2.85 million grant to provide consumer education in child care in 32 communities by Dayton Hudson, Target Stores, and Mervyn's is an example of this new trend. Similarly, companies are intervening in the child-care delivery system to improve the supply and quality of parents' choices. IBM, AT&T, and American Express have all launched major efforts to fund community child-care improvements. Future research should be conducted on the degree to which consumer education and quality improvement efforts affect parents' definitions of quality as well as the processes and outcomes of their child-care choices.

Obtaining Child Care and Parental Well-Being

There is little research investigating how the act of finding child care affects parental well-being. Those who have experienced it firsthand or who have observed it can attest to the stressful nature of this search process. One study that assessed close to 2,000 women before and after childbirth found that of those mothers with no problems arranging child care, 49% were very satisfied with their lives. Of new mothers with serious problems arranging child care, only 34% were very satisfied (National Council of Jewish Women [NCJW], 1987). There have been a few studies examining the relationship between the difficulty of finding child care and indicators of productivity. For example, a study of a representative sample of dual-earning parents with children 12 and under found that difficulty finding child care was predictive of absenteeism (Galinsky & Hughes, 1987). Further research is needed on how the process of selecting child care affects fathers' and mothers' well-being, labor force participation, and productivity.

MAINTAINING CHILD CARE AND
PARENTAL WELL-BEING

A second conceptual model related to maintaining child care and parental well-being should include the following factors:

Demographic Factors

As Mason and Duberstein state, there are a number of demographic factors of importance. First, is the sex of the employee. Because women play the major role in both finding and maintaining child care, they tend to be affected more strongly than men. In a study conducted by researchers from Portland State University, stress due to child-care problems was reported by 47% of the women with children under 12 as compared to 28% of a comparable group of men (Emlen & Koren, 1984). As a consequence of this greater responsibility, women are much more likely to miss work due to child care problems than are men. In one survey, 27% of the men reported missing work at least once in the previous three months due to child-care problems; the figure for women was almost twice as high: 49% (Galinsky, 1988a). It is interesting to note that when men take greater responsibility for child care, they are equally affected (Burden & Googins, 1986). In fact, Shinn, Ortiz-Torres, Morris, Simko, and Wong (1987) found that when men took on more child care responsibility, their well-being was even more vulnerable than women's. They state that:

> Although men more rarely missed work due to child care responsibilities, missing work for this purpose was more strongly associated with stressors and poor health and well-being for men than for women. We cannot tell from our data whether informal norms against men dealing with a child care problem were at work here. (p. 5)

Another significant factor is the age of the youngest child. In examining the research on parental well-being and child care, it is clear that there is an interaction between the sex of the employee and the age of the youngest child: Mothers with young children are tardy more frequently than other employees, they miss work more often, and they experience more work-family conflict (Emlen & Koren, 1984; Fernandez, 1986; Galinsky, 1988a).

Not surprisingly, several studies have found that the number of children is also a factor of importance in managing child care arrangements. For example, in one company, 66% of the mothers with three children were late to work at least once in a three-month period as compared to 50% of the mothers with only one child. Likewise, the number of children has emerged as a predictor of more unproductive time spent at work due to child-care problems (Galinsky, 1988a).

Job Attitudes and Conditions

The place of work in parents' lives and the feelings of having a choice about working and about the number of hours worked also figure in this conceptual model.

The two aspects of jobs that have been found to have the greatest impact on managing child care concern work schedule and work-family support. As Mason and Duberstein state, the number of scheduled and overtime hours makes a difference. So does schedule flexibility. In the study of new mothers in four states referred to earlier (Bond et al., 1991), analyses were conducted to test the notion of whether schedule flexibility makes it easier for mothers to manage their child-care arrangements. The researcher found that mothers with highly flexible flextime (those allowing daily variation in arrival and departure times) did, indeed, have less difficulty arranging child care and reported less work-family conflict and higher parental satisfaction than mothers with no flextime or mothers with moderate flexibility (policies allowing some control over hours but no daily variation; Staines, 1991).

Although no studies to my knowledge have examined the links between work–family support by supervisors and co-workers and maintaining child care, several studies have found that these work–family support factors are significant predictors of lower work–family interference, lower perceived stress, and fewer stress-related health problems (Galinsky, 1988b). It stands to reason then, that if the supervisor is supportive when the employee experiences child-care problems (a construct tapped by the supervisor work–family support measure used by the Families and Work Institute in previously mentioned research), employees would have less difficulty managing child care. Future analyses by the Families and Work Institute and others will explore these connections.

Child-Care Conditions

Different types of primary child-care arrangements have been shown to affect indicators of productivity. According to the research at Portland State University, parents (especially mothers) who used out-of-home care or care by their own child (*self-care* or *latch-key care,* as it is more commonly called) are more likely to miss work, arrive late, or leave early. Interestingly, fathers using latch-key arrangements had slightly higher absentee rates than did the corresponding group of mothers (Emlen & Koren, 1984). The type of primary child care has also been linked to stress. In the Portland State study, 36% of the men and 46% of the women who used out-of-home care reported child-care related stress. When using latch-key care, 50% of the women and 30% of the men reported stress.

Several studies have found a significant relationship between the number of child care arrangements that parents use for each child and the number of breakdowns in these arrangements. Simply put, the greater the complexity of the patchwork system of care that parents must maintain, the more likely that some aspect of this system will fall apart (Hughes, 1987; Shinn et al., 1987). In a nationally representative sample of men and women in dual-earning families with children 12 and under, 40% had experienced at least one breakdown of their child-care arrangements in the preceding three months. Twenty-seven percent of the men and 24% of the women had two to five child care breakdowns during that same time period (Galinsky & Hughes, 1987).

The leading causes of such breakdowns included having sick children or having a child care provider who quits or is sick.

When child-care arrangements break down, employed parents are more likely to be absent, to be late, to report being unable to concentrate on the job, to have higher levels of stress and more stress-related health problems, and to report lower parental and marital satisfaction (Galinsky & Hughes, 1987; NCJW, 1987; Shinn et al., 1987).

Although Mason and Duberstein assert that parents and child development experts do not fully agree about the components of quality that affect children. I would assert that there is a high degree of consensus about the most important factor: The relationship between the child-care provider and the child. This is the aspect of child care that parents define as most important (Hofferth et al., 1991); it is also the aspect of child care that professionals put forth as primary. This is the case in the accreditation standards for early childhood programs developed by the largest early childhood professional organization, the National Association for the Education of Young Children (NAEYC), based both on a literature review and a professional consensus-building process. The other facets of child care — such as group size, staff–child ratio, and training — make it more likely that the relationship between the child and provider will be individualized, warm, and caring (Bredekamp, 1984).

One study that investigated the impact of quality (as assessed by professional rating scales) and maternal well-being found that when child-care providers had a more detached style of interacting with children, mothers were less satisfied with the center and missed their children more. When the providers' style was chaotic, mothers also missed their children even more. In contrast, when providers were sensitive and responsive, mothers were more satisfied with the center, were more likely to believe that their children benefit from child care, and had fewer feelings of loneliness (Shinn, Phillips, Howes, Galinsky, & Whitebook, 1990).

The aspects of this provider–child relationship that are most salient to children's development are the caring relationship, the learning relationship, the disciplinary relationship, and the stability of the relationship (Galinsky, 1990). When the impact of turnover on parents was investigated, researchers found that the higher the staff turnover in the child's classroom over the previous 12 months, as reported by the center director, the more likely the mother was to be less satisfied with the center, to feel that her child did not benefit from child care, to feel less adequate as a parent, and to miss the child more while at work (Shinn, Phillips, et al., 1990).

I would agree with Mason and Duberstein on the lack of consensus between parents and child development experts about other aspects of quality. In a study that compared maternal child-care satisfaction with observer ratings of quality, mothers generally reported quite high levels of satisfaction with programs that were of relatively low quality. Mothers were, however, somewhat less satisfied with their child care when the global ratings of the preschool classrooms were poorer, and they were lonelier and missed their children more when the global assessments of the infant and toddler classrooms were lower. There were very small, trivial associations between satisfaction and actual group size and ratios. In contrast to expert opinion and some other studies (e.g., Hofferth & Wissoker, in press), the mothers in this study were slightly more satisfied with the center and felt slightly less inadequate as parents when the group sizes and ratios of children to teachers were larger. Staff training had no discernable impact on mother's well-being or satisfaction (Shinn, Phillips, et al., 1990).

This same study did find significant associations between satisfaction with the factors of child care that affect parents and parental well-being. These factors included the cost of the program, the location of the program relative to the home and the workplace, the hours it was open, its flexibility (e.g., if the parent had to bring the child in late), its rules (such as those concerning sick children), and parents' opportunity for providing input center decision making. When mothers were dissatisfied with these aspects of their child care arrangements, they were more likely to have higher levels of stress, more stress-related health symptoms, and more work–family spillover, and to come to work late more often (Shinn, Galinsky, et al., 1990).

Another aspect of child care that affects parents is the relationship between the parents and the provider. This facet of child care has been shown to affect children's development as well (Galinsky, 1990; Lally, Mangione, & Honig, 1988; Weikart, 1990). Negative support from teachers has been linked to higher work–family conflict; positive support from teachers, therefore, is important to family functioning (Galinsky, Shinn, Phillips, Howes, & Whitebook, 1990).

CONCLUSION

Mason and Duberstein' chapter provides an excellent review of the literature on child care and parental well-being, which I hope I have extended by my response. It is important to continue to refine the conceptual models that enable us to understand the complex web of relationships that exist. I agree that a worthwhile next step in research is to conduct longitudinal studies that investigate the impact of child-care availability, cost, and quality on men's and women's patterns of labor-force participation, but action to redress the well-known problems of child care must not wait for studies. We certainly know enough to assert that there will be dire consequences for children, parents, employers, and our future society if we do not continue our work to improve the quality of young children's care and education.

REFERENCES

Bond, J. T. (in press). The impact of childbearing on employment. In *Parental Leave and Productivity*. New York: Families and Work Institute.

Bond, J. T., Galinsky, E., Lord, M., Staines, G., & Brown, K. (1991). *Beyond the parental leave debate: The impact of laws in four states*. New York: Families and Work Institute.

Bredekamp, S. (Ed.). (1984). *Accreditation criteria and procedures of the National Academy of Early Childhood Programs*. Washington, DC: National Association for the Education of Young Children.

Burden, D., & Googins, B. (1986). *Balancing Job and Homelife Study*. Boston: Boston University School of Social Work.

Emlen, A., & Koren, P. (1984). *Hard to find and difficult to manage: The effects of child care on the workplace*. Portland, OR: Regional Institute for Human Resources.

Fernandez, J. (1986). *Child care and corporate productivity: Resolving family work conflicts*. Lexington, MA: D. C. Health.

Galinsky, E. (1986). Family life and corporate policies. In M. Yogman & T. B. Brazelton, (Eds.), *In support of families* (pp. 109–145). Boston: Harvard University Press.

Galinsky, E. (1988a, March). *Child care and productivity*. Paper prepared for the Child Care Action Campaign conference, Child Care: The Bottom Line. New York.

Galinsky, E. (1988b, August). *The impact of supervisors' attitudes and company culture on work family adjustment*. Paper presented at the annual convention of the American Psychological Association, Atlanta, GA.

Galinsky, E. (1989). The Parent/Teacher Study. In *Young children*. Washington, DC: National Association for the Education of Young Children. Vol. 45, No. 1 November 1989.

Galinsky, E. (1990). The costs of not providing quality early childhood programs. In B. Willer (Ed.), *Reaching the full cost of quality* (pp. 27–40). Washington, DC: National Association for the Education of Young Children.

Galinsky, E., & Hughes, D. (1987, August). *The Fortune Magazine Child Care Study*. Paper presented at the annual convention of the American Psychological Association, New York.

Galinsky, E., Shinn, B., Phillips, D., Howes, C., & Whitebook, M. (1990). *Parent/teacher relationships*. New York: Families and Work Institute.

Gamble, J., & Zigler, F. (1986). Effects of infant day care: Another look at the evidence. *American Journal of Orthopsychiatry*, 26–42.

Hayes, C. D., Palmer, J. L., & Zaslow, M. J. (1990). *Who cares for America's children? Child Care Policy for the 1990s*. Washington, DC: National Academy Press.

Hofferth, D. L., Brayfield, A., Deich, S., & Holcomb, P. (1991). *National Child Care Survey, 1990*. Washington, DC: The Urban Institute.

Hofferth, S. L., & Wissoker, D. A. (in press). Quality, price, and income in child care choice. *Journal of Social Issues*.

Howes, C., & Stewart, P. (1987). Child's play with adults, toys and peers. *Developmental Psychology, 23*, 423–430.

Hughes, D. (1987, August). *Child care and working parents*. Paper presented at the annual convention of the American Psychological Association, New York.

Hughes, D., Galinsky, E., & Morris, A. (in press). The effects of job characteristics on marital quality. Specifying linking mechanisms. *Journal of Marriage and the Family.*

Jackson, S., Zedeck, S., & Summers, E. (1985). Family life disruptions: Effects of job-induced structural and emotional interference. *Academy of Management Journal, 28,* 574–586.

Kontos, S. (in press). *Family child care: Out of the shadows, into the limelight.* Washington, DC: National Association for the Education of Young Children.

Lally, J. R., Mangione, P. L., & Honig, A. S. (1987). *The Syracuse University Family Development Research Program: Long range impact of early intervention on low-income children and their families.* San Francisco, CA: Center for Child and Family Studies, Far West Laboratory for Educational Research and Development.

Lally, J. R., Mangione, P. L., & Honig, A. S. (1987). Journal of National Center for Clinical Infant Programs, Arlington, VA.

National Council of Jewish Women (November, 1987). *Accommodating pregnancy in the workplace* (Report for the NCJW Center for the Child.) New York: Author.

Phillips, D. A. (Ed.). (1987). *Quality in child care: What does research tell us?* Washington, DC: National Association for the Education of Young Children.

Piotrkowski, C. S. (1979). *Work and the family system: A naturalistic study of working-class and lower middle-class families.* New York: The Free Press.

Piotrkowski, C. S., & Katz, M. H. (1983). Work experience and family relations among working class and lower middle-class families. In H. Z. Lopata & J. H. Pleck (Eds.), *Research in the interweave of social roles: Families and jobs* (Vol. III). Greenwich, CT: JAI Press.

Quinn, R. P., & Staines, G. L. (1979). *The 1977 quality of employment survey: Descriptive statistics with comparison data from the 1969–70 and the 1972–73 Surveys.* Ann Arbor, MI: Institute for Social Research.

Repetti, R. L. (1987). Linkages between work and family roles. In S. Oscamp (Ed.), *Applied psychology annual: Family processes and problems* (Vol. 7, pp. 98–127). Beverly Hills, CA: Sage Publications.

Shinn, M., Galinsky, E., & Gulcur, L. (1990). *The role of child care centers in the lives of parents.* New York: Families and Work Institute.

Shinn, M., Ortiz-Torres, B., Morris, A., Simko, P., & Wong, N. (1987, August). *Child care patterns, stress, and job behaviors among working parents.* Paper presented at the annual convention of the American Psychological Association, New York.

Shinn, M., Ortiz-Torres, B., Wong, N., & Simko, P. (1989). Promoting the well-being of working parents: Coping, social support, and flexible job schedules. *American Journal of Community Psychology, 17,* 31–55.

Shinn, M., Phillips, D., Howes, C., Galinsky, E., & Whitebook, M. (1990). Correspondence between mothers' perceptions and observer ratings of quality in child care centers. New York: Families and Work Institute.

Staines, G. L. (1990, November). Does flextime reduce work-family conflicts? *Paper presented at the APA/NIOSH Conference on Work and Well-Being: An Agenda for the 1990s.* Washington, DC.

Staines, G. L., & Galinsky, E. (in press). Parental leave and productivity: The supervisor's view. In *Parental leave and productivity.* New York: Families and Work Institute.

Voydanoff, P. (1988). Work roles, family structure, and work/family conflict. *Journal of Marriage and the Family, 50,* 749–762.

Weikart, D. P. (1990, February 26). Testimony at the Subcommittee on Education and Health, Joint Economic Committee.

Whitebook, M., Howes, C., & Phillips, D. (1990). *Who cares? Child care teachers and the quality of care in America: Final Report of the National Child Care Staffing Study.* Oakland, CA: Child Care Employee Project.

Zinsser, C. (1990). *Born and raised in East Urban: A community study of informal and unregulated child care.* New York: Center for Public Advocacy Research.

Child Care and Parental Well-Being: Bringing Quality of Care into the Picture

DEBORAH A. PHILLIPS
University of Virginia

Most of my research, and that with which I am most familiar, emphasizes the effects of child care on children (see Clarke-Stewart, this volume). My colleagues and I, as developmental psychologists, tend to be most interested in the developmental effects of variation in the quality of care, although the type of care and timing of entry into care have also received some empirical attention. The sociological literature, in contrast, typically addresses how market factors, such as the supply and costs of child care, affect women's labor-force participation, child-care choices, and fertility (Mason & Duberstein, this volume). There is very little interface between these two literatures. This means, for example, that sociologists tend to sidestep questions regarding the quality of child care, and that developmentalists tend to ignore questions about how child care affects adults. Herein lies the significance of the Mason and Duberstein paper. Their proposed model begins to integrate the psychological and sociological literatures by attending to the type and quality of child care, on the one hand, and by examining the psychological effects of child care on adults, on the other.

I have set four goals for this commentary. First, I make a few remarks about the context of child care in the 1990s, emphasizing elements that are likely to affect relations between aspects of care and parental well-being. Second, I examine a few of the assumptions in the Mason and Duberstein paper. Third, I critique their discussion of associations between child care and parental well-being. I close with some comments about child-care providers.

THE CONTEXT OF CHILD CARE IN THE 1990S

In Mason & Duberstein's opening paragraph, they refer to the distress and anxiety that often accompany reliance on child care. They attribute these reactions to the inability of some parents to find child care, to breakdowns in care, and to doubts about the quality of care that their children are receiving. I concur that these are tremendous sources of anxiety, but they are merely symptomatic of a society in which child care remains anathema to deeply held values about the desirability of exclusive maternal child care (McCartney & Phillips, 1988; Scarr, Phillips, & McCartney, 1989). Although reliance on child care has become the norm in our society—a fact that might affect criteria for the "best" ways to raise children—the increasing movement of care from the private sector of the home to market forms of care, particularly child-care centers, seriously challenges these values. Mason and Duberstein refer to these values when they discuss the standard of mother care against which all other forms of care are compared. When we examine parental reactions to child care, in general, and choices with respect to care by fathers and other relatives, in particular, a clear picture of the "paths through which child care affects well-being (p. 127)," requires attention to our society's values about maternal and nonmaternal care. Ironically, the inattention in the research literature to how child care affects parental well-being, is itself a reflection of a value system that is more consistent with judging parents for using child care than with seeking to understand how reliance on such care affects parents' psychological health.

The authors also raise the important, but largely ignored, issue of equity with respect to child-care choices and effects. This issue surfaces at several points in the paper, such as in the presentation of data concerning low-income parents' relatively high rates of dissatisfaction with child care (Kisker, Maynard, Gordon, & Strain, 1989; Sonenstein & Wolf, 1991). It emerges again in the authors' speculations about how single parenthood, particularly in the absence of other sources of human and financial support, may place unmarried mothers at particularly high risk of suffering psychological costs associated with combining work and parenting roles.

Income and racial distinctions have been granted far more attention in the sociological than in the psychological literature on child care, perhaps because we tend to think that these distinctions have their greatest effects on access to care and on payments for care—that is, sociological rather than psychological concerns. Recent data from the National Child Care Staffing Study (Voran & Whitebook, 1991; Whitebook, Howes, & Phillips, 1990), however, suggest that quality of care—the bailiwick of developmentalists—is also an equity issue. Specifically, we found a curvilinear relation between quality of center-based care and family income, such that middle-income families were using the poorest quality of care. Quality was measured with extensive on-site observations of the classroom and caregiving environment, with observed staff–child ratios, and with extensive data on caregiver qualifications and salaries. Each aspect of care was poorest in the centers in which the predominant enrollment was of children from middle-income families, with one exception: Actual caregiver–child interactions were more sensitive and less harsh in centers serving primarily high- and middle-income families compared to those serving primarily low-income families. I hope interdisciplinary conferences of this type will encourage greater attention to issues of equity in the psychological literature.

ASSUMPTIONS ABOUT CHILD CARE AND WELL-BEING

I now turn to some assumptions put forth by Mason and Duberstein. First, they emphasize the availability and affordability of child care as the key dimensions that affect parental well-being. Quality of care is encompassed under availability as a subjective element that parents consider when determining which options are on their list of choices. I am reluctant to assume that this is precisely how quality of care figures into the model. I would rather maintain quality of care as an independent contributor, with both objective and subjective elements, and examine whether and how parents both consider quality when they choose child care and are affected by variation in quality, apart from considerations of availability.

Second, it is assumed that satisfaction with child care is a measure of parental well-being. I am not aware of any data that either support or refute this assumption. There are, however, serious problems with satisfaction data, and this leaves me concerned about basing conclusions about how child care affects parental well-being on studies that rely exclusively on this outcome. As Mason and Duberstein note, satisfaction data are notorious for poor variability. Most nonpoor parents indicate that they are "very satisfied" with their child care. This not only makes it difficult to examine predictors and effects of satisfaction, but it leaves one wondering about what such questions are tapping. Some, for example, have speculated about the demand characteristics of questions about satisfaction. It is not easy for a mother to acknowledge — to herself or to others — that she is leaving her child in an arrangement that does not meet her standards for satisfaction. Are parents really satisfied with, or merely reconciled to, their child-care arrangements? It might be easier for mothers on Aid to Families with Dependent Children (AFDC) to admit to low satisfaction if they are using child care as a result of mandatory job requirements. To the extent that they did not choose to rely on child care, they may feel less responsible for its consequences. This is a methodological issue that deserves careful study before we base many more conclusions on available satisfaction data.

Moreover, satisfaction questions typically fail to distinguish different aspects of care: its convenience, its quality, its reliability. When these distinctions are made, somewhat more variability is obtained (Shinn, Phillips, Howes, Galinsky, & Whitebook, 1990). For example, parents using child care centers in the Atlanta site of the National Child Care Staffing Study were less than "somewhat satisfied" with the stability of the staff, but were highly satisfied with the location of the center. Interestingly, mothers' satisfaction with staff stability was highly negatively correlated with director reports of actual staff turnover. This suggests that parents do not make global judgments about their child-care arrangements. If this is the case, relating satisfaction to well-being is a complicated endeavor. At a minimum, investigators need to examine parents' satisfaction with different facets of care, as well as the relative importance they place on these different facets, prior to examining links to well-being.

Third, I want to commend the authors for an assumption that is *not* made, namely, that the well-being of mothers and fathers in a given family is positively correlated. In fact, the well-being of one parent may be traded off for the well-being of the other. For example, Mason and Duberstein cite data (from Baruch & Barnett, 1983) indicating that fathers benefit from situations in which mothers provide relatively more child care. Unfortunately, despite their recognition of trade-offs between mothers' and fathers' well-being, Mason and Duberstein conclude from these data that the father's well-being was not enhanced at the mother's expense because there was no association with the mother's reported role strain. This fails to consider other domains of maternal effects, including financial and professional consequences, self-esteem, and physical health.

A related assumption that is somewhat harder to resist is that the well-being of parents is positively correlated with the well-being of their children. In many cases, of course, this is true. The maternal depression literature is testament to this. Yet, Mason and Duberstein present data that efforts to provide exclusive parental care for children, accomplished primarily through shift work, take a toll on the parents by reducing marital satisfaction and increasing the likelihood of divorce. This is a clear case in which parents' efforts to increase their child's well-being (based perhaps on faulty assumptions about the relative benefits of exclusive parental care) cost them their own well-being. Over the long term, moreover, it is likely that marital strain will have negative effects on children.

CHILD CARE AND PARENTAL WELL-BEING

Although Mason and Duberstein conclude that child care availability and affordability affect the well-being of mothers and fathers, in my estimation the data are not in on this important question. They cite only one study that directly addressed this association (Ross & Mirowsky, 1988). Although problems with child care and lack of support from a husband predicted maternal depression in this study, we cannot rule out the possibility that depressed mothers report more child-care problems, including lack of support from their husbands, or that their depression actually contributes to child-care problems and low support. In other words, I suggest caution with respect to causal conclusions. It would be helpful to know more about the sample used in this study and about how child care difficulties were assessed. I have already noted that I don't place much faith in the data regarding satisfaction with child care, so I believe we are left with rather thin support for concluding that child-care availability and affordability affect parental well-being.

Aside from this conclusion, this section of Mason and Duberstein's chapter leaves me with the uneasy feeling that, although we know a great deal about quality of care when we define *quality* as what is good for children, we seem to know next to nothing about what aspects of care are good for parents. Mason and Duberstein report that parents are most satisfied with relative care, yet they drew a prior conclusion that reliance on relatives seems to be more a matter of economics than of preference. Parents without financial constraints seem to prefer center care, yet these data are based primarily on parents of preschoolers, and we know little about preferences of parents of infants and toddlers. Moreover, once care is selected, we really know very little about factors that promote what Mason and Duberstein refer to as "trust and confidence." What factors enable parents who use child care to believe that they have protected their child's well-being? I doubt that availability and affordability affect trust. Is it, then, the quality of care, as we typically assess it in the developmental literature? Is it the stability of care? Is it the parents' sense that the caregiver shares their values about childrearing? Is it cultural compatibility?

Another issue raised in this section concerns the utility of the role-strain construct. In many ways, this chapter may be seen as adding those stresses associated with child care to the role-strain literature. The unavailability and unaffordability of child care are cast as sources of stress and anxiety affecting women who combine work and family roles. This is a major contribution: Child-care problems have not been adequately considered in the work–family literature.

On the other hand, the broader role-strain literature is replete with contradictory findings that call into question the adequacy with which this construct has been conceptualized. For example, some investigators report high levels of anxiety and depression among working women (Sarbin & Allen, 1968). Others have found work to play a protective role for women, with women in the labor force reporting fewer health problems, less depression, and greater life satisfaction than women not in the labor force (Hofferth &

Moore, 1979; Hoffman & Nye, 1974; Kanter, 1977). Some have speculated that women who choose demanding work and family responsibilities are a self-selected group who have the capacities required to maintain multiple roles (Scarr, Phillips, & McCartney, 1989).

Unfortunately, many women do not choose work, and thus do not choose child care. An important question concerns the factors that predict well-being among this group of parents. A recent dissertation by Marlene Eisenberg (1991) suggests that the perception that there are no choices to be made with respect to roles and their associated responsibilities is a critical factor to consider in this area of research. Single mothers appear to feel trapped in their roles, with little or no possibility of relief, and this perception directly predicted these women's psychological well-being. This dimension of role choice/confinement was also a strong predictor of poor adjustment among married mothers.

What are the implications of these findings for Mason and Duberstein? First, they raise cautions about the magnitude of effects that should be expected from studies that link child-care problems to parental well-being, particularly when the analyses combine mothers with differing financial and social resources. Second, they call attention to the important mediating factor of parents' coping skills, a variable that is missing from their model. Third, they suggest that perceptions of role choice are critical to understanding links between parental well-being and child-care availability and affordability. Specifically, we need to go beyond assessing what child care arrangements are chosen or preferred and why, to assessing parents' perceptions that reliance on child care per se is a choice. I am also struck by the need to examine parents' perceptions that, given a change in circumstances or a breakdown in their child-care arrangements, they have enough maneuvering room to enable them to cope. For some parents, well-being may hang by a very thin thread, whereas for others, ample resources, flexible job requirements, and alternative child-care options may assure that well-being is a stable commodity.

A FEW WORDS ABOUT CHILD-CARE PROVIDERS

I could not help but notice that the guiding question for this session is, "What are the consequences of child-care practices and arrangements for the well-being of parents and providers?" So, where are the providers? I am not going to summarize the conclusions of the National Child Care Staffing Study (Whitebook, Howes, & Phillips, 1990), except to highlight that we know very little about the well-being of child-care providers. We do know that this profession is characterized by very low wages that fail to reflect the educational backgrounds of the providers. We know that center-based providers frequently change positions. We also know that these providers typically love the day-to-day demands of their jobs, but are highly dissatisfied with their pay and social status (see Phillips, Howes, & Whitebook, 1991). We have not, however, taken the next step of assessing the mental health of child-care providers, and relating their mental health to the well-being of the children in their care.

Mason and Duberstein touch upon these issues by including self-employment as a child-care provider among the options that some women consider. What are the stresses associated with providing care for one's own plus others' children? What are the implications of this choice for the stability of child care once the provider's children have entered school? Given the dismally low wages of child-care providers, what are the effects of this choice on these women's financial well-being and future career and earning trajectories? I hope that these issues find a more prominent place in future research and discussions.

REFERENCES

Baruch, G. K., & Barnett, R. C. (1983). *Correlates of fathers' participation in family work: A technical report* (Working Paper No. 106). Wellesley, MA: Wellesley College, Center for Research on Women.

Eisenberg, M. M. (1991). *Work–family interference, coping strategies, and subjective well-being in working mothers.* Unpublished doctoral dissertation, University of Virginia, Charlottesville, VA.

Hofferth, S. L., & Moore, K. A. (1979). Women's employment and marriage. In R. E. Smith (Ed.), *The subtle revolution: Women at work.* Washington, DC: The Urban Institute.

Hoffman, L. W., & Nye, F. I. (1974). *Working mothers.* San Francisco: Jossey-Bass.

Kanter, R. M. (1977). *Work and family in the United States: A critical review and agenda for research and policy.* New York: Russell Sage.

Kisker, E. E., Maynard, R., Gordon, A., & Strain, M. (1989). *The child care challenge: What parents need and what is available in three metropolitan areas.* Princeton, NJ: Mathematica Policy Research.

McCartney, K., & Phillips, D. (1988). Motherhood and child care. In B. Birns & D. Hay (Eds.), *Different faces of motherhood* (pp. 157–183). New York: Plenum Press.

Phillips, D., Howes, C., & Whitebook, M. (1991). Child care as an adult work environment. *Journal of Social Issues, 47,* 49–70.

Ross, C. E., & Mirowsky, J. (1988). Child care and emotional adjustment to wives' employment. *Journal of Health and Social Behavior, 29,* 127–138.

Sarbin, T. R., Allen, V. L. (1968). Role theory. In G. Lindsey, & E. Aronson (Eds.), *Handbook of social psychology.* Reading, MA: Addison-Wesley.

Shinn, M., Phillips, D., Howes, C., Galinsky, E., & Whitebook, M. (1990). *Correspondence between mothers' perceptions and observer ratings of quality in child care centers.* Unpublished manuscript. York University.

Scarr, S., Phillips, D., & McCartney, K. (1989). Working mothers and their families. *American Psychologist, 44,* 1402–1409.

Sonenstein, F. L., & Wolf, D. A. (1991). Satisfaction with child care: Perspectives of welfare mothers. *Journal of Social Issues, 47,* 15–31.

Voran, M., & Whitebook, M. (1991, April). *Child care quality and social class: Equity of access to quality care.* Paper presented at the meeting of the Society for Research in Child Development, Seattle, WA.

Whitebook, M., Howes, C., & Phillips, D. (1990). *Who cares? Child care teachers and the quality of care in America* (Final report of the National Child Care Staffing Study). Oakland, CA: Child Care Employee Project.

Child Care and Parental Well-Being: A Needed Focus on Gender and Trade-Offs

HARRIET B. PRESSER

University of Maryland

Adrienne Rich, in her 1976 book *Of Woman Born: Motherhood as Experience and Institution,* presented a provocative attack on motherhood and the family in its current patriarchal form. She explained in the foreword that she was not against either motherhood or the family *under nonpatriarchal conditions,* nor was she calling for a mass system of state-controlled child care. She then stated:

> Mass child-care in patriarchy has had but two purposes: to introduce large numbers of women into the labor force, in a developing economy or during a war, and to indoctrinate future citizens. It has never been conceived as a means of releasing the energies of women into the mainstream of culture, or of changing the stereotypic gender images of both women and men. (p. 14)

Here we are, some 15 years later, devoting extended discussion to the relationship between child care and parents' well-being. I am pleased to see this typically neglected topic among the four selected for this book. Although we explain the increasing demand for child care mostly in terms of women's greater labor-force participation, we do not devote sufficient attention — in terms of research or policy — to what child care means for women and for or on how attitudes toward child care reflect our conceptions of the appropriate roles for women or men.

I do not mean to negate the need to consider the effect of child care on children; such research is of critical importance and should continue to expand. If, however, we are to truly understand the complexities of the child-care problem and if we seek to maximize the potential contribution of *all* human beings in our society, regardless of gender, we need to frame the child-care problem in a societal context that includes a hard look at gender differences in childrearing responsibilities and the consequences of these differences for the economic and social welfare of all.

In juggling work and family roles, there are many tradeoffs that have to be made between one's own interests and those of one's child and spouse. The crux of the child-care problem, in my view, is that in making these tradeoffs, we expect women — more so than men — to put their families' interests before their own. As opportunities for rewarding activities outside the family have increased, women have become less willing to sacrifice their own interests for those of others (although they are still more willing than most men). Moreover, with the increase in marital instability, women's definitions of what is in their own interests, and those of their children, has changed. Over half of women who marry can expect to become divorced, leaving many as single mothers. There are also increasing proportions of never-married women who are single mothers. Although women's higher education and greater labor-force participation since the 1960s has generally postponed the timing of first births and reduced total family size, most women do not want to give up having children entirely. The tensions that result — among women, men, and children — because of the necessity to make some tradeoffs, and how these tensions relate to gender differences in views of sacrifice and fairness, need to be rigorously studied if we are to understand child-care decisions and their consequences for parental well-being.

The chapter by Mason and Duberstein provides us with an excellent overview of what we know thus far about the consequences of child care for parents, which is not that much. Moreover, the authors go beyond this fragmentary data base and model some hypothesized effects of child-care availability and affordability. This model represents a very important contribution in conceptualizing the relationship between child care and parental well-being. My comments reflect my interest in expanding this model even further.

It is interesting that as we move from left to right in Fig. 3.1, the research base for hypothesizing relationships becomes increasingly weaker, so that when we consider the ultimate outcome of child-care availability and affordability, which is well-being, we know almost nothing. This is the case despite the minimal constraints on the definition of *well-being*. It follows that we know virtually nothing about gender differences in parental well-being resulting from gender differences in child involvement; a few small studies are cited relating to role strain and depression, but that is all.

This raises the question of where gender fits into the model. As I noted earlier, I regard gender differences in making tradeoffs central to the child-care problem, and thus would like to see gender explicitly incorporated. One could view the process by which availability and affordability affect the well-being of men and women separately, and thus not specify it in the model, but this would exclude the important issue of the relationship between the well-being of mothers and of fathers as a consequence of child-care avail-ability and affordability. Indeed, it would be even more revealing to incorporate the well-being of children into the model, along with mothers and fathers, and consider the interrelationships of well-being for all three.

I am taking the prerogative as a commentator by calling for new ways of conceptualizing and conducting our research, without having to do the hard work of spelling it out in detail, but I have elaborated (in my commentary on Hofferth's chapter, this volume) on some examples of needed research based on my studies on shift work and fathers' involvement in child care that Mason and Duberstein have referred to. In this commentary, I discuss shift work in the context of *parental* well-being.

Despite the fact that employment in the evenings or nights, or rotating schedules is characteristic of one-fifth of all parents with young children, and that one in three dual-earner couples with young children in the United States includes at least one spouse who works these non-standard hours (Presser, 1989a), shift work continues to be treated as though it were a deviant case rather than a common lifestyle for parents with children. The different work schedules of spouses permit each of them to provide child care when the other is employed, and this is, in fact, how child care is arranged in almost all of these cases. This is why child care by fathers in the United States is quite substantial: For *all* dual-earner couples with preschool-aged children, 1 in 5 fathers provide the principal care for their children when mothers are employed, and virtually all of these fathers are employed.

What is the role of child-care availability and affordability for parents who share child care by working different shifts? How do parents take into account the costs and benefits of such an arrangement for themselves, their spouses, and their children? For example, although there may be psychological benefits that result from sequential parenting—and we have no research on this—these benefits may be offset by a less stable marriage, given the evidence of the lower quality of such marriages (Staines & Pleck, 1983; White & Keith, 1990). For the many men and women who work at night or on rotating schedules—excluding evening work or split shifts (Presser, 1990)—there is the additional consideration of negative health effects, such as digestive and sleep problems, that are directly linked to working late or changing schedules. Yet, parents may disregard these health costs because of non-health benefits.

Take, for example, the hypothetical case of a woman with school-aged children who works fixed nights. While the mother is at work at night, her sleeping children are being cared for by her sleeping husband, if she is married, or by a relative. The mother sleeps when her children are at school. Thus, she is home caring for her children when her children are home and awake. This schedule of employment maximizes maternal time with school-age children, and makes it more profitable to work by reducing, if not eliminating, child-care costs. The possible negative health consequences, or the risk to the marriage, may seem worth these benefits. Do such women, in fact, weigh the costs and benefits this way, when taking a night job? We have no idea.

The shift-work examples may seem unusual, but we must keep in mind that we are talking about a widespread phenomenon, especially when we include evening work. I have argued elsewhere (Presser, 1989a) that this mode of shared child care is largely a consequence of the growth of the service sector of our economy, which drives the growth in evening and night work. Thus, it may well be that it is changes in the labor market — that is, more job opportunities at nonstandard hours, particularly for women — that is increasingly pushing fathers to share child care, more so than changes in ideology. These considerations, however, go beyond Mason and Duberstein's model.

Returning to this model, it may be noted that marital status is not specified, yet the well-being of single parents, and especially single mothers, is a particularly problematic issue. It may be that differences in well-being by marital status can be explained by differences in family income relative to needs, time stress, social supports, and satisfactions — which *are* specified — but this remains to be seen.

I mentioned earlier that I would like to see more of a research focus on the issue of personal and interpersonal tradeoffs. This is particularly relevant with regard to how parents determine the time they spend in the workplace versus time with their children. Although to economists, time is money, to parents the obvious fact is that they cannot work more hours to buy more personal time with their children. Among married couples, one spouse can spend more time at the workplace to enable the other spouse to have more personal time with their children, but this is becoming less of an adaptation among couples: Different trade-offs are increasingly being made, and we need to explore how existing child-care arrangements and nonstandard work schedules result from these tradeoffs. The use of relatives for child care, particularly among single mothers, is of special interest in this context.

This relates to another issue: What about the well-being of relatives who provide child care? Should we incorporate them into the model? It is not only the staggered work shifts of mothers and fathers that permit familial sharing of child care, but grandmothers and mothers also often work different hours and share child care this way, particularly when the mothers are unmarried (Presser, 1989b). Should we not be concerned about the well-being of these grandmothers who have already raised their own children and are now juggling work and child care in order to care for their grandchildren? Not only are we reluctant to evaluate the quality of care by relatives, we are reluctant to study the well-being of relatives as a consequence of their child-care assistance. In the absence of such knowledge, we get a very incomplete picture of how child-care decisions are made and what their consequences are.

Can we look forward to more research on the consequences of child care for the well-being of parents in the 1990s? Sandra Hofferth (chapter 1, this volume) views the trend in the opposite direction: She believes the focus of child-care research in the 1970s was primarily on its consequences for parents, but that the 1980s saw attention increasingly focused on the consequences of both maternal employment and varying types of nonparental child care on children and society. I find this quite discouraging, not because of the growing interest in the consequences of child care for children, but because I do not regard the 1970s as having produced that much research on the consequences of child care for parents. The major child-care study in the 1970s, the National Child Care Consumer Study (NCCS; U.S. Department of Health, Education, and Welfare, 1976), did not address this issue. However, in a supplement to the June, 1977 Current Population Survey (CPS), a monthly survey estimating employment activity in the United States, the extent to which child care was a constraint on women's employ-ment was addressed. Several demographers, including myself, saw this supplement (which included fertility questions) as an opportunity to explore the possible relevance of child care in modifying the relationship between women's employment and fertility, which was then our prime focus (Presser & Baldwin, 1980). Thanks to the support of the Center for Population Research at the National Institute for Child Health and Human Development (NICHD), the Census Bureau reluctantly added several child-care questions to the June, 1977 CPS supplement. Although this was not a child-care study per se, these few questions became a major source of child-care data (U.S. Bureau of the Census, 1982). Five years later, in June, 1982 the Census Bureau again added child-care questions on its fertility supplement (U.S. Bureau of the Census, 1983), but it has not done so since. Fortunately, we now have other national sources of data on child care, such as the 1990 NCCS that Sandra Hofferth is involved in, but the extent to which they include questions that can address the consequences of child care for women — and men — is limited.

Again, what is needed is greater attention to the consequences of child care for both children and parents, and how the consequences to mothers, fathers, and children affect each other. This includes indirect effects. For example, would the children of single mothers have the health care they need if their mothers were not employed or were not employed full time? What does the increased earning power of mothers, facilitated by child care, mean for the welfare of other family members, fathers included?

We have made considerable progress in studying child care, but we have a long way to go. Let us consider child care "as a means of releasing the energies of women into the mainstream of culture," as I quoted from Adrienne Rich at the outset, and — I would add — as a means of releasing men's energies into the mainstream of nurturance. This should serve us all well, even our children.

REFERENCES

Presser, H. B. (1989a). Can we make time for children: The economy, work schedules, and child care. *Demography, 26,* 523–543.

Presser, H. B. (1989b). Some economic complexities of child care provided by grandmothers. *Journal of Marriage and the Family, 51,* 581–591.

Presser, H. B. (1990). The growing service economy: Implications for the employment of women at night. In G. C. Cesana, K. Kogi, & A. Wedderburn (Eds.), *Shiftwork: health, sleep and performance* (pp. 131–136). Frankfurt am Main: Verlag Peter Lang.

Presser, H. B., & Baldwin, W. (1980). Child care as a constraint on employment: Prevalence, correlates, and bearing on the work and fertility nexus. *American Journal of Sociology, 85,* 1202–1213.

Rich, A. (1976). *Of woman born: Motherhood as experience and institution.* New York: Norton.

Staines, G. L., & Pleck, J. H. (1983). *The impact of work schedules on the family.* Ann Arbor: University of Michigan, Institute for Social Research.

U.S. Bureau of the Census. (1982). *Trends in child care arrangements of working mothers* (Current Population Reports, Series P-23, No. 117). Washington, DC: U.S. Government Printing Office.

U.S. Bureau of the Census. (1983). *Child care arrangements of working mothers: June 1982* (Current Population Reports, Series P-23, No. 129). Washington, DC: U.S. Government Printing Office.

U.S. Department of Health, Education and Welfare. (1976). *Statistical highlights from the National Child Care Consumer Survey* (DHEW Publication No. OHDO 76-31096). Washington, DC: U.S. Government Printing Office.

White, L., & Keith, B. (1990). The effect of shift work on the quality and stability of marital relations. *Journal of Marriage and the Family, 52,* 453–462.

IV

What Policies Are Necessary to Meet the Need for High-Quality Child Care, and How Can the Policies Be Realized?

Policies to Enhance Access to High-Quality Child Care

REBECCA MAYNARD
EILEEN McGINNIS
Mathematica Policy Research, Inc.

Changes in the American labor market, the composition of American households, and federal welfare policies underscore the increased importance of nonparental care for young children. A growing majority of young children are now spending a significant portion of their day in the care of relatives, nonrelated family child-care providers, or center-based programs. For some families, the decision to rely on nonparental child care enables mothers to pursue their careers; for others, it enables them to achieve higher living standards; and for many others, it is simply a matter of economic necessity. The consensus among child development experts is that nonparental child care per se is not harmful to the development of children. However, the experts also agree that the quality of care for young children does matter (Clarke-Stewart, this volume), and that, as a society, we are underinvesting in our children (Hayes, Palmer, & Zaslow, 1990). Most notably, an enriched child-care environment can significantly enhance developmental outcomes among children from disadvantaged backgrounds (Hayes et al., 1990; Silverberg, 1988).

Despite this knowledge about the merits of quality child care, young children are being placed in care whose quality varies widely. Among all socioeconomic groups and in all regions of the country, some children are being cared for in enriching settings, and some are being cared for in low-quality settings; the majority of children are cared for in settings that are neither enriching nor likely to be detrimental to the welfare of the children

(Hayes et al., 1990; Hofferth, Brayfield, Deich, & Holcomb, 1991; Kisker, Maynard, Gordon, & Strain, 1989).

The inconsistent quality of care can be attributed, in part, to discrepancies between the features of care that parents value and those that child development experts deem important. As a group, low-income parents, in particular, tend not to be well-informed about the set of child-care options available to them and tend to select arrangements largely according to convenience and cost (Kisker et al., 1989). Alternatively, some of the inconsistency can also be attributed to the nature of the patchwork supply of care that has evolved in a largely unregulated market, in which supply and demand have increased rapidly without a consequent change in the prices that parents pay. Despite this increase in the child-care market, the popular perception is that parents believe that the supply of care, especially infant care, is inadequate and the cost of care is too high; providers charge that salary levels for child-care workers are too low to attract and retain enough high-quality staff; and child development experts express concern about low or nonexistent standards for care and about severe restrictions on access to high-quality care, particularly for children from disadvantaged backgrounds.

This chapter examines the rationale for policies to ensure access to high-quality child care, describes the available supply of quality child care and the problems that some parents encounter in procuring such care, and discusses the likely impact of current and proposed policies on the supply of and demand for high-quality care. We recommend a range of policies to stimulate the supply of and demand for quality care. Some of our recommendations — such as implementing minimum standards of quality, improving the information base available to parents, and promoting standards and training programs for caregivers — can be implemented relatively inexpensively. Policies to increase the affordability of care, to promote infrastructure development, and to encourage parents to select high-quality care are more expensive, yet are consistent with recent child-care legislation.

THE NEED FOR HIGH-QUALITY CHILD CARE

The dynamics of the American economy and society have changed the nature of child-rearing responsibilities; over half of all parents of preschool-age children now rely on one or more caregivers — most often a relative or an unrelated family day-care provider — to help raise their children. Between 10% and 20% of these caregiver settings are under state regulations (primarily day-care centers and larger family day-care providers). However, in both regulated and unregulated settings, we find that many children are cared for in environments that do not meet professional standards that describe the developmental needs of children, nor do they provide the range of choices necessary to meet the needs of parents.

Developmental Needs of Children

Child-care professionals define "quality" child care as care that promotes the physical, emotional, social, and cognitive development of children. Moreover, the factors that enhance the quality of the child-care environment are to be gauged along selected measurable and potentially regulatable qualities of the setting (Hayes et al., 1990; Kisker, 1990). Group size, staff–child ratios, and the qualifications of caregivers are associated with the level and quality of the interaction between the child and the caregiver. The stability and continuity of the caregiving arrangement are important determinants of a child's ability to develop secure attachments with parents and caregivers and of his or her capacity to adjust to schooling in the future. The structure and content of daily activities are associated with cognitive development. Finally, adequate space and facilities can have a positive effect on social interactions and development. The National Academy of Sciences Panel on Child Care Policy (Hayes et al., 1990) identified six criteria that represent the consensus on quality care:

- Minimum staff–child ratios that vary according to the age of the child, ranging from 1:4 for infants to 1:7 for preschoolers.
- Requirements that caregiver training include child development training.
- Structured activities that are flexible enough to give children freedom of choice.
- Organized and orderly space, with well-differentiated areas for different activities and for groups of children of different ages.
- For day-care centers, maximum group sizes in centers, ranging from 6 to 8 for infants to 16 to 20 for preschoolers.
- A moderate age range of children in family day care (e.g., a range of 6 to 24 months).

These six qualities of child care are desirable for all children, regardless of their backgrounds. However, for several reasons, the quality of care for children from disadvantaged backgrounds poses greater concern than the quality of care for other children. First, low-income parents are more likely than other parents to place their children in minimally adequate child care, primarily because their access to quality, enriched care is more limited. For example, a recent survey found that less than 6% of the children of low-income *working* parents participate in Head Start (Maynard, 1990), in part because most Head Start programs are only part-day programs and, in part, because even full-day Head Start programs tend not to cover the entire work day. Further, recent evidence from a survey of welfare-dependent adolescent parents, who are subject to mandatory school or work requirements similar to those being implemented under the Family Support Act of 1988 (FSA), suggests that this population is relying on child care by family day-care providers whose educational levels are exceptionally low (Kisker, Silverberg, & Maynard, 1990).

Second, the majority of children of working parents, including low-income children, are cared for by relatives or (in family day-care settings) by adults who have little, if any, formal training in early childhood education and child development. Relying on such caregivers or settings may not be particularly limiting for children from advantaged backgrounds, and it may not actually be harmful to children from low-income families, but it does imply lost opportunities to enrich substantially the child-care environment of poor children and possibly to mitigate some of their risks of subsequent school failure. Third, the incidence of physical, emotional, or learning problems is greater among low-income families, and access to care is especially limited for special-needs children. Finally, the freedom of choice among low-income parents is especially limited due to transportation problems, the affordability of some types of care, and the absence of the option to rely on maternal care.

Parental Needs for Child Care

Although parents express concern about the quality of their child care, their perspective on the features of child care that they consider acceptable differs substantially from that of child development professionals. These differences in perspective reflect the more basic needs of working parents and their ability and desire to pay higher prices for quality care (Leibowitz & Waite, 1988). In particular, the child-care choices of low-income parents are highly constrained by the location, hours, and dependability of their arrangements. That is, they tend to judge quality according to whether the environment is safe and healthy, whether it promotes learning (especially for older children), and whether it is convenient, including whether the child-care setting is within a 10- to 15-minute radius of home or work and whether it accommodates the mother's work schedule[1] (Kisker et al., 1989; Sonenstein, 1989). Only after such conditions are met do parents weigh aspects of quality that are considered important by child development professionals (Sonenstein, 1989). Thus, parents tend to select their arrangements according to more funda-

---

[1]Many jobs, but particularly low-wage jobs, involve nonstandard schedules. Furthermore, proportionately more low-income parents work part-time (two thirds versus one third of all working mothers), which restricts child-care options primarily to family day care (Maynard, 1990).

mental needs, rather than on the basis of a detailed knowledge of the features of their child-care options. For example, among a sample of low-income working mothers, less than half visited more than one provider before making their final selection (Kisker et al., 1989).

THE SUPPLY OF QUALITY CHILD CARE

Recent surveys of the supply of and the demand for child care reveal evidence of significant excess capacity in family day-care settings, but shortages of infant care in all types of settings and a tight supply of center-based care in general (Hofferth, 1991; Kisker et al., 1989). Exacerbating these shortages of care, the child-care market does not operate effectively to match parents with providers who meet their needs, and the quality of care is highly variable and often inadequate (Maynard, 1990). Moreover, despite the low average hourly costs of child care—$1.15 per hour for relative care and $1.40 per hour for center-based care (Hofferth, 1988)—the total cost of care consumes an average of 10% of family income (20% to 30% of the mother's income). For low-income families, child care often consumes as much as half of the mother's income (Maynard, 1990). Needless to say, parents must often limit their child-care search to care within their price range. In particular, the child-care choices of low-income families are often limited to relatives who charge little or nothing for their services (Hofferth, 1991) or to centers that receive Social Services Block Grant (Title XX) funding.

A major impediment to increasing the supply of quality child care is the real cost of providing such care. Child-care fees that seem high to the parents who purchase care are very low from the perspective of child-care providers. More importantly, they are substantially below the full cost of providing high-quality care. Family day-care providers often earn near or below minimum wages and do not recover any compensation for the wear and tear on their homes or for consumables (Kisker et al., 1989). Centers generally pay wages that are low relative to the qualifications of their staff, and often receive substantial support in the form of donated space, materials, and financial contributions, yet many of them are still unable to provide care that meets recommended quality standards.

Center-based care that approximates the quality of care recommended by the National Academy Panel or by the National Association for the Education of Young Children (NAEYC) is estimated to cost about $5,000 per year per child (or $2 per hour).[2] Family day care provided in a setting that both meets recommended standards for child–caregiver ratios and that compensates the

---

[2]This calculation encompasses an increase in the fees charged by providers to enable them to reduce staff turnover to acceptable levels.

provider at the minimum wage plus a 25% premium for nonlabor costs would cost about $3,400 a year per child (or $1.35 per hour; Kisker & Maynard, 1990); the cost of family day care with a more typical provider–child ratio of 1:2 would cost nearly twice as much.

CURRENT FEDERAL CHILD-CARE POLICIES

Until recently, the federal role in child care has been limited to a fragmented array of consumer, provider, and infrastructure subsidies that, together, consume less than 5% of the federal budget for social services, excluding health, Medicare, and Social Security (Robins, 1988). As shown in Table 4.1, the largest program, consuming two thirds of the federal child-care support, is the Child Care Tax Credit ($3.9 billion annually); Head Start, which usually provides only part-time care and was not implemented specifically to serve the child-care needs of working parents, has been the second largest program ($1.2 billion). Other *consumer-oriented* programs range from various public assistance and child-care disregard policies to child-care allowances and educational grant policies. Other *provider-oriented* policies include Social Services Block Grants to centers that serve children from low-income families, the Child Care Food Program administered by the U.S. Department of Agriculture, and special education and rehabilitation programs. Finally, the federal government has devoted about $3 million a year to programs directed at the child-care infrastructure: primarily resource and referral services and Child Development Associate (CDA) programs. Notably, despite the range of child-care subsidies provided by the federal government, it has played a minimal role in establishing standards for and regulating child care.

The Family Support Act of 1988 (FSA) was clearly the most significant source of new child-care policy. It includes several provisions that have significant implications for the supply of and demand for child care among low-income families. First, FSA instituted mandatory participation in the Job Opportunities and Basic Skills Training (JOBS) program for many Aid to Families with Dependent Children (AFDC) recipients with young children, including both adolescent parents and young custodial parents who have not completed high school, groups that tend to have preschool-age children. Second, FSA entitles AFDC recipients to child-care subsidies for approved JOBS activities and for self-initiated employment-directed activities, as well as for up to 1 year of post-AFDC transitional employment. Third, uncapped federal matching funds are available to pay for these child-care subsidies, covering child care provided by both family relatives and nonfamily providers. States may provide subsidies only to center-based and family day-care providers that meet regulatory standards.

Several other new pieces of legislation provide for significant increases in the resources devoted to improving the quality, affordability, and availability

TABLE 4.1

Estimated Federal Subsidies for Child Care*

Policies	Estimated Fiscal Year 1988 (in millions)	Fiscal Year 1980
Consumer Subsidies[a]		
Dependent Care Tax Credit	$3,920	$ 956
Dependent Care Assistance Plan	65	—
AFDC Disregard	44	60
Food Stamp Disregard	50	36
Housing Disregard	18	—
Support for Education		
(Pell grants, vocational)	66	1
	$4,163	$1,053
Provider Subsidies		
Social Services Block Grant	$ 591	$ 600
Child Care Food Program[b]	584	216
Head Start	1,200	736
Special Education and Rehabilitative		
Programs	219	39
Work/Welfare Programs	19	—
School-Age Programs	3	—
Provider Tax Incentives	6	—
	$2,619	$1,591
Infrastructure Subsidies		
Human Services Reauthorization Act	$ 2	$ —
Resource and Referral		
Child Development Associates Program	1	—
	$ 3	$ —
Total	$6,785	$2,644

Note. Data on federal subsidies for child care are imprecise. For FY 1980 and 1988, rely on estimates from the U.S. Department of Labor (1988), Besharov and Tramontozzi (1988), Robins (1988), and Kahn and Kammerman (1987). These do not include expenses for child care provided to government or military personnel. The Social Services Block Grant is an average from these sources.

*Hayes et al. (1990).

[a]These consumer subsidies do not include the general income support programs: personal tax exemptions, Aid to Families with Dependent Children, and the Earned Income Tax Credit.

[b]Includes $4 million for the Special Milk Program.

of child care (Table 4.2). These include the Child Care and Development Block Grant (CCDBG), the extension of the Social Security Act IV-A Child Care Assistance program to cover working poor families, and the reauthorization of the Head Start program. Other recent legislation increases the funds available to train providers, to support the activities of child-care resource and referral agencies, and to increase tax credits for low-income working families

TABLE 4.2
Summary of New Child-Care Legislation

	Child Care and Development Block Grant	Title IV-A (AFDC) Child Care Assistance	Title IV-A Child Care Improvement Grants	State Dependent Care and Development Block Grants	Head Start	CDA Scholarship Assistance	Refundable Tax Credits
Purpose	To provide funds to states to enable them to improve the affordability, availability, and quality of child care.	To help parents pay for child care if they are at risk of welfare dependency.	To improve and enforce child care licensing and registration standards. To train providers.	Funds may now be used to operate resource and referral agencies and school-age child-care programs.	To expand Head Start to serve all eligible children ages 3–5. To improve the quality of Head Start. To enable Head Start programs to serve full-day and full-year.	To expand CDA scholarship assistance. To expand the pool of persons eligible for scholarships.	To increase the value of tax credits to low-income working families with children. To provide credit for health insurance. To provide a newborn credit.
Appropriation for FY* 1991	$731M Begins 9/91.	$300M.	$13M.	$13.2M.	$1.952B.	$1.4M.	See below.
Authorization for FY 1992 and Beyond	$825M FY92. $925M FY93. "Necessary sums" FY94–95.	$300M/yr FY92–95 (Expected to be available after FY95.)	$50M/yr FY92–94.	"Such funds as needed" for FY92–FY94.	Increases to $7.6B by FY94.	Annual authorization.	$19 billion over FY91–95.
State Match	No.	Capped entitlement at 50–80%; NJ: 50% (FMAP)	10%.	No.	Community match at 20%.	No.	NA.
New Program State Allocation	Yes. Based on share of children under age 5; children who receive free or reduced-price lunches; state per-capita income.	Yes. Based on the number of children in the state.	Modification. Based on the number of AFDC children in the state. NJ: $400,000 in FY 91.	No. Unchanged.	No. Unknown.	No. Not yet determined.	Two new credits. NA.

196

Administrative Agency	HHS	HHS-FSA	HHS-FSA	HHS-ACYF	HHS-ACYF	HHS-ACYF	Treasury-IRS
Target Population	Financial assistance to families whose income is below 75% of state median. Quality and supply enhancements to providers and all parents.	Low-income working families with children under 13. "At risk" of dependency on welfare. States must define "at risk" until regulations are issued.	Child-care providers of children funded by IV-A.	General.	Head Start programs Groups of children who are served must include more than 10% handicapped; must not include more than 10% whose income is above federal poverty guidelines.	Persons whose income is at or below 130% of the lower living standard (average: $27,000).	Low-income working families with children.
Quality Enhancements	75% for: Family assistance, supply increase, quality improvements. 5% must be spent on quality improvements. 19% must be spent on increasing the supply of early childhood education programs and before- and after-school care programs. Providers who receive assistance must comply with health and safety standards and parent-access requirements.	None.	50% of grant must be spent on training providers. 50% on improving the monitoring and enforcement of standards for IV-A child care.	None.	Quality Set-Aside. 10% of FY91 funding must be spent on staff compensation. 50% on transportation, new staff, insurance, facility improvement, and training. 2% on training and technical assistance. Requires that Head Start classrooms have one teacher with CDA or ECE training.	Will expand CDA training to more low-income child-care providers.	Not addressed.

(continued)

TABLE 4.2 (*Continued*)

	Child Care and Development Block Grant	Title IV-A (AFDC) Child Care Assistance	Title IV-A Child Care Improvement Grants	State Dependent Care and Development Block Grants	Head Start	CDA Scholarship Assistance	Refundable Tax Credits
Health	States design and enforce health and safety standards as outlined in the legislation for providers funded by this program.	Not addressed.	No change.	Not addressed.	No change.	Not addressed.	Refundable credit for health insurance that includes a child.
Parent Involvement and Choice	Parents who receive assistance must have wide latitude for choosing providers. Programs that receive assistance must provide unlimited access by parents. Consumer education in choosing providers, licensing and regulation requirements, complaint procedures. Access to records of substantiated complaints.	Parents have wide choice of providers: licensed, regulated, or registered care, or a relative caring only for other relatives. Programs that receive assistance must provide unlimited access by parents.	Not addressed.	Not addressed.	$20M for Head Start transitional projects includes parent-involvement programs for Head Start graduates in elementary school. Head Start programs currently have parent-involvement components.	Not addressed.	Not addressed.

Note. Prepared by Christine Ross, Mathematica Policy Research, Inc.

*FY = fiscal year.

with children. Together, these new initiatives increased total federal child-care funding by over $1 billion (15% in 1991), and will increase it by substantially more in later years.

The CCDBG was authorized to improve the affordability, availability, and quality of child care. As much as 75% of the grant ($731 million for fiscal year 1991 and $4.5 billion over 5 years) can be used to provide child-care assistance directly to low-income parents; 20% is set aside for expanding supply; and 5% is designated specifically for quality enhancements.

The Title IV-A Child Care Assistance program expands eligibility for assistance to low-income families who need such care in order to be able to work and who would otherwise be at risk of becoming dependent on AFDC. A total of $1.5 billion has been authorized on a matching basis through 1996.[3] The Title IV-A Child Care Improvement Grants will provide about $63 million over 4 years to match state funds for instituting training programs for providers, improving state licensing and registration requirements for all child-care settings, and monitoring child care provided to children who receive AFDC.[4] The Head Start Reauthorization nearly doubles expenditures to support increases in the number of Head Start slots and the availability of full-day and full-year programs, and to institute quality enhancements, including staff training and program development.[5]

The other major policy change that will have a significant impact on access to care pertains to the expansion of child-related tax credits. Over the next 5 years, the earned income tax credit is being expanded to a maximum of about $2,000 for families with children, and a newborn credit is being offered to families that do not claim a child and dependent-care credit for a child under age 1. The legislation also institutes a refundable tax credit for child-related health insurance coverage.

RESPONSES TO VARIOUS TYPES OF POLICY CHANGES

The current array of child-care policies has affected both the supply of and demand for quality child care in undocumented ways. In this section, we discuss how changes in various types of policies are likely to affect the behavior of parents and providers, thereby altering the quality and use of available child care. We discuss six types of policies that have been the focus of the child-care policy debate of recent years. Three are consumer-oriented policies—consumer subsidies, income transfers, and parental leave—and three are provider-oriented policies—provider subsidies, provider training and service orientation, and regulations and standards.

---

[3]The match rate varies from 50% to 80%.
[4]Half of these grants must be used for provider training programs.
[5]The funding will increase to $7.6 billion by fiscal year 1994.

Consumer-Oriented Policies

Consumer Subsidies. The child-care subsidies provided to consumers through the income tax and the welfare systems primarily address access, parental choice, and, to a lesser degree, the quality of care. The primary effect of consumer subsidies is to increase the effective wage rates of parents and, hence, to mitigate the desirability of providing parental child care, thereby increasing the labor-force participation and child-care use of mothers. These subsidies can be especially influential in affecting the labor-force participation and child-care use decisions of low-income and welfare-dependent families. In addition, subsidy-induced lower effective prices of care, in theory, will enable and may persuade some parents to select higher quality care and to shift from informal and unregulated care to regulated care.[6]

Minimal real resource costs are associated with these consumer subsidies, insofar as the policies merely transfer income from economically self-sufficient families who do not use care to families in which the only parent or both parents work and rely on nonparental care. Nonetheless, the federal budgetary costs associated with these policies are substantial. For example, the estimated federal child-care subsidies paid out under JOBS totaled around $330 million for 1991. Public expenditures for the Child and Dependent Care Tax Credit in 1988 averaged $397 per family over the 7.9 million eligible families (Giannarelli & R. O. Barnes, 1989). These credits, which accrue primarily to middle- and high-income families, constitute by far the largest source of federal child-care subsidies.

Although the benefits of the current consumer subsidies accrue most directly to the parents of young children, taxpayers also derive benefits in the form of higher tax revenues and lower transfer program costs, because the subsidies should increase the labor-force attachment of parents. In addition, the higher work-related income of parents and the higher quality child care may promote secondary, long-range impacts.

Income Transfer Policies. Child allowances and refundable dependent-care tax credits are desirable because they increase the child-care options of parents without affecting their choice of parental versus nonparental care. Because such income transfer policies increase the disposable income of families, they eliminate income constraints that affect employment and/or child-care decisions. Although little empirical evidence is available on the likely net effects of the newborn tax credit and the refundable policies tax

---

[6]The available evidence to support this predicted response, however, is inconsistent (Hofferth & Wissoker, 1990; Leibowitz & Waite, 1988; Michalopoulos, Robins, & Garfinkel, 1991).

credit, we expect somewhat different responses among different subgroups of parents.[7]

We expect that parents who are currently on welfare will have little response to child allowances and refundable tax credits, because such subsidies will tend to substitute for or be dominated by the current welfare benefit. We expect that some low-income parents who are currently working and relying on nonparental child care will use their increased income to purchase more desirable care, and that others will use the increased income to reduce their employment hours. Some low-income parents might respond to the allowance by continuing their current child-care and employment behavior and spending the increased income on goods and services; others might be induced to enter the workforce and thus increase their demand for nonparental child care. We expect that some middle- and high-income families will opt for higher quality care, and that some will switch from nonparental to parental care.

Child allowances represent an intergenerational income policy whereby, once in steady-state, young families will be borrowing against their future income, and older families will be paying back their debts. The net losers under this type of policy are childless couples. To provide some perspective on cost, a child allowance policy that guaranteed a $750 benefit for every child younger than age 6 would have over 20 million beneficiaries and cost over $10 billion more than expenditures under our current dependent-care tax credit (R. O. Barnes, 1988).

Parental Leave Proposals. Parental leave policies have ranged from the very extensive paid-leave policies common in Europe to unpaid leaves of only a few weeks. Arguments in support of such policies are associated with the developmental needs of children, women's equity in the workforce, and the efficiency of the workforce (Frank, 1988). Leave policies would reduce the cost of parental care relative to nonparental care during the leave period, thereby encouraging more parents to take leaves from their jobs to care for their children. In particular, many child development experts feel that parental care should always be an option for the families of infants.

The existence of leave policies would encourage women to enter the workforce before they choose to start their families. The policy would also tend to mitigate the adverse employment effects associated with job disruption, and would tend to increase the proportion of parents who choose to interrupt their careers to care for their children, thus avoiding access issues

---

[7]The only rigorous evaluations of such policies were conducted in the late 1960s and early 1970s as part of the Negative Income Tax Experiments. Due to the significant changes in the labor-force participation of mothers of young children and the child-care markets, the relevance of these studies to current policy planning is questionable.

associated with quality child care. In the absence of wage replacement, however, a parental leave policy might be expected to have a minimal effect on the number of parents who choose to take leaves.

Parental leave policies also may affect the behavior of employers. On the one hand, the policies promote a greater attachment by workers to their employers, thereby increasing the stability of the workforce and promoting higher wage growth. However, they also encourage an increase in the incidence of employee leaves, thus imposing direct resource costs and possibly productivity losses on employers. The net effect may be to reduce the willingness of employers to hire and promote women of child-bearing age and, potentially, to reduce overall wages.

Provider-Oriented Policies

Concerns about the quality and supply of child care can be addressed most directly with policies that are directed at the providers of child care or related services. Such policies include subsidies to child-care centers and/or family day-care providers, subsidies to child-care training providers or trainees, support for service coordination and provider recruitment, and support to promote regulations and standards.

Direct Subsidies to Child-Care Providers. Direct provider subsidies currently constitute about 40% of the federal outlays for child care, primarily funds for Head Start programs and for child-care centers and family day-care providers that serve low-income children. Public subsidies to support entire programs, such as Head Start, focus on developing and enhancing program services for targeted families. However, the responses of families to these provider subsidies depend on the nature of the service being offered by providers and the degree of outreach to bring eligible families into the program.

Clearly, the aim of the new legislation is to greatly expand both the coverage of Head Start and its ability to serve the child-care needs of parents. The Head Start Reauthorization provides substantial funding increases to support new slots, to increase the number of full-day and full-year programs, to improve the training regimen for and credentials of teachers, to develop new programs (such as transitional projects and parent–child centers), and to support quality-improvement strategies, which include paying teachers higher salaries. However, even with the increased funding for Head Start, it will still only be able to provide services to well under half of the eligible children. Moreover, parents will continue to face the constraints imposed by the limited hours and weeks of operation of many Head Start programs.

The recent increase in provider subsidies available under the CCDBG and the Title IV-A Child Care Improvement Grants theoretically allow providers to lower their fees while maintaining the same quality of care, or to enhance the quality of their care while holding fees constant, or a combination of these two responses. The availability of subsidies might also induce others to enter the child-care market by increasing the potential financial returns to providers.

The benefits of these subsidies will tend to be shared by providers — who may realize higher wages, greater job stability, and an improved work environment — and by consumers — who would benefit from higher quality care, an increase in the supply of care, and possibly lower costs. In addition, these subsidies might yield longer term benefits, such as increases in the labor-force participation of mothers and improved outcomes for children.

Provider Training and Service Coordination Funding. Funding for provider training and service coordination is limited and available primarily through four modestly funded programs: Social Service and Community Development funding, Title IV-A Child Care Improvement Grants, the State Dependent Care and Development Block Grant Program, and the Child Development Associate (CDA) Scholarship Assistance Program. The net effect of these policies on the supply, quality, and use of child care is ambiguous. On the one hand, the greater levels of support for training will tend to increase the supply of providers, which should lower the price of care and stimulate an increase in the labor-force participation and use of child care by parents. On the other hand, the increase in the supply of *trained* providers will tend to increase the wages of child-care workers and thus the cost of care, which will tend to reduce labor-force participation and child-care use among parents.

The service coordination subsidies increase the supply of care by facilitating the entry of providers into the child-care market, and enhance the desirability and profitability of being a child-care provider. They are also expected to be critical to improving the quality of care and promoting more informed child-care choices among parents.

Regulations and Standards. Current regulations and standards, which are developed and administered at the state and local levels, generally emphasize the protection of the health and safety of children. New federal funds for regulation and monitoring, and the provisions that govern the use of federal CCDBG and Title IV-A child-care subsidies, will push states to improve their regulatory policies and practices. Proposals that encourage a more active federal role in minimum quality standards for care are still being discussed.

Stronger regulations will increase the cost of regulated care and thus tend to reduce the supply of care subject to the regulations or guidelines. That is, tougher regulations alone will discourage unregulated providers from entering the regulated market and could encourage some currently regulated providers to go "underground" or out of business. Thus, it is important that regulations be tied to technical assistance, resource and referral services, and other forms of consumer and provider subsidies in order to minimize their negative consequences.[8] Moreover, it is important that states have sufficient funds and incentives to enforce their regulations.

The impacts of more stringent regulations on the cost of care are also significant. For example, it has been estimated that the annual cost of providing minimally adequate care (similar to what is now available through the loosely regulated market) is about $2,600 per child, whereas the cost of providing care that meets the NAEYC Accreditation Standards is estimated at over $5,000 per child (Clifford & Russell, 1988). Certainly, a doubling of costs due to more stringent regulations could increase or reduce the use of care, depending on the cost/quality tradeoffs for parents.

RECOMMENDATIONS

Our long-range objective should be to improve the "patchwork" child-care system so that all parents who want to work outside the home have access to affordable, quality child care. The recent child-care legislation provides substantial opportunities to approach these goals.

Continue to Increase Financial Subsidies for Low-Income Families

The recent change making the child-care tax credit refundable will significantly increase the transfer of child-care subsidies to low-income families, particularly single-parent families, one third of whom would benefit (R. O. Barnes, 1989). At relatively modest cost, this policy change will reduce the average cost of child care for low-income families to nearer 15% of family income, rather than the current 20%.

The new federal child-care legislation will provide funds to states to increase consumer subsidies through vouchers or the purchase of service contracts. Whether states will be able to provide the matching funds necessary to access the additional Title IV-A funds available to them is unknown. The Congressional Budget Office currently estimates that states will access only about half of the $1.5 billion authorized over 5 years. However, still higher

---

[8]For example, in the case of the Department of Agriculture's Child Care Food Program, the financial benefits from meeting the standards of eligibility are substantial: over $500 per child per year (Besharov & Tramontozzi, 1988). This program seems to have been effective at encouraging providers to comply with the applicable standards.

subsidies would be necessary to provide all parents access to any care, let alone high-quality care.

Broaden the Mission of Resource and Referral Networks

Traditionally, resource and referral agencies have engaged primarily in coordinating resources and monitoring the regulatable indicators of quality, such as staff–child ratios and staff credentials. Their mission should be broadened so that they serve as a network that *promotes* improving nonregulatable indicators of quality, such as developmentally appropriate curriculum and staff–child interaction. In addition to improving the quality of the available supply of child care, resource and referral networks could play a critical role in improving the operation of the child-care market and facilities by promoting more informed decision making among parents and building the supply of quality family day-care providers. Such investments will be especially critical to the success of the Family Support Act and to the well-being of children whose parents participate in JOBS. For example, the JOBS program will not be successful at enrolling a significant number of parents of preschoolers unless better mechanisms are instituted for identifying the available child-care options. Referrals to poor-quality care could jeopardize the well-being of the children of participants. Recent legislation both targets some funds for service coordination and monitoring, and permits other funds to be devoted to these purposes. This change represents an important step toward improving the system.

Support Consumer Education

Although parents are aware of the importance of the teacher–child relationship, they do not necessarily know that low staff–child ratios, small group sizes, and staff education and experience are critical determinants of that interaction. Local child-care communities are in a good position to determine the most effective way to help parents become better consumers of child care. Possible avenues for disseminating information about quality care include the secondary school system, the media, resource and referral networks, and community-based organizations.

Promote Provider Training

Much more federal support should be directed at promoting training for providers, including training for family day-care providers. If we are to take full advantage of the opportunities presented by the JOBS program and by the Title IV-A Child Care Assistance Program to effect economic stability among low-income families, we must be concerned not only about the supply but also about the quality of available child care. Because most children of low-income working parents will be cared for by relatives and in family day-care settings, it is important that we focus attention on the quality of those types of care, as well as on the quality of the care provided by center staff. One fairly inexpensive and effective way to improve the quality of child care (including the care provided by parents themselves) would be to incorporate a child development curriculum into our secondary schools. Community-based refresher training and enrichment programs should also be offered on a regular basis, for example, through community colleges, community-based organizations, and local resource and referral agencies. Expanding the use of television-based training programs would also be a feasible option.

Support the Expansion of Infant Child Care

Public support for increasing the supply of both center-based and family day care for infants is necessary if current and projected demands are to be met. Without stimulating additional infant-care options, it may be difficult to achieve the intended level of school participation mandated under the Family Support Act for adolescent parents and young custodial parents who have not completed high school. Furthermore, many adult mothers of infants may become and/or remain welfare-dependent due to the lack of knowledge about realistic child-care options available that would enable them to work full-time. Other mothers, in striving for economic independence and/or because they face pressure from welfare programs to seek employment, may leave their infants in low-quality settings that affect them adversely.

The CCDBG funds will support some increases in the supply of care through vouchers or the purchase of service contracts. However, it is not clear whether states will target these funds in ways that promote the necessary expansion of infant care. Proactive steps must be taken to ensure that some of these funds are directed toward filling this critical need.

Ensure Minimum Standards of Care
That Can Be Regulated and Monitored

The majority of children in care are unprotected by state regulations because the majority of providers — small family day-care providers — are exempt from whatever regulations do exist. Moreover, in many cases, current regulations fall below professional standards of quality, and the enforcement of standards is generally very weak. It is critical that some mix of "carrots" and "sticks" be adopted to ensure that our children are being cared for in safe, healthy, and hopefully developmentally enriching settings. The enforcement of existing regulations should be strengthened not only through stricter standards, but also with active technical assistance to help providers improve the quality of care they offer. Steps should also be taken to encourage voluntary regulation by exempt providers, thus increasing the availability of information on the quality of providers, and promoting access to technical assistance services for a larger group of providers.

ACKNOWLEDGMENTS

We are grateful to Alan Booth, Alison Clarke-Stewart, Sandra Hofferth, Ellen Kisker, Christine Ross, and Karen Oppenheim-Mason for helpful comments on a draft of this chapter.

REFERENCES

Barnes, R. O. (1988, October). *The distributional effects of alternative child care proposals.* Paper presented at the 10th annual meeting of the Association for Public Policy Analysis and Management, Seattle, WA.

Barnes, R. O. (1989, April 19). *How effective are alternative child care tax credits at targeting low-income families?* Statement before the Committee on Finance, United States Senate. Washington, DC.

Besharov, D., & Tramontozzi, P. (1988, April 8). *The cost of child care assistance.* Washington, DC: The American Enterprise Institute.

Clifford, R. M., & Russell, S. D. (1988, April). *Financing programs for preschool-aged children.* Paper presented at the American Educational Research Association annual meeting, New Orleans, LA.

Frank, M. (1988). Costs, financing, and implementation mechanisms of parental leave policies. In E. Zigler & M. Frank (Eds.), *The parental leave crisis: Toward a national policy* (pp. 315–325). New Haven: Yale University Press.

Giannarelli, L., & Barnes, R. O. (1989). *Analysis of the ABC Bill and the Rostenkowski proposal* (Technical Memo). Washington, DC: The Urban Institute.

Hayes, C., Palmer, J., & Zaslow, M. (1990). *Who cares for America's children? Child care policy for the 1990s.* Washington, DC: The National Academy of Sciences Press.

Hofferth, S. L. (1988). *The current child care debate in context.* Bethesda, MD: National Institute for Child Health and Development.

Hofferth, S. L. (1991). *The demand for and supply of child care in the 1990s.* Washington, DC: The Urban Institute.

Hofferth, S. L., & Wissoker, D. A. (1990). *Quality, price and income in child care choice.* Washington, DC: The Urban Institute.

Hofferth, S. L., Brayfield, A., Deich, S., & Holcomb, P. (1991). *National Child Care Survey 1990.* Washington, DC: The Urban Institute.

Kahn, A., & Kammerman, S. B. (1987). *Child care: Facing the hard choices.* Dover, MA: Auburn House.

Kisker, E. (1990). The importance of quality in child care. In *Child care challenges for low-income families.* New York: The Rockefeller Foundation.

Kisker, E., & Maynard, R. (1990, May). *Quality, cost, and parental choice of child care.* Paper presented at the North Carolina Public Policy Conference on the Economics of Child Care, Chapel Hill, NC.

Kisker, E., Maynard, R., Gordon, A., & Strain, M. (1989). *The child care challenge: What parents need and what is available in three metropolitan areas.* Princeton, NJ: Mathematica Policy Research, Inc.

Kisker, E., Silverberg, M., & Maynard, R. (1990). *Early impacts of the teenage parent demonstration: child care needs and utilization.* Princeton, NJ: Mathematica Policy Research.

Leibowitz, A., & Waite, L. (1988). *The consequences for women of the availability and affordability of child care.* Unpublished paper prepared for the National Academy of Sciences' Panel on Child Care Policy.

Maynard, R. (1990). The child care market for low-income parents. In *Child care challenges for low-income families.* New York: The Rockefeller Foundation.

Michalopoulos, C., Robins, P. K., & Garfinkel, I. (1991). *A structural model of labor supply and child care demand* (Discussion Paper No. 932–91). Madison, WI: Institute for Research on Poverty.

Robins, P. K. (1988). *Federal financing of child care: Alternative approaches and economic implications.* Miami, FL: The University of Miami.

Silverberg, M. (1988). *Nonmaternal care: Implications for children and parents.* Princeton, NJ: Mathematica Policy Research, Inc.

Sonenstein, F. L. (1989). *The child care preferences of parents with young children: How little is known.* Unpublished manuscript.

U.S. Department of Labor. (1988). *Child care: A workforce issue* (Report of the Secretary's Task Force). Washington, DC: U.S. Government Printing Office.

Infant Care and Full-Time Employment

ANDREW CHERLIN

Johns Hopkins University

Although this commentary will deal mainly with infant care, let me, first, emphasize the good news about the effects of maternal employment and child care on children's development, in general, because I don't think it is amply recognized. In its 1982 report, the Panel on Work, Family, and Community of the National Academy of Sciences wrote defensively about the effects of maternal employment on children (Kamerman & Hayes, 1982). The panel concluded merely that no general statements could be made about the effects of maternal employment on children. The report rejected the idea that maternal employment had uniformly negative effects, but it went no further. I think we can now make a more positive statement. Most research conducted in the 1980s has shown no significant detrimental effects of maternal employment and out-of-home care on children age 1 and older. The best recent evidence can be found in two studies of data on the children of a national sample of adults in their 20s (Baydar & Brooks-Gunn, in press; Desai, Chase-Lansdale, & Michael, 1989). This survey of adults is called the National Longitudinal Survey of Youth (NLSY). The information on their children has come to be known as the "Children of the NLSY" data set. In 1986, the children of the respondents were given several standard psychological assessments, and the work histories of their mothers and fathers were obtained. The two studies focused on 3- and 4-year-olds; both sets of researchers concluded that the children's scores on a test of verbal ability and on a behavior problems scale were not affected by whether their mothers worked after their children turned 1. This was the first, large-scale, nationally representative data we have had on maternal employment, child care, and children's well-being. The parallel findings are the best evidence yet that maternal employment after a child's first birthday does not itself create a problem. Of course, if the child-care arrangement is poor, children can suffer; but, in general, mothers' employment doesn't harm children over the age of 1. That is an important statement for the debates about child-care policy.

That's the good news. The bad news is that there appears to be a negative effect of maternal employment during the child's first year of life on children's verbal ability and behavior at ages 3 and 4. The controversial findings of studies of infant attachment (Belsky & Rovine, 1988) are well-known. The Children of the NLSY data set provides the first information obtained from assessments of large numbers of 3- and 4-year-olds throughout the nation. Both the studies referred to earlier found lower verbal ability scores among at least some of the children whose mothers worked while they were infants (less than 1 year old), but little or no effects among children whose mothers went back to work after their children's first birthdays. The two studies used different statistical models; one study reported that 4-year-old boys from families above the poverty line whose mothers worked when they were infants scored about one half of a standard deviation lower on a verbal ability test, compared to boys whose mothers did not work when they were infants (Desai et al., 1989). The other study reported that white boys and girls aged 3 and 4 scored about one third of a standard deviation lower on verbal ability if their mothers had worked when they were infants; and 4-year-olds scored some-what higher on a behavior problems index (which was not computed for 3-year-olds). The effects were greatly reduced if the mother worked less than 10 hours per week (Baydar & Brooks-Gunn, in press).

No single data set, of course, can provide definitive answers to questions about employment, child care, and children's well-being. We can't tell whether these negative effects fade or are long-lasting. Moreover, these two studies suggest that there is no effect of maternal employment during infancy on children's ability or behavior problems among blacks (according to Baydar & Brooks-Gunn, in press) or among the poor (according to Desai et al., 1989), but the findings do suggest that for white, non-poor children, full-time maternal employment during infancy, and the associated child-care arrange-ments, may have negative effects for some children.

These findings pose a problem that is particularly acute in the United States because of our high levels of full-time employment among the mothers of infants. The published labor-force data are not detailed enough for a precise look at this part of the work force, but the U.S. Bureau of Labor Statistics (BLS) supplied me with some unpublished tabulations that provide some information. In 1990, 49% of women with a child less than 1 year old were in the labor force. As is well-known, this is a dramatic increase from, say, the mid-1970s. The rise in women's labor-force participation since World War II has occurred in stages: In the 1950s, mothers of school-age children had the highest rate of increase; in the 1970s, mothers of children under age 6 had the highest rates of increase; and in the 1980s, the rate of increase for the mothers of infants and toddlers (children under 3) was especially high.

Given the finding that the effect of employment may be reduced if the parent works part-time, it is important to ascertain the proportion of mothers of infants who work *full-time.* There are no tabulations of BLS data that allow this proportion to be calculated directly, but Howard Hayghe of the BLS (personal communication, 1991) did provide a tabulation of the proportion of all employed mothers, age 16 to 44, who were working full time in 1990: 79%. Most mothers in the labor force, in other words, work full-time. It is likely, however, that the percentage who work full-time is lower among the mothers of infants. If we were to suppose that this figure was 50%, then about one fourth of all mothers of infants in the United States would be working full-time. The actual figure could be somewhat lower or higher, but let us use this approximation.

It is my impression (and here again, statistics are difficult to come by) that in no other country in the West — and quite possibly in the entire world — does such a high proportion of the mothers of infants work full-time. Consider Great Britain. Demographic trends in Great Britain are the most similar, among European nations, to trends in the United States (Cherlin & Furstenberg, 1988). In 1988, according to tabulations supplied to me by Kathleen E. Kiernan of the Family Policy Studies Centre in London (personal communication, 1991), only 11% of mothers of children age 2 or younger were employed full-time. The percentage for mothers of infants, which is not available, would likely be lower still. In fact, among all British mothers of children less than age 16 (or age 16 to 18, in school, and living in the household), just 19% were working full-time, compared to 79% in the United States.

We often look to Sweden as a model of progressive family policy. In fact, more Swedish mothers of young children are nominally in the labor force than American mothers, but this total is misleading. According to information provided by Jan Hoem of the University of Stockholm (personal communication, 1989) about 84% of mothers with children age 2 or younger were in the labor force in 1988, but few of them are working full-time. Indeed, 38% of these "employed" women were absent from work because they had taken child-care leaves; they were not working for wages at all. Another 10% reported that they did not work at all in the past week because they were sick. So, about half of the employed mothers were home on any given week. Many of the others were working reduced hours under Sweden's generous parental leave policies, which allow parents to reduce their work hours until their children are 8.

The European countries have allowed mothers of very young children to remain at home through a mixture of income transfers to parents with dependent children and paid parental leaves for the care of infants and toddlers. These are popular programs whose benefits are used by many women who might otherwise work full-time. (Men are also allowed to take parental leave, but few do). Only in the United States, I believe, is the idea of continuous, full-time employment so entrenched, and only in the United States are parental leave policies so lacking and financial support for parents of young children so low.

In a recent conference paper, Sheila B. Kamerman and Alfred J. Kahn (1990) argued that discussions about child-care policy in the United States should pay more attention to the needs of children under 3 and their parents. This group, they state, remains largely invisible in the American child-care debate. I think this debate will, and should, emerge in the 1990s. There are two directions that social policy could take. Although these are not mutually exclusive, policies may emphasize one more than the other. The first direction is to provide better child-care options for the mothers of infants who work full-time outside the home. This could be done by improving the quality of, and expanding and subsidizing the supply of, out-of-home care for infants. The advantage of this direction is that it allows women to retain a continuous, full-time attachment to the labor force. This may be beneficial for their careers and their incomes in the long-term. It also would allow mothers from low-income families to bring home full-time paychecks.

There are costs to this direction, however. The largest cost may be financial: It is very expensive — more expensive than the care of older preschool children. The expense stems from the need to have more caretakers per infant than per 3-year-old. The National Academy of Sciences Panel on Child Care Policy recommended a ratio of not more than 4 infants per caregiver, compared to a recommended level of 5 to 10 3-year-olds per caregiver (Hayes, Palmer, & Zaslow, 1990). The second cost is the possible risk to some infants of having full-time nonparental care. Reasonable people can disagree on the extent of this risk and what to do about it; I think that there probably is an increased risk to middle-class and working-class children, at least among boys, and that we ought to factor this risk into our policy discussions.

The alternative direction is to subsidize parents so that they can stay home at least part-time during their children's first year of life. This is the direction nearly every Western developed country has followed. Kamerman and Kahn (1990) argued that Sweden has done the best job of crafting policies that allow parents to stay home and yet preserve gender equity. They write:

Sweden is characterized by high female labor force participation rates, high female labor force attachment rates, higher part-time employment rates for women than in most countries, relative equality of post-tax male/female wage rates, and high fertility rates for second and third births of educated women (p. 35).

I share Kamerman and Kahn's enthusiasm for the Swedish solution of extensive, paid parental leave and subsequent part-time employment, but we should recognize that there are some potential costs to this policy direction, too. Swedish mothers of young children work disproportionately in the public sector, providing Sweden's wide-range of social services. They work in jobs where it is easier to take a leave and return, they work in occupations in which wages do not rise much with age and experience, they work in jobs that are heavily female, and they can work six hours a day for up to the first eight years of their children's lives. In other words, they look very much like the American women in the pink-collar ghetto, although they are paid more relative to men, and they may hold jobs that are more respected.

Note that you cannot make Partner in a Stockholm law firm working six hours a day. The cost of the system is that its solution may impede the ability of well-educated mothers to rise up the managerial and professional hierarchies. In the short-run, the Swedish system still may be the best tradeoff public policy can make. Its adoption here would require that the United States legislate paid parental leaves for infant care (as most other Western countries have done). It would also require that part-time work with health insurance and other prorated benefits be more available.

This still leaves the problem that women (who probably would take parental leave much more often than men, given the experiences of other countries) may lose experience and continuity in the labor force and the associated promotions and wage increases. In order to ease that problem, I think, what is needed throughout the West is a reorganization of the structure of careers. What is needed is the acceptance for both women and men of the idea that it is acceptable and appropriate to take a leave from one's job or to work part-time for several years to take care of small children (and perhaps also aging parents). I acknowledge that this will be a difficult campaign, but there already is some increase in the number of men who have taken such career paths, and I think public acceptance is rising and will continue to rise. To mention just one sign of changing attitudes, the cover of the May 20, 1991, issue of the business magazine *Fortune* shows seven young children under the caption: "Can your career hurt your kids? Yes, say many experts. But smart parents — and flexible companies — won't let that happen." This upbeat line is still more of a recommendation than a reality, but it would have been unthinkable for *Fortune* to have run a cover story such as this 10 years ago. Also, should the drive for pay equity result in substantial gains for female workers, the added income will, I think, give wives more leverage to convince their husbands to share in the care of young children.

For now, in the United States I think it is important to work for (a) paid parental leave for infant care and (b) an upgrading of part-time work to a dignified option that provides health insurance and other prorated fringe benefits. Among Western nations, only the United States has no parental leave provision; and only in the United States do so many mothers of young children work outside the home full-time. We need to begin thinking about these and other changes in social policy that might ease the burdens on the parents of young children and help the children themselves by providing an option — part-time work or paid parental leave — that would allow them to spend more time with their children during the first year of life.

REFERENCES

Baydar, N., & Brooks-Gunn, J. (in press). Effect of maternal employment and child-care arrangements in infancy on preschoolers' cognitive and behavioral outcomes: Evidence from the children of the NLSY. *Developmental Psychology.*

Belsky, J., & Rovine, M. J. (1988). Nonmaternal care in the first year of life and the security of infant–parent attachment. *Child Development, 59,* 157–167.

Cherlin, A., & Furstenberg, F. F., Jr. (1988). The changing European family: Lessons for the American reader. *Journal of Family Issues, 9,* 291–297.

Desai, S., Chase-Lansdale, P. L., & Michael, R. T. (1989). Mother or market? Effects of maternal employment on the intellectual ability of 4-year-old children. *Demography, 26,* 545–561.

Hayes, C. D., Palmer, J. L., & Zaslow, M. J. (Eds.). (1990). *Who cares for America's children? Child care policy for the 1990s.* Washington, DC: National Academy Press.

Kamerman, S. B., & Hayes, C. D. (Eds.). (1982). *Families that work: Children in a changing world.* Washington, DC: National Academy Press.

Kamerman, S. B., & Kahn, A. J. (1990, November). *Innovative parenting policy and gender equity.* Paper presented at the Conference on Women, Work, and the Family: An Agenda for the 1990s, New York.

Keep Our Eyes on the Prize: Family and Child Care Policy in the United States, As It Should Be

SANDRA SCARR
University of Virginia

Maynard and McGinnis have presented a comprehensive look at the current and predictable policies that, at federal and state levels, will affect working families and their children. It is appalling to see how inadequate our support for families and their children is. These authors review family support policies and child-care policies that affect both consumers and providers. Parents' ability to choose and pay for their children's care and caregivers' incentives to enter the child-care profession and to improve the quality of their service are both addressed. They note the many problems in our "patchwork" system: problems of insufficient attention to quality and insufficient supply for low-income families. Recent legislation has made a step toward improving the ability of low-income families to pay for child care (using 15% rather than 20% of the family income) and some steps toward training caregivers and improving regulations. They note the seeming political impasse over parental leaves, even unpaid leaves, and the impact of this lack of policy on the unmet need for early infant care.

If we step back from the current morass of family and child-care policies in the United States, we can look at what other nations have done and continue to do for their working families. By comparison with other industrialized countries in the world, the United States neglects the most essential provisions that make it possible for parents in other countries to afford to rear children and to find and afford quality child care for their children.

TAX POLICY

Child-care policy must be understood as one provision in a large set of family supports that reduce the economic disadvantage of parents, compared to childless couples. Taxes are a primary consideration for most working, non-poor families: In the United States the dependent deduction declined in value from 1950 to 1990 by about two-thirds. This means that, just in terms of taxes, rearing children in the 1990s costs parents a great deal more (and non-parents a great deal less) than was true in earlier decades.

The phasing out of the dependent care credit for middle- and high-income families has lessened that benefit for millions of American families, but the same 1987 tax reform legislation increased the dependent care credit for the working poor. The focus of recent changes in tax laws has been just this: to increase the tax benefits of employment for the poorest families and to reduce benefits to the middle class.

Congress recently increased the earned income tax credit for the working poor, especially for parents of small children, and are expanding this mechanism to transfer some income to the poorest parents. Table 1 shows how this mechanism is being used to support more and more parents; the number of eligible families has increased from about 6.5 million in the Reagan era to about 12 million in 1989. The average amount of credit has also increased from less than $300 per family from 1981 to 1986 to almost $600 in 1990.

> In all, the IRS expects 13.8 million families to be eligible for the credit this year — more than one in every 10 households in the country. Treasury and congressional analysts estimate that the working poor will get an average of $700 a family, assuming they can figure out the new form. (Wessel, 1991, p. A16)

TABLE 1

Credit Where Due: The earned-income tax credit has become one of the major anti-poverty initiatives for the working poor.

Calendar Year	Total Amount (In billions)	Number of Families (In millions)	Average Credit
1981	$1.912	6.717	$285
1982	1.775	6.395	278
1983	1.795	7.368	224
1984	1.638	6.378	257
1985	2.088	7.432	281
1986	2.009	7.156	281
1987	3.931	8.738	450
1988	5.940	11.148	533
1989	6.695	11.918	562

Note. From Joint Committee on Taxation; Internal Revenue Service (Wessel, 1991).

In 1991, parents of infants were eligible for an extra "wee tots" benefit, designed to help mothers of babies less than 1 year old stay at home, or to help parents buy expensive infant care when they return to work. A second new provision was a special credit for parents who purchase health insurance for their children.

All in all, the earned income tax credit has become a major mechanism for partially offsetting the extra costs of parenthood for the working poor. It encourages participation in the labor force for both single mothers and married mothers whose husbands are in low-wage jobs, and it helps such parents buy better quality child care.

PAID PARENTAL LEAVE

In the summer of 1990, President Bush vetoed a plan for unpaid parental leaves at the birth or adoption of an infant. The legislation was bitterly opposed by the business community, especially small businesses represented by the U.S. Chamber of Commerce. The United States is the only industrialized country in the world that does not have mandated, paid, job-protected, maternal leaves following the birth of a child (Scarr, Phillips, & McCartney, 1989). By contrast, the paid parental leave policies of representative European countries are shown in Table 2.

Most countries compensate mothers for time away from employment in the child's first 4 to 9 months of life. The level of compensation varies from 50% to 100% of wages, but most pay mothers (and often fathers) 75% or more of their usual wage to stay home with the new infant. Furthermore, many countries have additional leave time that is compensated at lower levels to extend parental leaves up to a year or more.

The history of these paid maternal leaves (it is mothers who take more than 90% of the time afforded by these leaves) is that following World War II, with their economies in shambles, Europe realized that women were needed in the labor force to rebuild. If women were to be attracted to and retained in the labor force, some provision would have to be made for childbearing and early child rearing. In addition, most European countries had declining populations before the War, and adopted a consciously pro-natalist policy following the War. If women were expected to work and bear children, clearly governments were going to have to compensate them and make the combined roles attractive. Thus, paid, job-protected, maternal leaves became an instrument of government policy to rebuild economies and to increase the birth rate (in the latter goal they failed).

In the United States, after World War II women who had worked at all manner of jobs during the War were told to go home to make places in the work force for some 2 million returning veterans. Economists expected a massive recession and unemployment after the War; they failed to anticipate

TABLE 2
Paid Parental Leaves in Western Countries

Country	Date	Duration of Paid Leave	Available to Fathers Y = Yes	Supplementary Unpaid or Paid Parental Leave
Benefit Level at 100% Earnings[a]				
Norway	1984	4 months	Y	Y
Austria	1987	16 weeks		10 more months, at lower level[b]
F.R. Germany	1987	14 weeks[c]	Y	1 year at flat rate[d]
Portugal	1984	3 months		Y
Netherlands	1984	12 weeks[c]		
Benefit Level at 90% of Earnings				
Sweden	1987	9 months plus 3 months at flat rate	Y	up to 18 months; 6 hour work day, up to 8 years
Denmark	1987	24 weeks	Y	Y
France	1987	16 weeks[c]		up to 2 years
United Kingdom	1987	6 weeks + 12 weeks at flat rate		Y maternity leave
Benefit Level at 80% of Earnings				
Finland	1987	11 months	Y	Y
Italy	1984	5 months[e]		Y
Belgium	1984	14 weeks		
Ireland	1982	14 weeks		
Benefit Level at 75% of Earnings				
Spain	1982	14 weeks		
Israel	1984	12 weeks		
Canada	1984	17 weeks, 15 paid		
Benefit Level at 50% of Earnings				
Greece	1982	12 weeks		

Note. From S. B. Kamerman (1989).
[a]Up to a maximum covered under Social Security.
[b]Plus 2 years for low-income single mothers if they cannot find child care.
[c]6 weeks must be taken before expected birth; in other countries this time is voluntary.
[d]Last 6 months available only on an income-tested basis.
[e]100% paid for first 4 weeks; 2 months' leave before birth mandated.

the pent-up consumer demand for housing, automobiles, and refrigerators that fueled a tremendous boom in the United States economy in the late 1940s and early 1950s. Although most women did not leave the labor force, they were excluded from well-paying industrial jobs and returned to lower paid pink-collar occupations. The government withdrew any provisions that would encourage women to enter and stay in the labor force, especially after childbirth. Thus, the history of government policy toward women in the labor force is vastly different in Europe and the United States. From a 1990s' perspective, it certainly seems that they were right and we were wrong.

FAMILY ROLES

Another deterrent to mothers' participation in the labor force is the lack of full husband participation in home and child-care responsibilities. Garry Trudeau, in *Doonesbury,* so often captures family dilemmas, as he does in the following cartoon (Fig. 1).

By reversing the roles and having a female boss and an employee father who seems to have all of the planning and child-care responsibilities for his family, Trudeau captures the essence of women's problems in juggling work and home.

Data on time use by full-time employed husbands and wives — childless couples and parents — confirms Trudeau's view (Rexroat & Shehan, 1987). In families without children, wives work at combined job and home responsibilities about 52 hours a week, about 5 hours more than their husbands. When there is an infant or preschool child in the home, mothers work 16 to 24 hours more per week than fathers or a combined total of 80 to 90 hours a week. Figure 2 shows these data.

The old saying that "a woman's work is never done" could not be more true, especially if she is a mother.

CHILD-CARE PROVISIONS

It may surprise American parents to learn that in Europe parents pay no more than 5% to 15% of the true costs of their children's out-of-home care. In the United States, parents pay more than 90% of child-care costs, because we do not have a national policy that supports child care for working parents. Again,

FIG. 1.

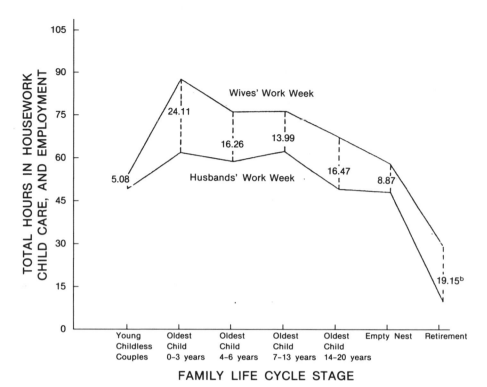

[a]Refer to Table 1 for definitions of family life-cycle stages.
[b]Stage 7 includes spouses who are not employed.

FIG. 2.   Mean Total Hours in Work Week for Husbands and Wives Who are Employed Full–Time, by Life Cycle Stage[a]

the European policy of publicly supported day care is part of a comprehensive family support system that is designed to attract mothers back to the labor force after the child's first year. In addition to maternal leaves, publicly supported child care is the other provision that is required to help mothers return to the work force when their children are less than school age. Most countries support child-care centers, although many also support family day care by paying the providers directly, providing training for them, and inspecting their homes for health and safety. Child care for preschoolers and after-school care for primary school children is simply an expected public expense, as is all of education. In this country, parents must support all of the costs of child care, unless they are poor, although middle-income families do get a small tax credit.

What is most surprising to Europeans who visit child-care settings in the United States is the lack of national standards. The fact that each state sets, and allegedly enforces, different regulations strikes them as very odd. How can it be that Georgia can have seven infants for each caregiver and Massachusetts can have half as many? Are the needs of infants in Georgia so different from the needs of infants in Massachusetts?

The fact that parents must pay nearly all the costs of child care in the United States has serious ramifications for our whole system, or nonsystem, of care. As Maynard and McGinnis estimate, the actual expenditure on child care in the country averages about $2,600 per year. To provide good care would require about $5,000 per year, which many parents cannot afford. In European countries the real cost of infant and preschool care is closer to $10,000 per child per year, because caregivers and teachers are paid a living wage, and European caregivers have health and social welfare benefits, just as any other citizen does. In this country, salaries of most child-care personnel are below the poverty level for a full-time job, and they have few, if any, benefits. The real costs of child care in the United States would triple if the women who care for children in centers and in their own homes were to make a decent wage, and have health, unemployment, disability, retirement, and other desirable benefits.

IMPLICATIONS FOR QUALITY

To provide a high quality system of child care in the United States will require massive infusions of public money. Parents cannot pay much more from their wages. This is especially true for low-income working families. Additional resources are needed for training, for better salaries and benefits to retain caregivers, for the expansion of Head Start into a child-care system, for direct subsidies to centers and family providers of care for the poor, for enforcement of regulations, and for much, much more.

In addition, we need minimum standards for care that receives public support. Because all care should receive public support, I argue for national minimum standards, above which the states could make improvements. Again, Doonesbury gets it right: High quality care cost money (Fig. 3).

It might not cost $400 a day to provide acceptably high quality care, but the real cost is much more than our system currently invests in the care of children.

We cannot afford to wait much longer before public monies are demanded for child care, as they were in the early century for free public education for every child. The demographics of maternal employment, inadequate wages for single breadwinners, and projections for the labor force all point toward the need for more and better child care. We can finance an improved system in a variety of ways: by increased subsidies to families, by direct payments to caregivers, by using public school mechanisms, and so forth, but we cannot

FIG. 3.

afford to let the current inadequate hodgepodge continue. The future of the nation rests on the adequate development of all of our children, and early care in quality settings is essential to that development.

ACKNOWLEDGMENT

This research is supported by a grant to the author (HD5R01HD27383).

REFERENCES

Kamerman, S. B. (1989). Child care, women, work, and the family: An international overview of child care services and related policies. In J. Lande, S. Scarr, & N. Gunzenhauser (Eds.), *Caring for children: Challenge to America* (pp. 93–110). Hillsdale, NJ: Lawrence Erlbaum Associates.

Rexroat, C., & Shehan, C. (1987). The family life cycle and spouses' time in housework. *Journal of Marriage and The Family, 49,* 737–750.

Scarr, S., Phillips, D., & McCartney, K. (1989). Working mothers and their families. *American Psychologist, 44,* 1402–1409.

Wessel, D. (1991, June 11). Paved with good intentions, tax writers' road to help the working poor turns into a maze. *The Wall Street Journal,* p. A16.

Child Care Policies: Changing to Meet the Needs

KATHY R. THORNBURG

University of Missouri

$\mathbf{A}$ll parents who want or need to work outside the home should have access to quality, affordable child care for their children, as outlined by Maynard and McGinnis. However, the cost, availability, and options of child care in their area create crises for many parents.

In May of 1991, 47 children were found in a basement in Chicago attended by one child-care worker. In 1990, in St. Louis, more than 100 children between the ages of 2 and 5 had only two caregivers in a church-operated child-care center. What possible effects might these child-care arrangements have on the future development and achievement of these young children? What changes are needed in our child-care policies to eliminate situations such as these?

My overall impression of the ideas expressed by Maynard and McGinnis is positive. They have summarized the current legislation and policies relating to child care well, and have made several important policy recommendations. I expand here on several of the issues they introduced. Specifically, I discuss the needs of low-income families, factors involved in child care — such as quality and cost, infant care — and resource and referral as they relate to the recommendations by Maynard and McGinnis.

In addition, I propose a familial view on child care and child development that may challenge us as we consider the content and scope of current child-care policy. This position encourages us to look at child-care policies from a broader framework: the comprehensive needs of the developing child as influenced by the changing family.

FAMILY NEED

Low-income families face a particularly difficult and complex struggle as noted by Maynard and McGinnis. The issue of child care is only one aspect of their multifaceted struggle.

When looking at the low-income population, it is critical to acknowledge the fact that risk factors (e.g., low-income, marital problems) work in an exponential manner in the young child's life. For example, one risk factor may not point to later problems, but two risk factors increase the likelihood of later problems fourfold. When there are four risk factors present, the chance of later problems is increased 20 times (Bogenschneider, Riley, & Small, 1991).

An example of this type of risk-factor impact is the socioeconomic level of young children with moderate neurological deficiencies. Bogenschneider et al. have found that middle-class children with moderate neurological deficiencies in early childhood do not suffer long-term problems in school. The quality of their home and school (supportive and stimulating) compensated for their deficiency. In low-income children, the problem was magnified and led to more severe problems in school.

These children are in need of comprehensive child-care programs (comprehensive in the same manner that Head Start looks at the total child within the family setting). Program components, such as quality care and education, dental and medical screening and services, and parental involvement, are all crucial. According to Copple, Cline, and Smith (1987), the Head Start children they studied were more likely to avoid serious school problems, were less frequently retained, and had better attendance records than their counterparts who did not attend the program.

QUALITY CARE

Research documents the success of high-quality early childhood programs and especially the comprehensive approach in helping low-income children. Evidence of the 25-year success of Head Start can be found in many longitudinal studies that cite the ongoing advantages of quality child-care programs. These benefits are found in the individuals' own lives (e.g., higher self-esteem, higher future aspirations, lower drug use, fewer teen pregnancies, and better academic performance), the lives of their families (seen in better family relations and increased volunteer work), and the community (resulting in fewer arrests and a higher employment rate).

The research clearly shows that young children respond in a positive manner to high-quality child care (Berrueta-Clement, Barnett, & Weikart, 1985; Illinois State Board of Education, 1985; Lazar & Darlington, 1982; Miller, 1989). A 19-year longitudinal study of the Perry Preschool Program of low-income children who attended quality part-day programs, found long-term comprehensive gains (Miller, 1989). One aspect of their study was a cost-effectiveness analysis of their child-care program. The gains or benefits of one year of quality care exceeded the cost seven times.

In another study of over 4,500 preschoolers, it was determined that children identified as at risk of failure in first grade, who had participated in at least three years of preschool, were as prepared for school as children not deemed at risk. At the same time, for at-risk children with only one or two years of preschool, the disparities in school readiness were pronounced (Committee for Economic Development, 1991). From experience and research, we know that effective comprehensive child-care programs can work proactively to combat the high-risk factors present in low-income families.

COMPREHENSIVE CARE

Policies directed toward the low-income population need to be comprehensive in their approach. The needs of the family, as well as the individual child and the child-care facility, must be considered. In light of our knowledge of the impact of high-quality child care, the need for child care in our society, and the special needs of the low-income population, we need to ask two questions when formulating effective policies: What makes a child-care program highly effective in meeting the needs of the population it serves? And how should the program be funded?

As Maynard (1990) pointed out, only 6% of children of working parents participate in Head Start, largely due to the part-day structure. Two early childhood programs that offer comprehensive child-care services to low-income families are the New Start/Head Start Program in Kansas City and the Dallas Model Preschool. These programs are able to offer full-day and full-year comprehensive child care due to multiple sources of funding. Both programs address educational, medical and dental services, parental education, and provide referrals to additional social services. In addition, teacher education and training are key components of these programs.

Funding for these programs combines federal, state, and private monies. In the Dallas Model Preschool, per pupil expenditure is $5,737, with Head Start providing the initial funding and Texas Instruments adding an almost equal amount. This program is open to all 4-year-olds in the elementary school zone (Committee for Economic Development, 1991).

The New Start/Head Start program provides a full-day program for 3- to 6-year-old low-income children whose parents are in job training, who are employed, or who are completing their education. Funding is provided by the federal government (Head Start), the state government (Department of Social Services) and several private foundations in the Kansas City area (KCMC Child Development Corporation, 1990). Federal policies should encourage programs such as those in Dallas and Kansas City by providing incentives to those who combine funding sources.

Five key factors are present in both programs: All eligible children benefit from the available care, the programs are full-day and full-year (when needed), parental needs are recognized, the programs offer high quality comprehensive services, and adequate funding has been secured. These five factors are key elements of successful child-care policy, and it appears there is a complementary relationship among the variables. For instance, secure funding provides for full-day, full-year quality child care which, in turn, has a positive impact on the child. Also, the needs of the parents may be met due to reduced stress, guilt, and conflict related to unpredictable or half-day child-care arrangements.

These five variables must be considered in formulating child care policy. We also need to recognize that the neglect of one item will likely weaken the effectiveness of the entire program due to their inter-relatedness. It is crucial that the goal of a comprehensive child care policy be to reduce the barriers that stand between families and quality child care.

COST OF QUALITY

Without compromising quality, the issue of cost needs to be addressed as each state begins to determine its level of support for child care. Child-care providers are in a crisis as directors and home providers struggle to keep their tuition within reach of many clients and still pay employees a wage above the poverty level. Clearly, low salaries are subsidizing our child-care system.

In an attempt to keep child-care costs affordable for low-income and some middle-income families, families who could afford to pay the true cost should be asked to do so. I fear that, as a society, greed has changed our values. As a director of a child-care center serving low- and middle-income families for the past 18 years, I have heard families who have a nice home, two cars, a summer home, a boat, and more, complain about child-care costs, those very costs that do not even cover the total child-care expense and are, therefore, keeping child-care provider salaries low. Those who can afford to pay the true cost should, and the government should subsidize only those who cannot. The subsidy should be at a level that approaches the cost of quality care. Only then will we be able to pay child-care providers more than poverty-level wages.

In a study conducted in Missouri, I found (Thornburg, 1988) the average hourly wage for directors of urban licensed child-care centers to be $7.30; teachers in those same centers reported earning $4.80. In the rural areas, directors and teachers earned $5.30 and $4.10, respectively. In this same study, I found that few child-care workers received job benefits. Directors fared much better than teachers; those who were employed by licensed facilities were more likely to have some form of a benefit package than those teaching in unlicensed centers. Approximately 60% of the directors in licensed and unlicensed centers received sick leave, holidays and vacation, and workmen's compensation. However, only about 40% of all child-care workers received benefits (health insurance, sick leave, holidays and vacation, retirement, life insurance, etc.). The results of another survey found that only 20% of the child-care providers received health benefits. A study of accredited centers reported that 64% of the child-care providers received health benefits (Willer, 1990).

This issue is well-summarized in a NAEYC position statement (Willer, 1990): "Early childhood professionals with comparable qualifications . . . should receive comparable compensation regardless of the setting of their job" (p. 51). This is a critical point to support when advocating funding as one compares child-care salaries with those of similar positions. For example, Willer reported that a degreed early childhood teacher in a licensed child-care center earns $14,100, whereas a public school teacher with the same credentials earns $28,900. An assistant teacher in a licensed center earns $10,200, and a teacher's aide in the public schools earns $14,664.

The issue of teacher salaries versus the cost of care to the parents may appear to be an arguable point (keep salaries low so parents pay less). It may be possible to raise salaries and provide benefits without increasing the cost to low-income parents due to the new federal child-care dollars. Perhaps program improvement and higher salaries could be attained with increased government funding (at least some of which could be conditional on staff improvement), charging true costs to those parents who can afford to pay, and increased private-sector funding. In other words, the true cost of quality care would be the joint responsibility of the federal, state, and local governments, the private sector, and parents.

Child care providers need the training and resources to provide quality care, and require government support. Greater financial subsidies, as outlined in the Child Care and Development Block Grant, is one way to help the parents while also addressing the true cost of child care. These subsidies can enable a provider to incorporate needed program or facility improvements, provide training opportunities to the staff, or increase teacher salaries. These subsidies need to be built into the system to ensure that the child receives quality and comprehensive care without having a negative impact on eligibility requirements.

INFANT CARE

Although infant care is in great demand today, the cost of providing it prohibits many child-care centers and day-care homes from entering the market. Maynard and McGinnis very aptly address this need in their discussion of teen parenthood, education, and the cost to parents. When parents are least able to afford quality child care, they are faced with the greatest cost of care. From this perspective, it seems necessary to support families.

The issue of parents caring for their own infants is often not considered when discussing infant care. Personnel policies such as flex-time, job-sharing, and part-time work help alleviate some of the need for full-time infant care. In addition, an effective parental leave policy could ease both the demand and the cost for infant care. Families would be encouraged and supported by the federal government, which would allow them to care for their infants and be assured of wages when they return to their jobs. Two key elements of an effective benefits package, according to Kamerman (1989) are "1) a guarantee of a right to leave work with assurance of full job, seniority, and benefit protection on return; and 2) a cash benefit that replaces all or part of the wages foregone while on leave" (p. 384).

Typically, European countries provide a 5- or 6-month leave paid at 90% of net wages. Kamerman (1989) proposed a policy that would, at minimum, allow mothers the right to paid disability at the time of childbirth for the standard 14 weeks that prevails in other industrialized countries. In addition, job-protected parental leave would cover another 4 months until the child is 6 months old. A certain number of days paid leave for the care of sick children should also be provided, according to Kamerman. A strong parental leave policy would lessen the demand and cost of infant care, as parents would be able to provide quality care for their own children. Of course, government expense for the parental leave policy would be significant.

RESOURCE AND REFERRAL

Another recommendation made by Maynard and McGinnis addresses the role of resource and referral networks. The high utilization of networks cannot be overemphasized because accurate information influences policy formation and parental decision making. The National Association of Child Care Resource and Referral Agencies (NACCRA) outlines the key elements of resource and referral agencies: to assemble and maintain a database on all types of care, to provide information and referral to parents, to provide resource development, to provide technical assistance and training, and to collect and analyze data. The mission of resource and referral is to be a vital link among all parties interested in families and child care. Resource banks should be developed and relevant information analyzed for parents, child-care providers, educators, and policy makers.

To have a positive impact on child-care policy, the role of resource and referral must emphasize resources including data collection, analysis, and dissemination in the areas of supply and demand, policy implementation and utilization, and child and family needs.

In many ways, resource and referral agencies that address each of these key elements also have an impact on Maynard and McGinnis' recommendations. A resource and referral facility would have the opportunity to influence policy in the area of low-income financial subsidies and infant care, provider training and high-quality child care, as well as parent information. It is important to ask each community with a resource and referral agency if work in each of these NACCRA recommended areas is being conducted and, if not, what changes could be made to increase and broaden the mission of their resource and referral agency.

Education is a key component of resource and referral as recommended by Maynard and McGinnis. Two separate areas that need to be addressed are (a) consumer education and (b) provider training. Consumer education is aimed at educating parents about the benefits of high-quality care and providing them with the information they need to make sound decisions regarding child care. Provider training is enhanced by the resource and referral agency by serving as a link between child-care providers and area training resources. These training and continuing education opportunities address concerns regarding provider qualifications.

The National Association for the Education of Young Children (NAEYC) recommends that child-care providers have a background in early childhood education and child development. Bredekamp (1989) reported that NAEYC's accreditation system has documented that developmentally appropriate prac tices occur more frequently when teachers have a combination of formal education and specific preparation in early childhood education. One study found that 26% of child-care teachers had not yet completed high school (Willer, 1990).

Considering the daily issues teachers face and the important role they play with each child and parent, it is essential to ensure continuing education. Because child-care providers are the natural disseminators of information on child development, it is important that teachers are well-trained, supported, and encouraged to keep current on the research in their field.

A good example of such a program working to provide education assistance to teachers, as well as to parents, is the Francis Child Development Resource Center at Penn Valley Community College in Kansas City. Primary funding is provided through a Francis Families Foundation grant. The primary goal of the grant is to ensure that technical assistance and training are available to all who work with children. Parents and family child-care providers have opportunities to gain knowledge in the areas of comprehensive child care, early childhood education, nutrition, and health screening. Providers can also learn about being effective parent educators and about using social services as referral agents.

This approach follows the philosophy that effective child care also addresses the needs of the family as a whole. In addressing such needs, any high-risk factor can be identified and appropriate services utilized. It is noteworthy that one key point of resource and referral is parent education, and the Francis Child Development Resource Center teaches providers to be effective parent educators. Many studies support the positive impact of a child's preschool attendance and the parents' attitude toward the child's education and future aspirations (Featherstone, 1986; Illinois State Board of Education, 1985; Lazar & Darlington, 1982).

PARTNERSHIPS

The essential ingredient for effectively solving our child care crisis is a federal policy that can give rise to broad-based community solutions. This crisis can only be resolved with cooperation from schools, corporations, private and public child-care providers, churches, family child-care homes, and other human service agencies. Policies that reflect the joint responsibility of the federal, state, and local governments as well as the private sector in meeting the true cost and need for quality child care, need to be developed and adopted.

An example of a multifunded agency is the New Orleans Council for Young Children in Need. With the objective of maximizing the potential of children in need, the council addresses issues from the prenatal stage through age 5. Their network of services (parent information, public awareness campaigns, policy and program advocacy, implication and evaluation) and provider support (aid with funding needs and coordination of services) is funded by the city, the public schools, and the Junior League with some start-up funds from the Greater New Orleans Foundation (Committee for Economic Development, 1991). This agency is a visionary example of a multifunded partnership that was formed to provide the quality services so desperately needed. Every possible source or partner must be recruited in the search for excellence.

STANDARDS

Standards of care, the last recommendation of Maynard and McGinnis, is directly affected by several of the other recommendations: education, training, comprehensive quality care, and adequate funding. As a nation, we speak of the need for quality care and the lasting benefits it provides, but too few children enjoy this right. Uniform high standards can begin to allow all children access to quality care, but there is a financial cost involved that must be understood by policy makers and parents, as well as providers.

Some states have developed adequate systems of governance for child-care centers and/or homes. Others have set standards for the child-care industry to govern itself in the form of self-reports. Some state governments have been timid about developing regulatory standards for child care. Thus, by default, it has fallen to the federal government to take action in this area. This phenomenon, however, is not unusual. The federal government has always acted in very restricted areas of education during periods of crisis and only when state and local governments will not or cannot take action.

Organizations such as NAEYC, the Children's Defense Fund, and the National Academy of Sciences Panel on Child Care Policy have provided suggestions and guidelines for developing standards at the national level. It is true that the national standards could force some centers to go "underground" or out of business, if the standards were directly tied to an incentive program or to the services of a resource and referral agency, but the negative impact on providers could be lessened while ensuring that children benefitted from the improved standards.

Responsibility for setting standards and regulating care is an issue to be addressed at all levels of government. Society is the beneficiary of higher quality care as long-term results are realized. In developing policies that seek to improve standards, it is important that a method of incentives be structured so as to encourage child-care providers to make changes and, having done so, to receive a direct benefit. Rather than linking the incentives to the eligibility-level of the children, the incentives should encourage centers to upgrade their care through improved teacher–child ratios, training, or building modifications.

This could help alleviate our two-tiered system of child care: one standard for those who can afford quality and a lesser one for those who cannot. Uniform standards would help create equality on all levels.

COMPREHENSIVE POLICIES

What is the federal government's role in reducing the barriers to quality child care? How can federal and state governments encourage private contributions to child care and what incentives can be offered to child-care centers to entice them to move toward high-quality programming?

One positive step in this direction is the recent announcement that the Department of Health and Human Services (HHS) has consolidated children's programs into one agency, the Administration for Children and Families. According to HHS Secretary Louis W. Sullivan, "For the first time the government will have a single agency bringing together the many child and family programs" ("U.S. agency," p. 8). This consolidation should help in the coordination of these children's programs. Our present system has funding from many different sources, as outlined so well by Maynard and McGinnis.

Neglectful situations, such as the ones in Chicago and St. Louis that I mentioned earlier, are the result of our policy shortcomings. As a country, we fail to provide appropriate child-care policies, services, and resources; as a result, we place our children in vulnerable situations with unsanitary environments, poor caregiver–child ratios, and lack of proper stimulation.

It is not difficult to assess the current child-care crisis or the needs of children and their families. Ample information is available in the areas of our nation's work force, family needs, demographics, quality of care, and available child care. We also have "American ingenuity" hard at work, as some communities are finding innovative ways to address local needs and concerns. These communities have based their model early child-care programs on current information, and their efforts are making a difference. Unfortunately, these communities and programs are few in number, and the needs of the vast majority of children and families are neglected.

Many communities are aware of their families' needs, but lack the resources or guidance to adequately address the child-care situation. The federal government can provide the guidance through a national child-care policy. Can programs be of high quality and not have strong parent education, health, and nutrition components? The policy must encourage comprehensive services and provide increased funding and incentive programs. With the federal government spearheading the effort, each state and local government can address its particular needs with complementary or supportive policies and services.

President Bush and our 50 state governors adopted six education goals in 1990. It is encouraging to note that the first goal, readiness for school, looks at children in a comprehensive manner. These goals, to be reached by the year 2000, will be directly affected by a child's early experiences. The first goal — for all children to enter school physically, intellectually, and emotionally ready to learn — can only be reached through comprehensive child and health care policies. Specifically, the objectives are as follows:

1. All disadvantaged and disabled children will have access to high quality and developmentally appropriate preschool programs that help prepare children for school.

2. Every parent in America will be a child's first teacher and devote time each day helping his or her preschool child learn; parents will have access to the training and support they need.

3. Children will receive the nutrition and health care needed to arrive at school with healthy minds and bodies, and the number of low-birthweight

babies will be significantly reduced through enhanced prenatal health systems (National Education Goals Panel, 1991, p. 1).

The first goal and its objectives address the developing child within the family unit in a comprehensive manner, with the child's physical, emotional, and intellectual needs in mind. To ignore the family is to say that the child exists in isolation. To neglect the child's needs for health care or adequate nutrition is to say that each family is fully self-supporting. We know this to be untrue: Children are greatly influenced by their families and, unfortunately, many families need a tremendous amount of support. The objectives, to have each child ready and able to learn by the time he or she enters school, can be realized only through massive changes in our national child-care and health policies.

Although we will always have a need for ongoing research, we have enough knowledge, task force reports, and goals to develop a comprehensive child-care policy. Our ongoing research can then address the ways to continually improve our policies and programs. It is not the lack of information on which to base policies that is the problem with child care today. It is, instead, internal turf battles and lack of funding.

Within our professions, we hear talk of profit versus non-profit centers, child-care homes versus child-care centers, schools versus child-care centers, and education versus custodial care. Some states are still debating whether church-operated child-care centers should have to meet safety standards. These issues must be resolved by child-care professionals.

Another major problem is the unwillingness of our elected officials to appropriate funds for the programs we know work. For example, in 1990 Congress passed a Head Start reauthorization act that projected funding levels to serve all 3- and four-year-old children by 1994. At President Bush's current proposed rate of funding, however, this goal will not be reached until the year 2171 (Edelman, 1991). The funding for the second year of the Child Care Development Block Grant is also under budget.

Our children will not wait to grow up, and family needs can not be put on hold. We have the knowledge to address the child care crisis effectively. It is time to develop strategies and tactics and to move with persistence. Only then will our children be ready to learn in anticipation of a promising future.

ACKNOWLEDGMENTS

I am grateful to Nancy Davis, Jacqueline L. Scott, and Linda Espinosa for their assistance in the preparation of this paper.

REFERENCES

Berrueta-Clement, J. R., Barnett, W. S., & Weikart, D. P. (1985). Changed lives: The effects of the Perry Preschool Program on youths through age 19. In L. H.

Aiken & B. H. Kehrer (Eds.), *Education studies review annual* (pp. 257–279). Beverly Hills, CA: Sage Publications.

Bogenschneider, K., Riley, D., & Small, S. (1991). *An ecological, risk-focused approach for addressing youth-at-risk issues.* Unpublished manuscript, University of Wisconsin-Madison.

Bredekamp, S. (1989). Regulating child care quality: Evidence from NAEYC's accredition system. Washington, DC: NAEYC.

Committee for Economic Development. (1991). *The unfinished agenda: A new vision for child development and education.* New York: Author.

Copple, C. E., Cline, M. G., & Smith, A. N. (1987). *Path to the future: Long-term effects of Head Start in the Philadelphia school district.* Washington, DC: U.S. Department of Health and Human Services.

Edelman, M. (1991, May/June). Kids first. *Mother Jones,* pp. 31–32, 76–77.

Featherstone, H. (1986). Preschool: It does make a difference. *Principal, 65,* 16–17.

Illinois State Board of Education. (1985). *Effectiveness of early childhood education programs: A review of research* (ED 260 825). Springfield, IL: Department of Planning, Research and Evaluation.

Kamerman, S. B. (1989). Toward a child policy decade. *Child Welfare, LXVIII,* 371–389.

KCMC Child Development Corporation. (1990, February 26). *New Start and Francis Center grants total $1.15 million.* Kansas City, MO: Author.

Lazar, I., & Darlington, R. (1982). Lasting effects of early education: A report from the consortium for longitudinal studies. *Monographs of the Society for Research in Child Development, 47*(2, Serial No. 195).

Maynard, R. (1990). *The child care market for low income parents.* New York, NY: The Rockefeller Foundation. (ERIC Document Reproduction Service No. ED 323 025)

Miller, G. (Ed.). (1989). *Giving children a chance: The case for more effective national policies.* Washington, DC: Center for National Policy Press.

National Education Goals Panel (1991). *Building a nation of learners: The national education goals report.* Washington, DC: U.S. Government Printing Office.

Thornburg, K. (1988). *Missouri Child Care Study.* Columbia, MO.

U.S. agency for children to be set up. (1991, April). *St. Louis Post Dispatch,* p. 8.

U.S. Department of Labor, Bureau of Labor Statistics. (1990). *Occupational outlook handbook, 1990–91 edition.* Washington, DC: U.S. Government Printing Office.

Willer, B. (1990). Estimating the full cost of quality. In B. Willer (Ed.), *Reaching the full cost of quality* (pp. 55–86). Washington, DC: National Association for the Education of Young Children.

Author Index

Subject Index